Pity Transformed

CLASSICAL INTER/FACES

Also available

Lucretius and the Modern World
W.R. Johnson

Plato's Progeny
Melissa Lane

Translating Words, Translating Cultures
Lorna Hardwick

PITY TRANSFORMED

David Konstan

Duckworth

This impression 2004
First published in 2001 by
Gerald Duckworth & Co. Ltd.
90-93 Cowcross Street, London EC1M 6BF
Tel: 020 7490 7300
Fax: 020 7490 0080
inquiries@duckworth-publishers.co.uk
www.ducknet.co.uk

© 2001 by David Konstan

All rights reserved. No part of this publication
may be reproduced, stored in a retrieval system, or
transmitted, in any form or by any means, electronic,
mechanical, photocopying, recording or otherwise,
without the prior permission of the publisher.

A catalogue record for this book is available
from the British Library

ISBN 0 7156 2904 2

Printed and bound in Great Britain by
Antony Rowe Ltd, Eastbourne

Contents

Acknowledgements	ix
Introduction: Pity as an Emotion	1
1. Pity and the Law	27
2. Pity versus Compassion	49
3. Pity and Power	75
4. Divine Pity	105
Conclusion	125
Appendix: Aristotle on Pity and Pain	128
Notes	137
Bibliography	159
Index	175

To Pura
and to Tupi and Jon,
Geoff and Christine,
and the little ones,
Alexandra and Zachary.

For Mercy has a human heart,
Pity a human face.
     William Blake

Angels out of mercy
Do not heed our prayers
Strings of accidents touch
Start and stop our tears
Never however do angels meddle
Theirs is to tell what has to be.
     Alan L. Boegehold

Acknowledgements

In this book, I draw upon several articles of mine that have been published elsewhere; these are identified in the bibliography as Konstan 1998, 1999, 1999a, 2000a, 2000b, 2000c, 2000d, 2001 and 2001a. I am grateful for permission to make use of these materials here. I wish also to acknowledge the institutions at which I first presented these papers (or parts of them) as talks, including the Boston Area Colloquium in Ancient Philosophy, Brown University, Cambridge University, the Center for Hellenic Studies in Washington, D.C., the Classical Association of England and Wales, Columbia University, Oxford University, Royal Holloway/University of London, the Societat Catalana d'Estudis Clàssics (Barcelona), the Universidad Internacional Menéndez Pelayo de Santander, the Universidade de São Paulo, the Universidad Nacional de Educación a Distancia de Madrid, the Universidad Nacional de La Plata, the Université de Paris XII (Val de Marne), the University of Durham, Washington University in Saint Louis (courtesy of the John H. and Penelope Biggs Resident Lectureship), and Yale University. I regret that I cannot thank each of the many friends and scholars who commented helpfully on these occasions and on others in which I delivered one or another version of the above.

    I am also deeply indebted to my colleagues at Brown University for their constant support, and to the University itself for two sabbatical semesters during which I was able to research and write the larger part of this book. I cannot fail to express my gratitude as well to colleagues at Cambridge University, where I spent a delightful term preparing the final draft, and at the University of Edinburgh, where I made final revisions. Simon Goldhill, in particular, read the complete draft and gave me valuable comments as well as timely encouragement. The series editors, Susanna Braund and

Pity Transformed

Paul Cartledge, provided the inspiration to undertake so challenging a project as well as help along the way. I would also like to thank Deborah Blake, who was all that an editor should be.

I have learned much from colleagues who generously shared their work and thoughts with me when they became aware that I was investigating pity in antiquity. My thanks to them, and, never belatedly, to my teachers at Columbia University. Let it not be thought invidious if, on this occasion, I single out two, William M. Calder III and the late Howard N. Porter, who in different ways provided models of what it is to be a scholar.

Finally, I thank my wife, Pura, who has shared in every aspect of my life throughout the period in which I worked on this book.

D.K.

Introduction

Pity as an Emotion

> Until recently, many scholars refused to believe that the categorization of 'emotions' can differ from language to language and insisted that at least some 'emotions' must be linguistically recognized in all languages. There can no longer be any doubt, however, that this is not the case. (Wierzbicka 1999: 24)

> This philological study takes as its point of departure the word; it depends not on facts, but rather on the expression of a specific area of experience (Burkert 1955: 10).[1]

This book is a case study of an emotion in a comparative context. The emotion in question is pity, although, to discuss pity adequately, it will be necessary to touch as well on such cognate sentiments as compassion, sympathy, empathy, mercy, clemency, forgiveness and generosity; for 'the way people interpret their own emotions depends, to some extent at least, on the lexical grid provided by their own language' (Wierzbicka 1999: 26). My focus will be on how pity was represented and understood in the ancient Greek and Roman world over a period of more than a thousand years, from the archaic age of Greece, represented chiefly by the Homeric epics, to the emergence of Christianity as the official religion of the Roman Empire in the fourth century AD. As one might expect, pity was not a simple or uniform concept throughout classical antiquity. Even in a single place and time, the meaning of pity might vary from one context (e.g. religion, the courtroom) or social group (women, soldiers) to another – or even among individuals, for example Plato and Aristotle. Over the course of an entire millennium, and in an empire like that of Rome, which embraced a great variety of influential cultures including Hebraic and Egyptian, the notion of pity naturally underwent fundamental changes.

The mobility of the ancient idea of pity puts in doubt whether a single modern term could cover all the senses of the ancient. In fact, one may legitimately wonder to what extent English emotional concepts correspond at all with ostensible equivalents in Greek and Latin. As David Wiles (1997: 6) has observed à propos Aristotle's theory of tragedy, there is no reason to assume that 'pity and fear ... are the same, whether felt by a fifth-century Athenian or a twentieth-century Englishman'.[2] Anthropologists and comparatists have identified various notions in contemporary societies that defy an easy translation into English. To take but one example, in her account of her sojourn with the Ifaluk, a people dwelling on a tiny atoll in the South Pacific, Catherine Lutz describes her perplexity concerning the Ifaluk term 'fago', which she parses as 'compassion/ love/ sadness'. 'This concept required,' she writes, 'more than did most other Ifaluk emotional concepts, an effort to disentangle my own native emotional understanding from theirs' (1988: 119). At first, the situations in which the Ifaluk used the word 'fago' baffled her, and inspired her attempt at a deeper kind of translation from the Ifaluk's system of emotional meaning to her own.[3] Again, Michelle Rosaldo (1984: 142) affirms that 'the Balinese no more feel "guilt" than we feel *lek*, the Balinese emotion closest to our "shame" '; might we not find, on close inspection, that Greek and Latin terms are equally untranslatable into simple English equivalents, and vice versa?

The matter is further complicated by the fact that in English too, the meaning of 'pity' and related terms is by no means entirely stable. For example, we commonly regard pity as crucial to moral sensibility: to call people pitiless is to fault them for a lack of elementary humanity. At the same time, however, pity may carry a note of contempt: witness a recent book on the rights of the disabled that bears the title *No Pity!*.[4] So too, the Greek adjective *oiktros*, 'pitiable', carried two senses, as the first-century BC historian Diodorus Siculus (15.6) makes clear by way of an amusing anecdote: when the tyrant Dionysius (fourth century BC) asked the poet Philoxenus for his opinion of some verses of his that narrated

Introduction: Pity as an Emotion

particularly pathetic events, Philoxenus replied, 'Pitiful!'. It is unproductive to eliminate such tensions and contradictions by stipulating a restricted or univocal meaning for the concept – what Wierzbicka optimistically calls 'the *invariant* of a given "emotion concept"' (39) – whether in English, Latin or Greek. Emotional terms, like other complex ideas, are not always self-consistent in their uses, and the task of the researcher is to display rather than suppress the range of relevant meanings. Indeed, there are occasions, as we shall see, when sharp differences of opinion among ancient writers hinge precisely on the polysemy of the terms for pity.

Different parts of speech deriving from the same root may also have distinct nuances, as may the same term in different phrasal combinations. Take the case of 'sympathy' versus 'sympathize': one may sympathize (or be in sympathy) with the position of a political party without feeling sympathy for it (cf. Árdal 1966: 56-7). The situation is still more intricate when one is working across languages. Thus, in English we customarily speak of 'self-pity', whereas 'self-compassion' sounds odd. In Spanish, however, it is just the reverse: one may say *autocompasión*, but *misericordia* is not used reflexively. This difference in usage will prove informative when we come to examine the idea of self-pity – and the lack of it – in classical Greek and Latin.

As if all this were not enough, a further obstacle in comparing modern and ancient notions of pity is the uncertainty over whether pity is to be classified as an emotion at all in the several lexicons. In classical Greek and Latin, there is a virtual unanimity, at least among pagan thinkers, that pity – or, more precisely, the terms we habitually render into English as pity – is indeed an emotion; or rather, we find pity subsumed under the general rubrics that we regularly translate as 'emotion' (the situation is somewhat more complicated with Christian writers). Thus, Aristotle, in his discussion of the *pathê* (plural of *pathos*, the closest term in Greek to our 'emotion') in the *Rhetoric*, includes along with pity analyses of anger, which he defines as the response to an insult or slight, calm (or, more precisely, calming down), love and hatred, fear, confidence, envy, spite, rivalrousness or emulation, indignation and shame. Yet modern classifications of the emotions are remarkably reticent about pity. Several investigators have attempted to isolate an array of basic or universal emotions; while the inventories vary, they tend to single out such sentiments as happiness, sadness, interest, disgust, acceptance, anticipation or expectancy, and panic, along with rage or anger and fear – but never pity.[5] Some theorists hold that the more sophisticated emotions, among them those apparently peculiar to human beings like guilt or jealousy, are generated by combinations of the basic responses. Thus, Robert Plutchik classifies hate as the combination of anger and surprise, guilt as joy plus fear, and envy as sorrow mixed with anger.[6] Although Plutchik's eight basic emotions generate several dozen amalgams, including such compounds as curiosity, awe, despair, remorse, stubbornness, pessimism, hopefulness, resentment, resignation, anxiety and fatalism, some of which, like curiosity and fatalism, may seem to be at the margins of what are ordinarily described as emotions, pity does not have a place in his taxonomy.[7]

The problem of how to classify pity raises the question of the definition of emotion as such. I consider some modern views in what follows, but we must recognize that the concept of emotion is bounded by a variety of other notions such as feeling, mood and disposition – the last bordering on the semantic sphere of ethics – and the frontiers are not always clearly marked. For each of these concepts, definitions vary substantially: one investigator stipulates that 'Moods are but generalized emotions,' while another pronounces that 'Emotion states that last for more than a few hours are referred to as *moods*, particularly when the subject is unaware of how the state started.'[8] A person who readily gets angry may be described as having an irate temper or disposition (Aristotle treats this condition under the heading of *êthos* or character); such an individual is prone to exhibit the emotion anger when provoked by a relevant stimulus. Seneca, in turn (*On Anger* 2.6.3-4), distinguishes between a person who is *iracundus*, that is, permanently angry, and *iratus*, angry at a particular thing. So too we may distinguish between the temperament of a person who is normally inclined to feel pity, and the emotion pity that is elicited in response to perceived suffering. Both Greek and Latin have adjectives to denote such a disposition (*eleêmôn, misericors*), although current

Introduction: Pity as an Emotion

English is deficient in this respect (we make do with 'merciful' and 'compassionate'). A disposition, moreover, in Greek as in modern thought, may have a normative function that we do not necessarily ascribe to emotions as such: one ought to be capable of pity – it is as bad in Greek as in English to be called pitiless (see Conclusion) – even if the occurrent emotion, as an involuntary response, cannot be a matter of duty or obligation.[9]

Even if pity is best described as an emotion rather than a mood or state, however, shall we say the same about clemency or compassion? 'Clemency' in English, like 'mercy', has an associated adjective, 'clement', but no verb; we shall see that a similar difference characterizes certain expressions in Greek and Latin. Such patterns afford a clue to the folk status, at least, of affective terms, whether in English or ancient tongues, and popular belief is raw material for the historian, if not always for the physical scientist.

Mapping the ancient Greek and Latin terms commonly rendered as pity – principally, *eleos* and *oiktos* in Greek and *misericordia* in Latin – onto English or other modern languages is thus a delicate and sometimes messy business, but the intricacy of the task is not cause for despair. We cannot correct our intuitions about the meanings of classical terms by means of live interviews and interactions with the ancient Greeks and Romans, as Catherine Lutz could with the Ifaluk. We do, however, have many thousands, even millions of pages of written documents against which to test our presuppositions, provided we are alert and open to possible disparities, and we may sometimes observe that the ways the ancients describe emotions, or emotional responses to stimuli we think we recognize, diverge sufficiently from what we expect to cast doubt on any easy equation between their experience and ours. The realization that others have seen things differently expands our own moral vision, and is one of the rewards of an investigation such as this.

Despite the absence of pity from modern catalogues, a knowledge of recent theories of the emotions is important to the study of ancient Greek and Roman conceptions. We are accustomed to the conventional contrast between reason and passion, and the idea that they are mutually exclusive has achieved the status of common sense in modern culture. In his study of the basis of feeling in the brain,

Antonio Damasio (1994: xi) writes: 'I had been advised early in life that sound decisions came from a cool head, that emotions and reason did not mix any more than oil and water'; Damasio adds that he had even 'envisioned separate neural systems for reason and emotion'. Such a view is not entirely alien to ancient thought. In the second century AD, the novelist Chariton described how Dionysius, a highly cultivated man and regent of the Greek city of Miletus, struggled with his desire for a beautiful woman who was in his power: 'Then one could see a contest between reason and passion [*logismou kai pathous*]' (2.4.4), and comparable expressions may be found in Plato and elsewhere (Nussbaum 1993a). Nevertheless, even a cursory examination of Aristotle or the Stoics (e.g. Seneca *On Anger* 2.1.4-5) on the emotions indicates that this opposition is foreign to their way of thinking, and theirs was the prevailing view among philosophers in antiquity. In Aristotle's account, the emotions involve a generous component of judgment and evaluation (see Appendix); for the Stoics, the emotions were nothing but. Such an approach, which emphasizes the role of cognition in emotions, would appear indispensable to an understanding of a complex, ethically charged emotion such as pity. What is more, it has come to be the dominant interpretation of the emotions today.

It was not always so. Charles Darwin's seminal treatise, *The Expression of the Emotions in Man and Animals* (1965 [orig. 1872]), in many ways launched the modern investigation of emotions; Jon Elster (1999a: 48) describes it, along with William James's 'What is an Emotion?' (1884), as 'the first studies of the emotions using scientific methodology', and its influence is still apparent in the new and unproven discipline of evolutionary psychology. Darwin connected the baring of teeth, growls, bristling of fur, and other such responses in animals to human expressive reactions, which he took to be evolved (but not always functional) forms of primitive adaptive behaviours. As recently as fifteen years ago, the entry on 'Emotion' in *The New Encyclopaedia Britannica* (Grastyán 1986: 348) reported that 'Investigation into so-called emotional phenomena increasingly is being directed toward objective biological evidence', thanks in large measure to Darwin's pioneering work, and that it has tended to focus on manifest strategic behaviours such as aggres-

Introduction: Pity as an Emotion

sion, fright and fawning, as well as stress responses, involuntary crying and laughing, sleep patterns and the like.

There is indeed some evidence that certain physical expressions are instinctive and cross-cultural, and these may have origins in earlier stages of the evolution of our species. According to one recent study, 'No society exists wherein people express anger with the corners of the mouth going up, and no person has ever lived who slits his eyes when surprised. An angry person appears angry to everyone worldwide, and likewise a happy person, and a disgusted one.'[10] So too, Paul Ekman, the most prominent neo-Darwinist investigator of emotional expression, writes (1980: 137-8; cited in Wierzbicka 1999: 168): 'Regardless of the language, of whether the culture is Western or Eastern, industrialized or preliterate, these facial expressions are labelled with the same emotion terms: happiness, sadness, anger, fear, disgust and surprise.'

Yet the labels 'happiness', 'sadness', and so forth are hardly indifferent to *language*. When the corners of the mouth of an ancient Greek turned downward, it was not 'anger' that was signalled but (presumably) something that in Greek was called *orgê*, which Aristotle, as we have seen, defined as a response to belittlement – and to nothing else. Injury or harm as such, for example, might induce hatred, according to Aristotle, but not *orgê*. Did the ancient Greeks, then, also turn the corners of their mouths downward when they experienced hatred? Do we? If there was no term in classical Greek that corresponded exactly to the English 'anger', what does it mean to say that 'an angry person appears angry to everyone worldwide'? As Wierzbicka (1999: 168) puts it: 'From [Ekman's] perspective, English lexical categories such as "sadness" or "anger" appear to cut nature at its joints ..., whereas the lexical categories of languages like Ifaluk or Pintupi ...' – or Greek and Latin – 'can only correspond to "blends". ' In effect, she concludes, Ekman and his colleagues 'absolutize the English folk-taxonomy of emotions' (171; cf. Harré 1986a: 4-5).

Whatever the case may be with anger or surprise, neither Darwin nor anyone since, to my knowledge, has identified a characteristic and universal expression, whether in humans or animals, associated with pity, although Aaron Ben-Ze'ev (2000: 110) observes that 'chimpanzees, and maybe some other kinds of higher animals, can clearly be said to show compassion', and Aristotle includes pity among emotions that are not independent of the body (*On the Soul* 1.1, 403a16-27). Pity differs from a response such as surprise precisely in the degree to which it necessarily involves judgment and other cognitive operations that are learned and socially conditioned, and it accordingly demands an approach that takes account of beliefs and values as well as of physiological excitation. Indeed, to the extent that surprise resembles a mere reflex, like being startled, one might hesitate to categorize it as an emotion at all, not to mention such reactions as involuntary crying, sleep patterns, and related phenomena surveyed in the *Encyclopaedia Britannica* article (cf. Ortony, Clore and Collins 1988: 4). Such behaviours are, in turn, absent from the classifications of emotions or *pathê* elaborated by the ancient Greeks and Romans.

Even within those sentiments about which there is broad agreement in labelling them as emotions, it may be advisable to discriminate different kinds or classes. Paul Griffiths (1997: 8) points out that the neo-Darwinian approach to the emotions developed by Ekman (1982) and others, which investigates responses under carefully controlled laboratory conditions, deals with a limited range of phenomena corresponding to the English terms 'surprise', 'fear', 'anger', 'disgust', 'contempt', 'sadness', and 'joy'; these are typically 'short-term, stereotypical responses involving facial expression, autonomic nervous system arousal, and other elements'. While Griffiths does not deny the universality of such affective reactions, even if they do involve 'some specialized learning algorithms', he argues that a 'quite different account is needed of higher cognitive emotions such as envy, guilt, jealousy, and love' (9; cf. 228-9; Griffiths omits to mention pity). Indeed, he goes so far as to recommend that the term 'emotion' be 'eliminated from our psychological vocabulary' (15) because of its ambiguity.

Despite the important work of Ekman and his associates, the main approaches to the emotions that have emerged over the past three decades or so place the emphasis, as we have said, squarely on the cognitive or evaluative component, and this has opened the way to a deeper understanding of both modern and ancient emo-

Introduction: Pity as an Emotion

tional concepts such as anger, shame and pity. For example, William Lyons (1980: 70) defines an emotion as having three parts – cognitive (or perceptual), evaluative and appetitive – and argues that the evaluative aspect is just what distinguishes one emotion from another. In a similar vein, Lazarus, Kanner and Folkman (1980: 198) define emotion as 'consisting of cognitive appraisals, action impulses, and patterned somatic reactions' and go on to assert: 'Emotions and cognitions are thus inseparable.' They point out that human emotions differ from those of animals lower on the evolutionary scale insofar as 'they depend on shadings and meanings that are absent or minimal in infra-human animal life', with the result that 'sociocultural forces have a far more powerful influence on human than infra-human emotions' (200). Robert Solomon (1984: 249) puts the case for 'a cognitive theory of the emotions' forthrightly: 'an understanding of the conceptual and learned appetitive functions of emotion is all that there is in identifying and distinguishing them from each other and from non-emotions.' Cognitive qualities thus assume a primary function in identifying and differentiating the broad and variable range of human emotions.[11]

Some theorists have gone so far as to deny that emotions involve anything other than cognition, in this respect recalling the radical intellectualist doctrine of the Stoics (and perhaps the Epicureans as well: cf. Philodemus *On Anger* col. 6; Fowler 1997: 25-7). Thus, Robert Solomon (1993: viii) underscores the thesis of his book that 'emotions are judgments' (cf. xvii, 15, 60, 125-6), although in practice he seems to admit other elements as well. So too, Richard Lazarus (1991: 353) holds that 'cognition is both a necessary and sufficient condition of emotion'. This is not the occasion on which to enter into an extensive analysis of theories of the emotions, but the advantage of an approach that takes account of cognitive aspects is that it permits interesting comparisons across cultures in a way that exclusive attention to expression and the search for universals has not. If emotions depend at least in part on beliefs, then they have a history analogous to that of the cultures or societies that have generated them. The cognitive approach also enables a fruitful dialogue with the Aristotelian and other ancient views of pity in which, as I have indicated, the evaluative dimension is crucial, as classical scholars have increasingly recognized since the pioneering work of William Fortenbaugh.[12] It is not that the ancient writers wholly neglected expression; a chapter in the *Problemata* attributed to Aristotle, for example, has been characterized as providing 'a list of the symptoms of fear in man that rivals in extent that found in Darwin or any other modern writer',[13] and ancient treatises on physiognomy stressed the importance of the eyes and other facial features in identifying human character traits, including emotional dispositions.[14] But expression, like internal physiological alterations such as respiration or the flow of blood round the heart, was normally secondary to cognitive processes in classical discussions of the passions, and nowhere more so than in the case of pity.

A number of modern theories – perhaps the majority – maintain that emotions are processes. Typically, they begin with a stimulus (usually an event in the outside world), and end in a response, which may be an instinctive expression of the sort Darwin and Ekman have investigated but may also take the form of an action, most often conscious and deliberate. As Joseph LeDoux puts it (1996: 127): 'At the neural level, each emotional unit can be thought of as consisting of a set of inputs, an appraisal mechanism, and a set of outputs.' One commentator offers a sequence of five components that are constitutive of an emotion: '(1) *objects, causes, precipitating events*, (2) *appraisal*, (3) *physiological changes*, (4) *action tendencies / action / expression*, and (5) *regulation*.'[15] Keith Oatley (1992: 22, summarizing Frijda 1986) provides a somewhat different formula in a schematic diagram: 'event coding → appraisal → significance evaluation → action readiness → action.' Between the stimulus and the overt reaction lies the difficult part, namely what goes on in the organism that experiences the emotion. An organism encounters an object and reacts in a way that we perceive as emotional (we have yet to define just what constitutes it as such): what happens between the initial perception and the final response?

A sophisticated, though still controversial, analysis of one emotion, namely fear, has been offered by Joseph LeDoux on the basis of neurological evidence for the functioning of the brain. LeDoux recognizes that emotions have an important cognitive dimension: 'subjective emotional states, like all other states of consciousness,

Introduction: Pity as an Emotion

are best viewed as the end result of information processing occurring unconsciously' (37; cf. 268). But information is of two kinds, and each follows its own neural pathway: 'The perceptual representation of an object and the evaluation of an object are separately processed in the brain .... It is, indeed, possible for your brain to know that something is good or bad before it knows exactly what it is' (69). More particularly, 'a fear reaction system ... involves parallel transmission to the amygdala from the sensory thalamus and sensory cortex. The subcortical pathways provide a crude image of the external world, whereas more detailed and accurate representations come from the cortex' (165). LeDoux offers (284) as an illustration of the process our reaction to the sight of a snake-like object on the ground: we recoil instantly, and only afterwards discriminate whether the stimulus was truly a live and dangerous serpent rather than what we know to be a harmless variety or even a stick. At this stage, we moderate or control our original response; as LeDoux puts it: 'One of the reasons that cognition is so useful a part of the mental arsenal is that it allows this shift from *reaction* to *action*' (175).[16]

It is not implausible that the kinds of stimuli that evoke pity also travel by diverse pathways to the brain, where they reunite to form the complex response that we identify as the emotion. The sight of human suffering might, for example, cause us spontaneously to wince or avert our eyes, while only subsequently do we recognize that the condition is undeserved and worthy of efforts to ameliorate it. Seneca, in his treatise on anger, distinguished between protoemotions (*propatheiai*), which are involuntary responses such as a shiver, and emotions proper, which can be 'stopped or altered by our rational powers if we consciously suspend the process and apply critical scrutiny to the presentation which sets it in motion' (Inwood 1993: 176; cf. Schiesaro 1997: 105-6; Sorabji 2000: 66-75). If pity should turn out to involve an initial aversive reaction followed (and revised) by assessments processed in the higher cognitive centres of the brain, it might help to explain why pity was classified as a painful emotion by Greek thinkers, and even why Aristotle connected it with fear (for the latter, see Appendix). Again, it might account for the paradoxical association between pity and contempt or even disgust, and how it may happen that 'disgust overwhelms

11

pity' (cf. Miller 1997: 8-9, 32; Hume 1906: 381). Of course, it cannot be assumed that the Greeks and Romans saw the same affinity between pity and contempt. Aristotle held that we feel pity for those who are similar to ourselves, albeit less fortunate, and Robert Solomon (1993: 207) concurs: 'It is true, of course, that one can pity another only when he or she (or perhaps, it) is in a sorry state while one is himself in a relatively satisfactory state. But this judgment of fortune and misfortune is possible only within the framework of a more general judgment to the effect that the parties are of equal stature.' Nevertheless, many scholars hold that the beneficiaries of Julius Caesar's clemency – to take one example – considered themselves demeaned by it, on the grounds that clemency is extended *de haut en bas*. Whether this is so can be decided only by a careful examination of the evidence (see Chapter 3).

If avoidance or revulsion is indeed a primitive response to suffering in others, which is overridden by higher cognitive assessments in the production of pity as an emotion, instinctive sympathy or empathy may in turn enable an unreflective participation in the pain (or joy) of another. This view has a distinguished pedigree in the theories of David Hume, Adam Smith, Jean-Jacques Rousseau, and Arthur Schopenhauer, for example, where the terms for sympathy and pity are not always sharply distinguished. Thus, Edmund Burke affirms that 'sympathy must be considered as a sort of substitution, by which we are put into the place of another man, and affected in many respects as he is affected'.[17] Hume, in turn, contends that the thought of another's passion may acquire 'such a degree of force and vivacity, as to become the very passion itself' (*A Treatise of Human Nature* 1906 [orig. 1739-40]: 317, cited in Árdal 1966: 43). He goes on to argue (369) that it is 'easy to explain the passion of *pity* from the preceding reasoning concerning sympathy. We have a lively idea of everything related to us. All human creatures are related to us by resemblance. Their persons, therefore, their interests, their passions, their pains and pleasures must strike upon us in a lively manner, and produce an emotion similar to the original one .... If this be true in general, it must be more so of affliction and sorrow. These have always a stronger and more lasting influence than any pleasure or enjoyment.'

Introduction: Pity as an Emotion

The weakness in relating pity so closely to sympathy (in Hume's sense of the term) is that pity does not in fact require that we experience an emotion identical to that of the pitied. As Árdal remarks (1966: 55): 'We may pity a justifiably jealous husband, without being ourselves jealous'; pity is one emotion, the grief or despair of the sufferer is another. But perhaps Hume meant that we share the pain involved in another's jealousy without experiencing the complete emotion, a distinction that is relevant to Aristotle's conception, not of pity, but of compassion (see Chapter 2).

For philosophers in the tradition represented by Hume and Smith, sympathy bridged what was perceived as an otherwise absolute distance between isolated selves, given that human consciousness was understood to contain nothing but what is given by the senses. As Schopenhauer explains, 'everyone is given to himself *directly*, but the rest are given to him only *indirectly* through their representation in his head' (1995 [orig. 1840]: 132). How, then, do I come to care for or even understand the affliction of another person? Only if, according to Schopenhauer, 'in the case of his *woe* as such, I suffer directly with him, I feel *his* woe just as I ordinarily feel only my own .... But this requires that I am in some way *identified with him*, in other words, that this entire *difference* between me and everyone else, which is the very basis of my egoism, is eliminated, to a certain extent at least' (143-4). The name Schopenhauer gives to this radical identification is sympathy or compassion (*Mitleid*). Though it is, for Schopenhauer, the basis of morality, it precedes evaluations of desert, in this respect differing radically from Aristotle's definition, which stipulates that pity or *eleos* is elicited only by undeserved misfortune (see Chapter 1 and Appendix). There also exist in ancient Greek words that are morphologically analogous to sympathy and *Mitleid*, in that they too are compounds beginning with a prefix meaning 'with' (*sun-* in Greek, which yields the 'sym-' in 'sympathy'; cf. the Latin *con-* or *com-* in *compassio*, a term introduced into Latin by Christian writers); while these terms did not entail moral judgment in the way that pity commonly did, they were generally limited, as we shall see (Chapter 2), to relations between intimate friends or relatives. Neither they nor pity, however, were exploited to address what in modern philosophy is known as the problem of other minds – an issue with which Greek thinkers were not deeply preoccupied.

Max Scheler, in his great phenomenological investigation into sympathy, discriminated the several ways in which two people are said to experience the same emotion. They may simply respond identically but independently to the same situation, as when siblings learn of a parent's death; this is what Sally Planalp (1999: 61) calls 'emotional coincidence'. Sometimes, an expressed emotion is infectious or contagious, like laughter even when we haven't heard the joke (Scheler 1954 [orig. 1923]: 14; Planalp 1999: 62); as Horace puts it (*Art of Poetry* 101-2), 'the human face weeps with those who are weeping and laughs with those who are laughing'. Infants are known to experience distress at the sound of other children crying, whether through 'motor mimicry' (the imitation of expression) or 'reflexive crying', which depends on other kinds of cues (Hoffman 1978: 230). Animals too have an empathic capacity, which some researchers ascribe to the so-called 'reptile brain', a primitive part of our triune cerebrum: 'The reptile brain, capable of reading the world and altering internal physiology to meet changing conditions, contains the germ of emotion .... A mammal can detect the internal state of another mammal and adjust its own physiology to match the situation – a change in turn sensed by the other, who likewise adjusts' (Lewis, Amini and Lannon 2000: 63). But this is not pity; indeed, Seneca already distinguished mimetic reactions to laughter or sadness from true emotions (*On Anger* 2.2.4-5).

Whatever the case with animals or neonates, developmental psychologists indicate that very young children are capable of empathy or 'the ability to feel the emotions of another' and are said to manifest a 'visceral understanding of' another's plight (Denham 1998: 32, 33). Such responses take two forms: 'sympathetic reactions to another person's distress and personal distress reactions'; in the latter, a child experiences discomfort at the sight of a companion's suffering, and, attentive to its own affect, may panic or run away, whereas children who feel sympathy 'are likely to behave prosocially', that is, be helpful. Although the grounds of this distinction are not entirely perspicuous, it suggests the twin impulses of aversion and commiseration that give pity its complex character. 'There

Introduction: Pity as an Emotion

are two kinds of pity,' wrote Stefan Zweig (1982: vi). 'One, the weak and sentimental kind, which is really no more than the heart's impatience to be rid as quickly as possible of the painful emotion aroused by the sight of another's unhappiness ...; and the other, the only kind that counts, the unsentimental but creative kind, which knows what it is about and is determined to hold out, in patience and forbearance, to the very limit of its strength and even beyond.'

Over and above reactions to instinctive cues such as smiles or tears, more advanced children can respond to the suffering of others by identifying imaginatively with their situation (cf. Scheler 1954 [orig. 1923]: 39-41). 'Empathy occurs when you see the situation from the other person's point of view, leading you to feel the other person's feelings' (Planalp 1999: 64) – but at a certain distance: 'you may empathize with someone else's embarrassment ..., but you know that you are identifying with his emotions. You are not feeling them directly yourself. You feel his embarrassment, but he is the one who is making a fool of himself' (ibid.). Planalp gives the name of sympathy to the final stage in the differentiation of self from other in emotional commmunication: 'Whereas empathy is feeling *with* another person ..., sympathy is feeling *about* another person's situation' (66).[18] Thus one may 'empathize with someone who has brought on her own sorrows (you feel her sorrow), but you may have no sympathy for her (her situation does not justify sorrow in you)'. With this last proviso concerning merit or desert, Planalp's definition of sympathy approaches the Aristotelian view of pity (the term 'pity' is avoided in modern studies of behaviour, doubtless for its suggestion of superiority or haughtiness), which for its part too posits a distance, rather than identification, between the pitier and the pitied; Aristotle, as we shall see (Chapter 2), goes so far as to deny that pity obtains among close kin.

Psychological research on sympathy has been largely concerned to determine how and when mature social behaviour emerges in children, with a view to the clinical treatment of empathic deficiencies in teenagers and adults. Instinctive responses to distress are a precondition for emotions proper, such as sympathy in Planalp's sense, which depends upon a rich understanding of suffering and responsibility. Adult emotion, then, is a learned capacity, and accordingly exhibits considerable variation across cultures. As Hildred Geertz (1959: 225) observes: 'The range and quality of emotional experience is potentially the same for all human beings .... In the course of the growth of a given person, this potential range of emotional experience becomes narrowed, and out of it certain qualitative aspects are socially selected, elaborated, and emphasized' (for an overview of biology versus culture in the formation of emotions, cf. McNeal 1999; Hinton 1999b). It has fallen to anthropologists and sociologists to investigate the interaction between emotion and social structure.

Within a given population, emotions are typically associated with particular social roles. There are conventions that determine who may express anger and who not, who is the subject of pity and who the object, and these positions reflect relations of power. As Planalp puts it (1999: 147): 'Power and status are especially important and may be the real forces underlying emotional expectations based on sex, age, race and occupation. In general, greater power and higher status tend to give people more emotional freedom.' Nicolas Malebranche, a neo-Cartesian philosopher of the seventeenth century, observed that while the expression of some passions has a mimetic effect, one person's fear inducing fear in another, others engender a complementary response: 'It is necessary ... to be humble and timid ... when one is in the presence of a person of high rank, or of a proud and powerful man. For it is almost always advantageous to the body's welfare if the imagination submits in the face of sensible *grandeur*.'[19]

In the novel composed in the second or third century AD by Achilles Tatius, the heroine, who has been kidnapped and sold into slavery, falls at the knees of her owner and pleads (5.17.3): 'Pity me, mistress, woman to woman – a free woman by birth, but now a slave at Fortune's whim' (cf. Dionysius of Halicarnassus *Roman Antiquities* 8.40.3). In a fine paper, Denise McCoskey (1998) contrasts this episode with the American slave Harriet Jacobs' autobiographical account of her relationship to her vindictive mistress, Mrs Flint: 'Yet I, whom she detested so bitterly, had far more pity for her than [her husband] had.'[20] McCoskey suggests that, whereas 'Mrs Flint vio-

Introduction: Pity as an Emotion

lently denies any similarity to Harriet' (36), in the Greek novel 'the unity of gender proves to outweigh any class distinctions' (35-6). We ought not to overlook, however, the heroine's claim to have been born free: anyone in classical antiquity might, by a turn of chance, end up a slave, and the young woman is both appealing to the commonplace that vulnerability to like misfortune is a condition for pity and asserting her status by birth.[21] As McCoskey notes, Clytemnestra recognizes no such bond of gender between herself and the slave Cassandra in Aeschylus' *Oresteia* – but then Cassandra was Trojan, not Greek. Similarity as a condition for pity might work to exclude certain classes from the circle of fellow feeling. For example, pity in no way inhibited the torture of slaves as the obligatory condition for their giving evidence in court (further discussion in Chapter 4).

The defeated and defenceless were always potential objects of pity, but women and children, along with the aged, were deemed to be especially deserving of it because they were considered weak by nature (cf. Lucretius 5.1017-23; Appian *Mithridatic War* 148; Josephus *Jewish Antiquities* 2.26, 14.480; *Jewish War* 1.352, 2.496; on orphans, 1.556, 560). Pliny, in his *Natural History* (8.48), explains that 'the lion alone among wild animals exhibits clemency toward suppliants: it spares those that are laid low and, when it is raging, roars at men rather than at women, and never at children unless driven by great hunger' (cf. Seneca *On Clemency* 1.5.5). In this way, social practice is projected onto nature.

A radical version of the social interpretation of emotions treats emotion entirely as a function of social position; one theorist, for example, describes anger as 'a socially constituted syndrome – a transitory social role, so to speak' (Averill 1982: viii; cf. 6, 30, 33, 66, 315; Oatley 1992: 208; for an overview, see Gergen 1985; Hinton 1999a: 8-9). Emotions may be assigned the further purpose of disposing people 'to behave in such ways as to confirm the judgment of our society', that is, its 'cultural prescriptions, proscriptions, attitudes and values' (Scruton 1986: 27; cf. Armon-Jones 1986). Don Fowler was certainly being over-optimistic when he remarked (1997: 17) that 'we are all constructionists now', but few deny that the more complex emotions, at least, are constituted as much by culture as by biology.

It is circular, of course, to argue that emotions are evaluative in nature and hence particularly subject to social determination when one has excluded in advance from the category of emotion responses that are not evaluative, but there is nothing wrong with singling out for investigation the group of emotions that depend essentially on judgment – and these may turn out to include almost all the usual candidates (despite Griffiths' doubts). In any case, we have seen that Greek and Roman theorists were inclined to focus on the cognitive aspect of emotion, in part because they tended to study the passions in relation to rhetoric and persuasion, which involve arousing and subduing emotion in others by means of argument rather than physical stimuli. In addition, the forensic context naturally encouraged attention to the relationship between emotion and merit or justice. Pity figures importantly in the rhetorical tracts, and I shall refer regularly to Aristotle's penetrating discussion of pity in his *Rhetoric*, which set the terms for subsequent technical treatments in classical antiquity (a detailed treatment of Aristotle's view may be found in the Appendix).

It is well to keep in mind, however, that different purposes may motivate distinct kinds of analysis: the aim of a treatise on public oratory is not that of a manual of child psychology, a national history, or an epic poem, and the constraints of discipline and genre may explain divergences in the way pity or compassion is treated, whether in classical antiquity or modern times. Indeed, Aristotle's emphasis on the evaluative component of pity and the role of desert may have slighted a different sense of pity, also current in Greek thought, as an elementary response to suffering or misfortune as such (and thus closer to Planalp's 'empathy').[22] Aristotle himself points to this tension when he observes that pity has two opposites, envy and indignation (the significance of this is discussed in Chapter 1), and he begins the *Rhetoric* with a swipe at the uncritical side of emotion, remarking that 'one ought not to warp a juror by leading him to anger or envy or pity' (1.1, 1354a24-5), for that is like bending the ruler with which one intends to measure something. The possible interplay between two diverse notions of pity has a bearing on an ancient debate concerning the role of pity in historiography (see Chapter 3). Moreover, it provides a salutary illustration of why Griffiths' proposal to split the concept of emotion, whatever its value

Introduction: Pity as an Emotion

in experimental psychology, may hinder the work of interpretation if it causes us to ignore the way multiple meanings inhabit the Greek and Latin emotional lexicon as well as our own, not least in regard to pity.

The approach of the present study is historical, but it is worth mentioning that a historical view of the emotions is not the same as a teleological or progressivist view. Particularly in the case of emotions such as pity and compassion, which occupy a central place in Christian thought, we ought to be on guard against assuming in advance that a primitive selfishness gradually gave way to a more universal and ethical ideal of human sympathy. The notion of divine compassion has a particular salience in the Jewish Bible and in the Christian New Testament that emerged in the context of Jewish theology (and subsequently in Islam), and this tradition intersected in productive ways with the rather different conception of the role of pity current among pagan intellectuals (see Chapter 4). But this amalgam did not necessarily represent a psychological or moral advance. In an article entitled 'The Discovery of Pity' (1936), Francis Burgess affirmed that 'in scanning the chronicles of the progress of mankind over the centuries one can see how, with frequent failures, set-backs, and discouragements, the reign of law and of that greater influence, pity for the less fortunate and the weak, have gradually and assuredly strengthened ... at least', Burgess adds, 'among the men and women of our own race' (282, 286). While such ameliorist views are less frequently expressed in scholarly literature today, at least in so bald and partial a manner, they remain a staple of popular and even learned opinion.

The relatively new area of research on the history of manners, for example, may be seen as a variation on the progressivist model. Norbert Elias located the origins of modern ideals of control over emotional expression in the shift from the relative autonomy of feudal lords to the courtly society that emerged under absolute monarchs, above all in seventeenth- and eighteenth-century France (Elias 1983, 1994; cf. Hirschman 1997 for the transformation of passions into interests as a mark of modern civilization). Whatever the merits of Elias' analysis for this specific period, to which he devoted his most exact research, it should not be taken as a general model of human development from an initially uninhibited display of emotionality to the stiff upper lip endorsed by Victorian public etiquette, especially for males.[23] It is true that Homeric heroes are given to copious weeping under the influence of grief, anger, or indeed pity, and there is a temptation to set the tears of Achilles against the impassive reaction to misfortune that is sometimes taken today to be a sign of virile restraint.[24] After the Serbian accord with NATO, Mirlan Petrovic, a colonel in the Serbian police force, replied to a reporter's question concerning his feelings at abandoning Kosovo: 'I am a professional and I don't have emotions. If you want to know about emotions, ask bishop Artemio.'[25] But emotion too is governed by protocols that are grounded in rational values and beliefs. Stephen White (1998: 140) observes of mediaeval social etiquette: 'More than an emotional response to a past political act, a display of anger also involves a quasi-juridical appraisal of the act and of the person or persons deemed responsible for it.' Under appropriate conditions, a show of emotion was not so much spontaneous as obligatory. For what it is worth, it has also been argued that in classical Athens, as opposed to the world of Homer, open weeping, particularly by men, had already come to be frowned upon (van Wees 1998), and that norms for the display of grief at funerals differed for men and women (Stears 1998: 120-1).

Following Elias, H.P. Dreitzel (1981: 211) affirms confidently that, in regard to nudity, sex, excretion and eating, 'the European historical development over many centuries points in the same direction: towards a greater distance from our "animal" nature'. What is more, he adds: 'The same can be said about the direct expression of emotions.' He offers as a case in point the 'sudden outbreaks of aggressive emotions' in the Middle Ages, 'which are unknown today or else understood in pathological terms' (213), and illustrates the change in attitude with reference to the treatment of animals: 'during the sixteenth and seventeenth centuries it was a popular custom in Paris on the occasion of street festivals to look at the spectacle of a large heap of cats caught in a net being burned alive. Characteristically, in our days we have to go to countries on the periphery of Western culture to experience a spectacle even vaguely similar: bullfights and cock-matches may be mentioned

Introduction: Pity as an Emotion

here.' Now, the idea that modern Spain is marginal to 'Western culture' betrays a curious perspective on the history of Europe. One will have to drive classical Athens as well to the edges of the 'Western' tradition on Dreitzel's view, since cock-fighting was a popular sport there (particularly, perhaps, among the aristocracy).[26] Moreover, if one includes strictly human spectacles, the sport of boxing seems considerably more violent and aggressive than the bullfight. But Dreitzel's argument is instructive for revealing the uncritical association between incremental restraint in the expression of emotion and compassion in the public sphere.

There is also an alternative story about pity, according to which it is more characteristic of simple than of complex societies. Rousseau, in the *Discourse on the Origin and Foundation of Inequality among Mankind* (1967 [orig. 1754]: 203), asserted that 'commiseration must be so much the more energetic, the more intimately the animal, that beholds any kind of distress, identifies himself with the animal that labours under it. Now it is evident that this identification must have been infinitely more perfect in the state of nature, than in the state of reason.' Nor is this view wholly extinct. Writing of the Pintupi Aborigines in the Western Desert of Australia, Fred Myers (1980: 357) observes: 'few of the accounts about Aborigines illustrate cruelty or torture; many are the accounts of their kindness to unfortunate Europeans. "Compassion" or "pity" seems a highly adaptive quality among people whose resources are somewhat unreliable. Men told me they would never send visitors away from their own waterholes in time of drought. Such action was unthinkable: "We would feel compassion for them." ' I do not doubt the description of the Pintupi, but I would question whether scarcity inevitably inspires generosity or a sense of fellow feeling.

Recently, there has been considerable discussion about the capacity for compassion in the modern world, often informed by political agendas that look to harnessing or mobilizing what is considered to be a socially useful emotion when practised by individuals as opposed to governments (again, the word pity is eschewed in these controversies). Marvin Olasky's *Renewing American Compassion*, which has a foreword by the conservative United States congressman Newt Gingrich, explains that 'Sermons for several hundred years equated compassion with personal involvement that demanded firm standards of conduct among recipients of aid' (1996: 35-6), and recommends a return to personal beneficence in place of state welfare programs. While he was Leader of the Social Democratic Party in Great Britain, David Owen wrote *A Future that Will Work: Competitiveness and Compassion* with a view to encouraging greater voluntary efforts to assist the needy (1984: 122). On the other hand, it has been argued that volunteer work may have 'the effect of placing limits on charitable feelings, assigning clear roles to be fulfilled, and so protecting people from being made unbearably miserable by the misery they see' (Zeldin 1994: 249; cf. Wuthnow 1991: 194-9).

An excess of pity may take the form of a generalized melancholy over the state of things: *Weltschmerz* is a pathology of compassion, just as undirected or free-floating anxiety is of fear. Anxiety is sometimes explained as a symptom of repressed or displaced fear; repressed pity does not seem to have excited the interest of psychoanalysis, although Zeldin (1994: 243) maintains that 'Since the world began, compassion has been the most frustrated of emotions, more so than sex.' Alternatively, overexposure to suffering, for example as a consequence of media coverage, has been thought to induce 'compassion fatigue' (Moeller 1999). But perhaps pity and compassion are extinguished not at the continual sight of misfortune as such but rather through despairing of our ability to ameliorate it. The narrator in Herman Melville's 'Bartleby the Scrivener' meditates:

> My first emotions had been those of pure melancholy and sincerest pity; but just in proportion as the forlornness of Bartleby grew and grew to my imagination, did that same melancholy merge into fear, that pity into repulsion. So true it is, and so terrible too, that up to a certain point the thought or sight of misery enlists our best affections; but, in certain special cases, beyond that point it does not. They err who would assert that invariably this is owing to the inherent selfishness of the human heart. It rather proceeds from a

certain hopelessness of remedying excessive and organic ill (cited in North 1999: 29).

For pity to be excited, it must have a reasonable chance of achieving its purpose; otherwise it is paralysed or dissipated.

Although I shall touch on it only in passing, the ancients too were conscious of what we may call the dynamics of pity. Cicero quotes an adage in connection with the danger of overplaying the appeal to a jury's pity: 'nothing dries more quickly than a tear' (*On Invention* 1.109). Quintus Curtius (first century AD) describes a pathetic scene in his history of Alexander the Great, in which a band of four thousand Greeks who had been mutilated by the Persians ponder whether to return to Greece or settle where they are. Euctemon of Cyme argues against going home: 'those who place high hopes in the pity of their kinfolk are ignorant of how quickly tears dry up; no one faithfully loves one who disgusts him, for disaster is piteous and happiness is proud' (5.5.11-12). The Athenian Theaetetus replies, however, that 'he deserves every sort of evil who blushes at an involuntary one; for he bears a sad opinion of mankind and despairs of pity because he himself would deny it to another'.

The ancient Greeks and Romans were capable of great cruelty. Judicial torture, which was obligatory, as we have noted, for evidence given by slaves in classical Athens and imperial Rome, seems to testify to a profound failure of compassion in regard to the suffering of fellow human beings, comparable to the brutal punishments meted out to slaves in the United States prior to emancipation, and to lynchings afterwards. The extermination or enslavement of entire populations in the course of war was sufficiently commonplace to be recorded without remark by ancient historians (see Chapter 3). At the same time, as we shall see, Greeks and Romans took pride in their capacity for pity and their humanity toward the vanquished or afflicted. In what follows, I do not attempt to award merit points to the ancients for the quality of their mercy, nor to tot up examples of exceptional behaviour in regard to cruelty or compassion. For one thing, our evidence is too patchy to warrant confidence in the statistics that a survey of the sources, which are mainly anecdotal, might furnish. Besides, in reviewing so broad and varied a period in cultural history as classical antiquity, one must expect a wide range of local variation which can, at this distance, scarcely be documented (were Thebans more merciful than Athenians? Egyptians than Romans?). Finally, such comparisons presuppose that we can measure ancient and modern pity and its contexts with a common yardstick. This is a legitimate ambition for some purposes – it is sometimes right to condemn practices that are customary in other cultures but not our own – but it is not the primary aim of a historical investigation, which is to appreciate how other peoples' ways of life differ from our own.

If this book is historical, however, it is not a conventional history. It respects chronology, but it does not straightforwardly follow the transmutations in the idea of pity or compassion from their earliest mentions in the Homeric epics to their manifestation in late antiquity, when they are transformed by the Christianization of the Roman Empire. In part, this is to avoid giving the impression of an evolution from a primitive to a more advanced stage in moral awareness over the course of classical civilization. In part, too, it is because the idea of pity did not develop or change in a uniform way. Pity, as I have said, was and remains a complex concept, and it sometimes underwent an alteration in one sphere, such as politics or judicial practice, without a corresponding change in others, for example in relation to slaves or children. Nor do I imagine that I have captured every dimension of ancient pity within these pages. Some aspects have simply escaped me; others have proved recalcitrant to systematic research. A standard historical format might have conveyed the impression that the present effort is exhaustive, and that I have succeeded in adequately tracing the trajectory of so subtle and labile a concept as pity in classical antiquity.

Rather, the chapters that follow offer a series of soundings, in which instances of pity and compassion are examined in various contexts, always with a view, consistent with the intention of the Classical Inter/Faces series, to seeing how a comparison of modern and ancient attitudes may be illuminating for the understanding of both. I begin with a consideration of appeals to pity in courts of law, in an effort to understand why the ancient practice of appealing to the pity of the judge or jury, which was endorsed by every handbook

Introduction: Pity as an Emotion

of rhetoric, differs so radically – to all appearances – from modern judicial procedure. In the next chapter, I examine the scope or range of pity: whether pity depends on an intimate identification with another person or, on the contrary, entails a certain distance between the pitier and the pitied. I then look to the relationship between pity and power, especially in the context of war; here, I inquire into the kinds of circumstances that elicit pity, and ask to what extent pity can serve, or did serve, to ameliorate the suffering and dependency of others. Finally, I turn to the issue of divine pity, and consider whether pity is possible on the part of a being so superior to his fellows, or so perfect, as to be invulnerable to mortal suffering. In the Appendix, which is more narrowly philosophical in character, I investigate in detail the text that has, in many ways, served as my point of departure for the study of every aspect of Greek and Roman pity, namely, Aristotle's treatment of this passion in the *Rhetoric*. Here, I raise the question of just what it is about pity that qualifies it, in Aristotle's view, for inclusion among the list of *pathê* or emotions, and indicate how Aristotle's analysis differs from modern treatments.

In the course of these chapters, I touch upon a variety of other topics associated with the idea of pity. Among these are the role of merit or desert in the construction of the emotions, and hence the relationship between pity and justice; the possibility of self-pity and the connection between pity and the gaze or the position of observer; the correlation – if there is one – between democracy and pity on the one hand, and slavery and pity on the other (the two issues are not wholly independent); whether there is pity for the dead; pity as a response to literature, especially tragedy, and the question of literary identification; the relationship between pity and clemency; pity as a basis for charity; and so forth. Various kinds of texts are exploited, as the subject under consideration may demand: courtroom orations, drama, histories, funerary inscriptions, philosophical and theological treatises. My object is not so much to capture the essence of pity, whether ancient or modern, as to exhibit its several facets and stimulate further reflection on this grim and subtle passion.

1

Pity and the Law

One of the more conspicuous differences between ancient and modern trial procedures is the admissibility, in the courts of classical Greece as well as Rome, of appeals to pity – the so-called *argumentum ad misericordiam*. Efforts to arouse the pity of judges or jurors were not only permitted, they were a regular and practically obligatory feature of defence speeches, and sometimes employed by plaintiffs as well; they were common enough in fifth-century BC Athens to be satirized by Aristophanes (*Wasps* 572, 975-8). Rhetorical handbooks, which generally speaking were designed for forensic oratory, went into great detail concerning the methods and tropes for inciting the jury to pity. Much the greater part of what survives of a treatise composed (it appears) by one Apsines,[1] in or about the third century AD, is devoted to this subject, and while Apsines' elaborate subdivisions are almost absurdly minute, Cicero himself, in his youthful manual *On Invention* (1.107-9), did not hesitate to list, and pedantically enumerate, no fewer than sixteen different modes or *loci* for eliciting pity. One should emphasize, Cicero advises, (1) the contrast between present evils and past goods, (2) the duration of evils, (3) the many kinds of loss incurred, and (4) their squalid and ignoble character; above all, (5) one must make them visible to the eye, as though one were at the scene itself, and not just hearing about it. It is good also (6) to note that the reversal of fortune was unexpected, (7) to remind the jurors that they too have children, etc., (8) to mention the offices, such as proper burial, that one was prevented from performing, (9) to apostrophize inanimate items, (10) remark on one's weakness or isolation, (11) commend one's burial to the jurors, (12) deplore the loss of dear ones, (13) note the ingratitude of those who did the harm, (14) assume a suitably humble demeanour, (15) show that one's complaint is more at the fate of others than one's own, and finally (16) indicate that one has pitied others, and is bearing one's own misfortune nobly. 'For often,' Cicero concludes, 'courage and high-mindedness, which bespeak seriousness and authority, avail more in arousing pity than humbleness and pleading.' One ought not, in any case, to dwell too long on stirring up the jurors' emotions, for 'nothing dries more quickly than a tear' (Cicero ascribes the aphorism to the rhetor Apollonius).

Aristotle, of course, had already treated the techniques for rousing pity in the second book of his *Rhetoric*, where he takes up the topic of the emotions, and Aristotle himself reports that the subject had long since been a favourite with writers on rhetoric; the so-called *Eleoi*, or 'Pities', attributed to the sophist Thrasymachus, was very likely a collection of practical examples.[2]

In the modern courtroom, on the contrary, such appeals to emotion are not only suspect, they are normally prohibited. In the United States, Rule 403 in the Federal Rules of Evidence, which falls under Article IV: 'Relevancy and its Limits', concerns the 'Exclusion of Relevant Evidence on Grounds of Prejudice, Confusion, or Waste of Time'. In their commentary on this rule, Stephen A. Salzburg, Daniel J. Capra and Michael M. Martin explain: 'Evidence is not "prejudicial" merely because it is harmful to the adversary. After all, if it didn't harm the adversary, it wouldn't be relevant in the first place. Rather, the Rule refers to the negative consequence of "unfair" prejudice. Unfair prejudice is that which could lead the jury to make an emotional or irrational decision, or to use the evidence in a manner not permitted by the rules of evidence.' The assumption is that an emotional judgment is inadmissible in a trial because it impedes jurors from arriving at impartial conclusions concerning fact on the basis of the evidence itself.[3] Even relevant evidence may induce an emotional response in jurors, and may, for this reason, be excluded under Rule 403. To be sure, the exclusion of evidence that is germane is a measure of last resort, and in order to overcome the presumption in favour of its admission, 'the negative countervailing factors must be demonstrably greater than the probative value of the evidence'.

The emotions in general, and pity in particular, have long been assumed to serve only as a distraction from rational argument, and

1. Pity and the Law

to dispose a jury to draw erroneous conclusions from the evidence.[4] As Douglas Walton (1997: 1) writes in his book devoted to this kind of argument: 'The *argumentum ad misericordiam*, or appeal to pity, is standardly listed as one of the fallacies in twentieth-century logic textbooks.' Walton illustrates this tendency by citing, among other sources, a textbook entitled *How to Argue: An Introduction to Logical Thinking* (Crossley and Wilson 1979: 40), where the appeal to pity or, as the authors parse it, 'playing on your feelings', is described as 'a technique for bypassing one's thinking abilities'. Insofar as the *argumentum ad misericordiam* names a specific logical fallacy, its salient feature, according to Walton (2), is generally reducible to lack of relevance.[5]

Scholars have explained the apparent difference between ancient and modern legal practice in regard to appeals to pity in two ways. On the one hand, Greek and Roman jurisprudence is charged with exhibiting a far more generous attitude toward irrelevancy and outright fallacy in argument than is tolerated in the modern courtroom. Thus, the comment in an excellent recent manual of Greek history (Pomeroy et al. 1999: 345): 'Though rules of time were stringently observed, rules of evidence were few, and defendants themselves were not discouraged from speechifying about their past services to the polis or from parading their vulnerable children before the jury.' On the other hand, the rejection of emotional appeals in modern legal practice is sometimes criticized as unduly restrictive, and some scholars have defended the emotions as having an important and respectable role in the formation of judgments. On this view, ancient styles of argument are held to be compatible with modern strictures on argument or even downright superior, insofar as they enable a better appreciation of all the circumstances relating to a specific case (cf. Stocker 1996: 93, citing Brennan 1988: 17). The recent victims' rights movement in the United States, for example, has supported a constitutional amendment that 'would give such victims the right to notice and to attendance at all public proceedings "relating to the crime" and ... to be heard and to submit written statements at proceedings involving release from custody, acceptance of a plea bargain, or sentencing', among other entitlements (Henderson 1998: 588). Others have argued for 'reconstructing the role of the judge as an empathic, contextually sensitive, and compassionate individual who immerses [him/herself] in the stories of others'.[6]

In what follows, I take a different approach to understanding the role that appeals to pity played in ancient forensic oratory. Before comparisons are drawn between classical and modern views, it is wise to determine the extent to which the central terms under discussion are in fact analogous. An examination of the meaning of the Greek term *eleos* and its Latin equivalent, *misericordia*, suggests that, while they may in many instances reasonably be translated as 'pity', they have a penumbra of associations that are missed by the modern English word, and which, when taken into account, alter the picture we might otherwise form of appeals to this emotion in the Greek and Roman contexts. In this connection, I consider also the significance of certain related ideas, including *sungnômê*, which is commonly rendered as 'pardon' or 'forgiveness', although expressions such as 'indulgence' are also found in cases where 'pardon' is manifestly inappropriate, and *metameleia*, which is translated variously as 'regret', 'repentance', and 'remorse'. These issues will take us to the heart of how moral categories function in ancient argumentation.

When, in modern treatments, the arousal of pity is regarded as an inappropriate form of argument at law, it is because it is assumed that judgments based on pity are in principle indifferent to the issue of guilt or innocence. A jury may be moved to acquit a person who, on a rational review of the evidence, would be deemed guilty, if it is induced to dwell, for example, on the unfortunate childhood of the defendant, or to take into account other pitiable or mitigating conditions. Contrariwise, pity for a plaintiff who has been the victim of a particularly violent assault may dispose a jury to convict the accused, even where the evidence might have appeared insufficient on a rigorously logical examination. But classical definitions of pity almost invariably treat the question of desert as being of central importance: it was taken for granted, as we shall see, that pity is elicited only by unmerited suffering.[7] How, then, does pity influence a judge or jury to come to a verdict that is independent of the rights and wrongs of the case?

We may perceive the different status of appeals to pity or emotion

1. Pity and the Law

then and now by considering the place accorded to them in the judicial process. In the United States, guilt or innocence in a wide variety of criminal cases is decided by a jury; the penalty, however, is assigned by the judge, in accord with sentencing guidelines that were generally quite flexible, although since 1986, when federal sentencing guidelines were drawn up, maximum and minimum penalties have been prescribed which judges are obliged to respect except for special reasons.[8] For some crimes, which historically have included capital crimes, a mandatory sentence is or at one time was prescribed by law. As Jeffrey L. Kirchmeier (1998: 350) explains, however, 'One problem with the mandatory death penalty was that juries, fearful that guilty but sympathetic defendants would be put to death, often would ignore the law and find such defendants not guilty.' As a result, as early as 1838, the legislature of the State of Tennessee gave juries 'discretion in capital cases once they found a defendant guilty of murder'. Other states followed suit, and in 1897 the United States Congress passed an act allowing juries in capital cases to qualify a guilty verdict by the phrase, 'without capital punishment'. By the year 1963, all states in which a death penalty could be imposed by a jury 'also gave the juries discretion to give mercy to a defendant convicted of a capital crime'.

When, a little over twenty years ago, the death penalty was reintroduced in the United States, a post-verdict phase in capital crimes, in which a jury decided on the nature of the penalty, became a regular part of capital trials.[9] Naturally, procedures for the penalty phase of a trial differ from those of the liability phase. During the liability phase, the defendant is presumed innocent, and only that evidence which is materially relevant to the question of culpability can be presented to the jury. As we have seen, even such evidence, if it is deemed likely to arouse unfair prejudice in the minds of the jurors, may be disallowed in federal courts under Rule 403. After a defendant has been convicted, however, he or she is legally guilty, and the rules of evidence are accordingly different. To take one example, Theodore Eisenberg, Stephen P. Garvey, and Martin T. Wells write: 'South Carolina's capital-sentencing scheme is like that of many other states. The capital trial is bifurcated into a guilt phase and a penalty phase. If the jury finds the presence of at least one statutory aggravating circumstance, the defendant becomes "death eligible". Having made the finding, the jury can sentence the defendant to death or life imprisonment. Finally, South Carolina law, like the law of most other states, provides the jury with a list of aggravating and mitigating circumstances to guide its sentencing decision' (Eisenberg et al. 1998: 1603).

Mitigating circumstances relate exclusively to the sentencing phase. Some of the conditions stipulated by the South Carolina statute are that the defendant 'has no significant history of prior criminal conviction' for violent offences, the defendant committed the crime when suffering from 'mental or emotional disturbance', and the defendant 'was provoked by the victim into committing murder' (ibid.: 1604). The code of the state of Virginia (sec. 19.2-264.4[B]) provides that 'Evidence which may be admissible [in the sentencing phase] ... may include the circumstances surrounding the offense, the history and background of the defendant, and any other facts in mitigation of the offense.' The Virginia Supreme Court has taken a very liberal view of the jury's latitude in recognizing mitigating circumstances. In 1899, it declared: 'How far considerations of age, sex, ignorance, illness or intoxication, of human passion or weakness, of sympathy or clemency ... should be allowed weight in deciding the question whether the accused should or should not be capitally punished, is committed by the act of Congress to the sound discretion of the jury, and of the jury alone.'

At this stage of the proceedings the question of the defendant's, or rather, the criminal's expression of remorse takes on particular salience. As Eisenberg et al. (1998) remark: 'Although South Carolina law does not list remorse as a mitigating circumstance, a capital defendant nonetheless enjoys a constitutional right to proffer in mitigation "any aspect of [his] character or record and any circumstances of the offense". Along with most, if not all, other jurisdictions, South Carolina accordingly appears to treat remorse as a mitigating factor in capital-sentencing proceedings.' Various studies have demonstrated that the appearance of remorse is a crucial factor in sentencing. Scott E. Sundby, in an article entitled 'The Intersection of Trial Strategy, Remorse, and the Death Penalty' (1998: 1560), in which he made use of the data for California drawn

1. Pity and the Law

from the Capital Jury Project ('a nationwide study of the factors that influence the decision of capital jurors on whether to impose the death penalty'), notes that 'The interviews of jurors who served on a jury that imposed a sentence of death ... strongly corroborated earlier findings that the defendant's degree of remorse significantly influences a jury's decision to impose the death penalty.' Sundby found further that 'the earlier the defendant personally expresses some type of acceptance of responsibility for the killing, the greater the likelihood that the jury will be receptive to later claims of regret' (1586). This latter factor puts at a disadvantage those defendants who insist from the beginning of the trial – that is, in the liability phase – upon their innocence, and therefore refuse to express remorse. If they are intent upon appealing the verdict, it will not be in their interest to display remorse even in the penalty phase. The situation has a certain Catch-22 quality, although that issue is beyond the scope of our concerns here. What I wish to emphasize is that remorse is relevant in the penalty phase of a trial, when it may inspire the compassion or mercy of the jury. Indeed, mercy would not be relevant before the verdict. As Malla Pollack (1998: 551) observes in a subtle paper on the incompatibility of mercy with a rights-based system of justice: 'One can only be merciful to the guilty. If guilt ends all consideration, mercy is dead.'

I wish to introduce one last point of modern law, before returning to the role of pity in the ancient forensic context. This concerns the role of pardon or clemency. Juries may exhibit compassion or mercy in the sentencing phase of a capital trial, as we have seen. Even in coming to a verdict of guilty or not guilty, juries cannot be prevented from ignoring precedent and deciding in favour of a defendant, if, for example, they deem that the law in question is inappropriate, or that the action in question is intrinsically good or beneficial. In the United States, such a judgment is described as jury nullification.[10] Douglas Cairns (personal communication 19 February 1999) informs me of a British parallel in the 'recent case concerning the civil servant, Clive Ponting, who was the source of the information that Margaret Thatcher had lied to parliament on the sinking of the Argentinian warship, the General Belgrano, during the Falklands war. Ponting did not dispute the facts, but claimed a higher duty to conscience; the judge directed the jury to convict, but they decided to acquit. In such cases, though, the prosecution retains the right to appeal.' But such an act does not constitute a pardon. Pardoning, or clemency, is exclusively in the domain of the executive rather than the judiciary branch of government. The framers of the United States Constitution regarded clemency as a prerogative, with its origins in the capacity enjoyed by the English king to 'extend his mercy on what terms he pleases'.[11] Thus, due process is not held to apply to executive clemency.

The above considerations concerning relevance of evidence, remorse and pardon are of course not automatically transferable to the conditions of ancient legal procedure, which was in many respects 'desperately foreign'.[12] As we have seen, it was customary to appeal to the pity of the jurors in the peroration of a defence speech,[13] and rhetoricians developed a whole array of devices by which to enhance the effect of such an appeal. Is petitioning for pity the same thing as a request for mercy? If it is, can one say, with Malla Pollock, that 'One can only be merciful to the guilty'? In this case, would not a defendant in a Greek or Roman court have effectively proclaimed his guilt in advance of the jury's verdict? Something is obviously amiss in this line of reasoning.

In seeking to arouse the jurors' pity, Greeks and Romans did not imagine that they were conceding guilt. Rather, as I suggested earlier, the opposite is the case: pity was generally presumed to be aroused not by the spectacle of misfortune as such, but rather by that of undeserved misfortune. To cite an early example of a formula that is repeated in one form or another throughout classical antiquity, Aristotle's definition of pity in the *Rhetoric* runs: 'Let pity, then, be a kind of pain in the case of an apparent destructive or painful harm *in one not deserving to encounter it*, which one might expect oneself, or one of one's own, to suffer, and this when it seems near' (2.8.2). Correspondingly, defendants did not seek the jury's pardon, at least not in the modern legal sense of that term; an act can be pardoned only after it is deemed a crime by a guilty verdict, not before. It is for this reason too, I believe, that there is virtually no reference to remorse in the speeches of the Greek orators. As Douglas Cairns (1999: 171-2) defines the concept, 'Remorse ... is a

1. Pity and the Law

species of regret over actions for which one considers oneself responsible, which one wishes one had not performed, and whose damage one would undo if one could.' There can be no question but that the Greeks were familiar with the idea. But, as Cairns observes (176), 'it is perhaps surprising that the topic is so scarce in the functioning legal system of Athenian democracy'. Cairns goes on to suggest some reasons why this should have been the case, among which he mentions the amateurish and adversarial nature of judicial proceedings, and the role of a large popular jury, 'which received no legal guidance' before coming to a decision. As a result, Cairns says, there was 'little incentive (indeed little opportunity) for a defendant to plead guilty, hoping that his remorse will secure a more lenient sentence'.

Cairns is broadly right about the peculiar characteristics of the classical Athenian system of justice, which was often more like a public wrangling for status among upper-class citizens bringing high-risk suits than an impartial attempt to secure justice.[14] A guilty plea, however, would not normally require a defence speech, and so it is perhaps not surprising that we do not possess transcripts of cases in which the defendant failed to contest the charge against him. Where the accused sought to affirm his innocence, it cannot have been good strategy to express remorse and thereby accept responsibility for the offence. As Aristotle puts it (*Rhetoric* 1.6, 1358b32-3), a litigant 'would never concede that he has done wrong, for if he did there would be no need for a trial'. In one respect, however, Athenian trial procedure did bear a curious resemblance to modern procedure in the United States in relation to capital crimes. That is, in a broad variety of situations, not restricted to those in which the death penalty was an option, Athenian trials were divided into two parts: a liability phase, in which the question of guilt or innocence was decided, and which resulted either in conviction or acquittal; and a penalty phase or *antitimêsis*, in which the convicted party might recommend a counter-penalty or *antitimêma* to that demanded by the prosecution, and it was up to the jury to decide between the two.[15] Surely, the latter stage is that in which one might expect to encounter expressions of remorse, and a request for the mercy of the court.

Unfortunately, there survives only a single example of an Athenian penalty-phase discourse, and that one is a free rendition, rather than a verbatim report, of the speech in question, and has also the peculiar feature that the condemned party continued to insist on his innocence, and made little effort to win the favour of the jury even at this stage of the proceedings. I am referring, of course, to Socrates' *Apology*, as transmitted to us by Plato. According to Plato, Socrates first suggested that he be rewarded for his allegedly criminal behaviour by being feted as a state hero, and only afterwards proposed a small fine in answer to the death penalty sought by his accusers; when Plato and others offered to stand surety for a larger amount, Socrates consented. Xenophon, in his *Apology* (23), denied that Socrates either consented to propose a counter-penalty or allowed his friends to offer one, 'but he actually said that to propose a counter-penalty was the part of a man who conceded that he committed an injustice'. I am not concerned here to adjudicate between the two accounts so much as to indicate that Socrates is the last person one might expect to have demonstrated signs of remorse for his behaviour, since he persisted to the end in a posture of open defiance of the verdict. This cannot have been the response of all, or even most defendants in the penalty phase.

Remorse, then, if it was expressed at all in classical Greek and Roman trials, may have been largely confined to arguments concerning sentencing, rather than the verdict proper. In this respect, ancient practice will have conformed to modern. The difference between the two is that ancient pleaders enjoyed far greater freedom to bring up in the liability phase matters of character, service to the community, and other extenuating (or aggravating) circumstances that are excluded in courts today as irrelevant to the determination of guilt, although they are allowed in the sentencing part of capital and other trials. The appeal to pity comes under this heading as well, of course; however, given the close connection between pity and desert in ancient thought, this liberty ought not to be construed merely as a device to circumvent the factual question of guilt and innocence. Rather, it was another means by which a defendant insisted on his innocence, and asked that it be recognized.

We thus return, after a longish detour, to the question of logical fallacy: if an appeal to pity was a way of summoning attention to the

1. Pity and the Law

defendant's innocence, in what respect did it depart from the kinds of reasoning that ought to enter into a judgment based on the merits of the case? We have remarked in the Introduction that the radical opposition between reason and emotion, on the basis of which pity and other feelings are frequently treated as inimical to rational evaluation, is more characteristic of modern than of classical thought, although, in the past two or three decades, philosophers as well as social scientists and psychologists have again come to appreciate the cognitive or evaluative dimension of the emotions, in this respect returning to the kind of analysis we find in Aristotle and the Stoics.[16] David Hume had already observed that passion 'must be accompanied with some false judgment, in order to its being unreasonable; and even then it is not the passion, properly speaking, which is unreasonable, but the judgment' (Hume 1906 [orig. 1739-40]: 415-16). Some scholars have argued that emotion is indeed necessary to certain kinds of reasoning, whether to focus the attention or as an efficient means for processing complex data: 'Because of our uncertain knowledge and multiple goals, many of the problems we face have no fully rational solution. Emotions are a biological solution to this problem' (Oatley 1992: 162). As vehicles of values, emotions may also be seen as preconditions to a sense of justice: 'Justice begins not with Socratic insights but with the promptings of some basic emotions, among them envy, jealousy, and resentment ..., but also, of course, those basic feelings of sharing, compassion, sympathy and generosity' (Solomon 1990: 33). When Aristotle identified the object of pity as an 'apparent destructive or painful harm in one not deserving to encounter it', he was incorporating into the definition of the emotion both values and judgments, on the basis of which one deems that the circumstances of another are miserable and unearned. Pity did not consist for Aristotle in an identification with the suffering of another irrespective of desert (for this, classical Greek had other terms; see Chapter 2); rather, it required a certain measure of detachment or distance from the pitied, which opened up a space for ethical discrimination.

Let us turn now to the consideration of some actual ancient cases, beginning with a peroration in which there is not an explicit attempt to evoke pity in the jurors. Lysias 21 is a defence speech written for the son of one Eucrates, who was accused of malfeasance in office, including the charge of having taken bribes. What survives is the concluding oration, in which the young man expatiates upon his civic-mindedness and generosity toward the city; the detailed rebuttal of the specific charges will have been made earlier, perhaps by more experienced *sunêgoroi*, that is, co-speakers in the defence (for their role in trials, see Rubinstein 2000). The defendant explains that he has never shrunk from personal hardship in the city's behalf, nor did he take pity on his own family when risking his life for his country in war. In return (*anth' hôn*), he demands *kharis* (25) of the jury, that is, grateful recognition of his services, which he insists he deserves (*axiô*), as opposed to being condemned on such charges (*toiautais aitiais* presumably means such absurd or spurious charges), which would deprive him of his property and civic rights, and send him and his children wandering penniless in foreign lands (commentary in Todd 2000). The speaker's intention is to contrast as sharply as possible what his character and history of service to the state ought to earn him with the harsh consequences of a negative verdict. He is not for a moment suggesting that he be spared on the basis of his good deeds or character, *in spite of* the wrongs he may have committed while holding public office. Rather, he is making vivid to the jury what losing his case would mean for himself and his family, precisely on the assumption that he is innocent. His object is not to ask for mercy, in the sense in which mercy presupposes guilt (cf. Ben-Ze'ev 2000: 332-3); it is to make sure that no irrelevant motive, such as personal hostility, political partisanship, or favour toward his accuser, may induce the jury to convict him, by making clear what is at stake if they do so. It is a way of charging the jury to take seriously the power at their disposal, and be certain that they do not do grave harm, as they can, on the basis of insufficient evidence, when the charges involving bribery are all the more implausible in light of his history of selfless service to the city.

Because Eucrates' son does not ask specifically for pity, his argument may seem more compatible with our ideas of relevance: he may appear simply to be reminding the jurors of their sworn duty. Let us take a glance, then, at the conclusion to another partially preserved defence speech in the Lysianic corpus (4), delivered in

1. Pity and the Law

response to a charge of a premeditated attack on a fellow-citizen. Here again, the speaker ends the presentation of his case by pointing to his previous behaviour, which, he claims, offers no reason to suppose that he would have acted violently in the instance under consideration. 'Thus I supplicate and beseech you, by your children and wives and the gods who protect this place, pity me ...; for I do not deserve [*ou gar axios*] to be exiled from my city, nor does he deserve to exact so great a penalty from me for wrongs he says he suffered, but did not' (20). Once again, there is the strongest possible affirmation of innocence, combined with a plea for pity, which is as it should be: pity is only for undeserved misfortune, not for misfortune as such. The appeal to pity is not a means of distracting the jurors from the evidence relevant to the case, but rather of enjoining them to judge in accordance with the facts and with justice, and not heedlessly impose a penalty that will cause an innocent man to suffer gravely, and thus in truth be pitiable (cf. also Lysias 7.41).

Analogously, when a defendant asks the jurors for *sungnômê*, it is not mercy, or undeserved pardon, that he is seeking, but rather a favourable disposition toward a just case. The connection with the root sense of *sungignôskô*, that is, to have the same opinion or *gnômê* as another, was not, I think, wholly lost in the classical period. Lysias 31 is an accusation, brought before the *boulê* or council of 500, against the election of a man named Philon to the council; the speech was delivered a short time after the restoration of the democracy in 403 BC. Among the charges is that Philon failed to participate in the struggle against the violent regime of the Thirty Tyrants. Those who were prevented from doing so because of some private misfortune (*sumphoras idias*, 10), the speaker says, deserve to meet with a certain *sungnômê*; but those who acted in this way *gnômêi*, that is, intentionally, are not worthy of any *sungnômê* at all, because they did what they did deliberately. *Sungnômê*, the speaker continues (11), is due only to those who, if they behave wrongly, do so involuntarily. Here, *sungnômê* is not pardon or acquittal; it is more like a shared attitude. One who acts badly from deliberate judgment, that is, *gnômê*, cannot expect to encounter a comparable disposition or *sungnômê* among upright jurors; however, in a case in which someone acts, or fails to act, for reasons such as ill health or extreme poverty, his *gnômê* may still be presumed to be correct, and one can with justice share it. To be sure, in many contexts it is preferable to render *sungnômê* as 'indulgence', or even perhaps as 'forgiveness', but in legal arguments, and in particular when a defendant appeals for the *sungnômê* of the jury, one must understand that such a plea does not entail admission of culpability. Like pity, it depends rather on the assumption of innocence.

If pity in classical antiquity was in fact closely associated with just deserts, and not conceived of as a raw emotion evoked only to disarm reason and circumvent legitimate evidence, what of the suspicions that the appeal to pity aroused among the Greeks themselves? For they too, and not just modern commentators, entertained doubts about the validity or admissibility of such pleas in court. For example, in the defence speech on behalf of Polystratus (20), attributed to Lysias but written, it appears, around 410 and thus before the beginning of Lysias' career as a logographer, Polystratus' son, defending his father against the charge of collusion with the oligarchic regime of the Four Hundred, points to his own and his brother's services to the democracy, for which he demands the recompense he deserves (*tên axian kharin*, 31; cf. 33: *axioumen heuriskesthai kharin*). 'But,' the speaker adds, 'we see you, gentlemen of the jury, when someone puts his children on the stand and weeps and laments, both pitying his children, should they lose their civic rights on his account, and dismissing the crimes of the fathers on the children's account, though you do not yet know whether they will turn out good or bad when they grow up' (34). This looks like the standard argument against the legitimacy of pity in the courtroom: that some extraneous concern, such as that for the welfare of innocent children, should have such weight with the jurors that they acquit someone who is manifestly guilty.

But the case is not so straightforward. First of all, the speaker's design is to draw a contrast between regard for young children, who may, despite their vulnerability and innocence, yet prove to be unworthy of the city's concern, and that for a man of established worth such as the speaker's own father. Thus, he has no hesitation about saying in practically the next breath, 'but rather pity both my father, who is aged, and ourselves' (35), and summing up resound-

1. Pity and the Law

ingly: 'we beg you by whatever goods you may each possess, that those with sons pity us for these, and those too who are our age-mates or our father's, pity and acquit us' (36). But if the speaker is so free in beseeching pity of the jury for himself, it is not just because his father has proved his mettle, as opposed to still infant children, but that it is just his father's commitment to the democracy, and that of the family as a whole, that is at stake in the trial. Thus, pity for both father and sons is justified, according to the speaker, precisely because they are innocent of the charges brought against them. Since this makes all the difference, the speaker sees no inconsistency in asking for it in his own behalf, right after denouncing such an appeal on the part of one who has committed an injustice.

In his attack upon the younger Alcibiades (son of the famous general) for desertion of his post, Lysias sums up the treacherous history, as he perceives it, of the entire clan and declares: 'Deem him a hereditary enemy of the city and condemn him, and do not count pity or *sungnômê* or favour (*kharis*) more than the established laws and the oaths you swore' (14.40). The point, once again, I think, is that just as the entire family, and the accused in particular, deserve no gratitude from the people because they have done them nothing but harm, so too they are not worthy that the jurors should entertain their point of view or feel pity, because of their criminal characters and deeds. It is not that the emotion of pity is being condemned as in principle irrelevant, but rather that it is, in this instance, the wrong emotion, or is misplaced; as Lysias says elsewhere (6.55): 'those who have died unjustly are worthy to be pitied, not those who have died justly' (cf. 22.21, 11.9-11, 18.1, 28.11; Isocrates *Plataïcus* 52). Thus, in the next speech, possibly written for delivery by a *sunêgoros* in the same trial (cf. Rubinstein 2000: 27), the plaintiff asserts: 'And if any one of you, gentlemen of the jury, thinks that the penalty is great and the law too harsh, you must recall that you have not come here as lawmakers on these matters, but rather to vote according to the established laws, nor to pity those who do wrong, but rather to be angry with them and to come to the aid of the entire city' (15.9). The speaker is evidently warning against the possibility of what today is called jury nullification – that is, setting the law aside because it seems excessive or otherwise inappropriate, given the overall circumstances of the case. But in admonishing the jurors to reject pity, he specifies that this is the wrong sentiment to entertain toward those who have committed an offence, for they deserve not pity but rather anger (more on this opposition in Chapter 3). The speaker is not requesting a dispassionate judgment, but one in which the jurors' emotions are the right ones in respect to the deserts of the accused. So too, Demosthenes (24.170-1 *Against Timocrates*; cf. 175-6) insists that people should hate (*misein*) rather than be gentle toward the wicked, and 'pity the weak [and presumably innocent] but not permit the strong to be insolent' – a remarkable anticipation of Anchises' famous injunction to the Romans in *Aeneid* 6.853 to 'spare the defeated and subdue the proud'.

There may have occurred to the reader the well-known passage in Plato's *Apology* in which Socrates, toward the end of his first speech, that is, in the liability phase of the trial, explains why he has decided not to bring in his children and family and plead for the pity of the court, as most other defendants do even in cases of less consequence (34b-c). Socrates professes to fear that his behaviour may be construed as a sign of arrogance, and that the jurors may as a result cast their votes in anger (*met' orgês*). Socrates recognizes here that an appeal to pity may neutralize the jurors' anger, though he suggests that any anger they feel is due not to their response to the crimes for which he has been charged – such anger, if well founded, would not be illegitimate – but simply to his refusal to humble himself before them. Socrates' first reason for not resorting to the pity argument is that it is a sign of effeminacy and cowardice: since no one is immortal, death is hardly so dreadful a thing to suffer (35a); this view was the more plausible in that Socrates was already old, and pity was usually reserved for an untimely death (see Chapter 2). If the punishment does not constitute a misfortune, then to be sure the jury has no reason to feel pity, whether or not the defendant is ultimately innocent or guilty.[17] But Socrates then adds that it is not just to beg for acquittal, but one ought rather to teach and persuade the jury – persuade rationally, that is to say (35b-c). Socrates may well have believed that an innocent defendant should not dramatize in court the pitiableness of an unjust condemnation, since any departure from a discussion of the abstract principles of

1. Pity and the Law

justice must inevitably mislead the jury. But he had a different idea of what constitutes a rational argument from that of his fellow Athenians.[18]

I have been arguing that pity, in the classical conception, like anger for that matter, was not something separate and apart from judgments concerning justice and desert, but rather presupposed the innocence (or, in the case of anger, the guilt) of the accused party. For this reason, an appeal to pity was not accompanied by expressions of remorse, nor a request for pardon or forgiveness; it was designed rather to make vivid to the jury the consequences of condemning an innocent person. Thus, the Greeks and Romans did not attempt to arouse pity by dwelling on their unfortunate childhood, for example; they were not explaining how they acquired criminal tendencies – quite the contrary. Nor were they seeking to alter the description of the events themselves: in their narratives, Greek and Roman pleaders exploit logical probabilities with Aristotelian acuity. The ancient view of pity as involving an appreciation of merit rendered the forensic appeal to pity something distinct from what it appears to be in the modern courtroom, since it was taken for granted that one should be pitiless toward those who deliberately committed an unjust act. It is not merely the judicial systems that are incomparable, but the notion of pity too.

Let me indicate the limits of the claims I am making here. I do not doubt that defendants who humbled themselves before the jurors and begged for pity might have sought to flatter their pride, and to dispose them favourably to themselves on these grounds. Nor do I think that defendants who were guilty as sin could not and did not avail themselves of the appeal to pity, and thereby secure a favourable verdict. I am merely arguing that if they did succeed in doing so, the underlying strategy was not just to induce the jurors to lay aside their judgment concerning guilt or innocence and exonerate the defendant solely on sentimental grounds, but rather to reinforce the idea that the defendant was innocent, and just for that reason was to be pitied in the event of a vote to condemn rather than acquit. Since pity was warranted only on the assumption of innocence, an appeal to pity constituted an implicit claim of innocence.

At the beginning of his *Rhetoric*, Aristotle remarks that those who have previously composed manuals or *tekhnai* for speeches (*tôn logôn*) have treated only a small part of the subject. Only proofs (*pisteis*), Aristotle holds, are properly a technical (*entekhnon*) part of rhetoric, and these consist principally of enthymemes, or arguments based on probable or plausible premises. But other writers, Aristotle complains, have nothing to say about these forms of deduction, but discuss rather topics that are outside the issue (*exô tou pragmatos*): 'for slander and pity and anger and such affects of the soul are not about the issue, but rather are directed at the juror' (1354a16-18). Aristotle adds (as noted in the Introduction) that 'one ought not to warp a juror by leading him to anger or envy or pity' (1354a24-5), for this is like bending the ruler with which you wish to measure something. Aristotle claims further that 'the part of one who is litigating is nothing other than demonstrating that the thing [*pragma*] exists or does not exist or happened or did not happen' (1354a27-8).

Given this preface, which seems to conform nicely to modern standards of evidential relevance, it comes as something of a shock to recall that Aristotle devotes the better part of the second book of the *Rhetoric* to the means of rousing the emotions of jurors. But one need not wait so long in the treatise to encounter a positive assessment of appeals to passion in the art of persuasion. In the second chapter of Book 1, Aristotle explains that 'of proofs, some are non-technical and others are technical [*entekhnoi*]' (1355b35-6). In the non-technical category – those kinds of proofs that do not depend on rhetoric as an art – are such things as witnesses and evidence produced by torture. 'Of proofs provided by speeches, in turn, there are three kinds: some are in the character of the speaker, some in how the listener is disposed, and some in the speech itself' (1356a1-4), by which Aristotle means the techniques of demonstration. As far as the listeners are concerned, the object, Aristotle says, is to move them to emotion by one's speech or *logos*, 'since we render judgments differently when we feel pain or joy or affection or hatred' (1356a15-16). This line of argument appears openly to contradict the strictures on what is proper to the art of persuasion laid down in the first chapter, and Jonathan Barnes in the new *Cambridge Companion to Aristotle* (1995: 263) flatly describes the opening sections of the *Rhetoric* as incoherent.[19]

1. Pity and the Law

Aristotle was justifiably proud of his work in logic, including the sub-class of syllogisms he called enthymemes, and it is no wonder that he wished to give pride of place to this branch of technical knowledge at the beginning of his *Rhetoric*. He goes on to affirm that laws ought to be so precisely defined as to leave as little as possible to the discretion of those who sit in judgment (1354a31-4): nothing more, that is, than to ascertain the facts of the case, or rather, as Aristotle puts it, 'what has or has not been, will or will not be, is or is not' (1354b13-14). The inclusion of 'what will or will not be' in this list should be alarming for those who want to recruit Aristotle in support of modern conceptions of evidentiary relevance on the basis of the first chapter of the *Rhetoric*: it would appear that Aristotle has in view arguments about the likely future behaviour of the defendant. Besides, his concern here seems to be as much with the separation of legislative and judicial powers as with forms of pleading. However that may be, having celebrated briefly the importance of the enthymeme – his own particular discovery – for establishing the truth of a matter, or, more precisely, 'the truth and what is similar to the truth' (1355a14), as Aristotle puts it (since enthymemes are based on merely plausible premises), Aristotle proceeds directly to the broader conception of persuasion that includes disposing the jury favourably by working on its emotions. What we perceive as a radical tension between demonstration of fact and eliciting emotion evidently did not have the same salience for Aristotle.[20]

But it may be that, in condemning the appeal to pity at the opening of the *Rhetoric*, Aristotle had in mind a notion of pity different from the one he was to advance in the body of his treatise – a view that ignored or played down the element of desert, and looked rather to the suffering as such and the impression it might make on people who who were themselves vulnerable to such a plight, irrespective of whether it was merited. Aristotle himself points out (as we observed in the Introduction) that there appear to be two different emotions that are regarded as opposites to pity: on the one hand envy (*phthonos*), and on the other indignation or *nemesis*. Indignation is pain at the undeserved success of another, whereas the pain associated with pity is motivated by undeserved suffering (2.9, 1386b9-12). Both emotions, Aristotle notes, are marks of good character, since people ought neither to prosper nor to suffer unworthily. But envy too is opposed to pity, since it is, Aristotle says, 'a disturbing pain resulting from the well-being of another' (2.9, 1386b18-19; cf. 2.10, 1387b22-4), as opposed to pain at another's misfortune. Envy, however, as Aristotle goes on to explain, is not elicited by the fact that the other is undeserving of good fortune, but simply by the fact that he is one's equal or similar (2.9, 1386b19-20).

The contrast between pity and envy was a commonplace before Aristotle (cf. Pindar *Pythians* 1.85; Lysias 2.67, 24.2). But the contrast with indignation may, I think, have been Aristotle's own contribution. Indeed, the element of desert too was clearly part of the tradition concerning pity before Aristotle wrote (cf. Euripides *Suppliant Women* 233, 304, 328; Ničev 1985): it was a staple of trial speeches, as we have seen, and Isocrates affirms in one of his few forensic discourses that 'one must pity those who are unjustly at risk' (*On the Chariot* 48.6; cf. *Plataïcus* 52.4; *Against Callimachus* 62). Plato too is explicit on the matter: 'When people believe that they are experiencing misfortune by Nature or by luck, nobody gets angry or advises them or lectures them or punishes them in the hope of changing them. Instead they feel pity towards them' (*Protagoras* 323d; cf. Aristotle *Nicomachean Ethics* 3, 1114a25-28; Garland 1995: 2).[21] But in a formal defence of the rhetorical manipulation of the emotions Aristotle may have felt the need to place particular stress on the evaluative component in pity. In the subsequent tradition, both Greek and Latin, it was nevertheless the opposition of pity to envy that prevailed, due in part no doubt to the influence of the Stoics, who reduced it to a neat formula: pity is pain at another person's ill fortune, envy is pain at another's good fortune (e.g. Andronicus *Peri pathôn* 2 p. 12 Kreuttner = *SVF* 3.414). Cicero puts it elegantly in the *Tusculan Disputations* (3.21): 'to pity and to envy befall the same person, since the same person who is pained at the adverse circumstances of another is pained also at the favourable circumstances of another' (cf. *On the Orator* 1.185; cf. 2.206, 2.216; Ben-Ze'ev 2000: 338-40).

In the *Poetics*, where Aristotle defines pity and fear as the two

1. Pity and the Law

fundamental emotions elicited by tragedy, he explains that these passions are not excited when we see thoroughly bad men ruined: 'for such a plot may involve a "philanthropic sentiment" [*to philanthrôpon*], but neither pity nor fear, for the one concerns a man who is undeservedly unfortunate, while the other concerns a man who is similar [*homoios*]: pity concerns the undeserving man, fear concerns the one who is similar' (13, 1453a2-6; cf. Ničev 1981: 78).[22] The meaning of *to philanthrôpon* in this context is not entirely clear, and it has been argued (not convincingly, in my view) that the phrase may merely mean that such a peripety is morally satisfying.[23] In later Greek, however, *philanthrôpia* signifies humane sympathy, and a connection with pity is already present in the treatise *On Virtues and Vices* 5, 1250b32-5 (cited in Apicella Ricciardelli 391-2), which is part of the Aristotelian corpus although probably not by Aristotle himself. I suspect that the term reflects a recognition on Aristotle's part that extreme distress may excite a kind of commiseration or fellow-feeling independently of the merits of the sufferer. So too, Aristotle acknowledges that tragic pity may be excited by the sheer *pathos* of the events portrayed (*ouden eleeinon ...plên kat'auto to pathos*, 13, 1453b18).[24]

That pity might bypass a judgment of desert continued to generate a certain uneasiness. When Cicero observes (*On the Orator* 2.109) that 'one ought to pity those who are in trouble [*miseriis*] on account of fortune, not [their own] evil', the 'ought' (*oportet*) suggests the problem with appeals to *misericordia*, for a vivid representation of a defendant's wretchedness may obfuscate the question of merit. As Seneca (first century AD) puts it in *On Clemency* (2.5.1): 'pity looks not to the case, but to the condition' (*misericordia non causam, sed fortunam spectat*). Livy (first century BC) describes how, when the people of Tusculum (in Latium) were accused of encouraging the enemies of Rome to make war against the city (323 BC), 'they came to Rome with their wives and children. This multitude, having altered their attire and in the guise of defendants, went round to the several tribes, throwing themselves before everyone's knees. And so, pity had more weight in gaining them pardon from punishment than did their case in clearing them of the charge' (8.37.9-11). So too, the younger Pliny wrote a letter to his friend Arrian, who had retired from public life, concerning a case in the senate that offers, he says, a salutory lesson in the need for strictness (*seueritate exempli salubre*, 2.11.1-2). Marius Priscus was accused of abuses as proconsul (governor) of the province of Africa. Pliny and Tacitus represented the provincials. The issue was whether Priscus should be tried only for extortion, or for his other crimes as well. Fronto Catius, a man highly skilled in eliciting tears, spoke in behalf of Priscus and let out all the stops, or, as Pliny puts it, filled his sails with the wind of pathos (*miseratio*, 2.11.3-4). Finally, the consul designate judged in favour of a wider hearing, and won unanimous approval: 'thus one sees from experience that the initial onslaught of partisanship [*favor*] and pity is keen and forceful, but they gradually settle down as though quenched by reason and good sense' (2.11.7; cf. 6.29.9-10).

Whereas Aristotle regarded the emotions, pity included, as a natural and healthy part of human life, the Stoics developed a radical attack on the passions in general, which they regarded as an assent to an erroneous proposition, and they condemned pity in particular as being incompatible with reason and impartial judgment. Both schools, however, recognized evaluation as an essential component of pity. But there was another, less theorized conception of pity as an unmediated response to suffering as such.[25] These senses were not neatly discriminated in ordinary usage then, any more than they are today. We may disambiguate them for purposes of analysis, but they coexisted in the Greek and Latin vocabulary. After Aristotle, orators continued to employ and defend the appeal to pity in the courtroom, but the practice had now become intellectually problematic, and discussions of the *argumentum ad misericordiam*, for example by Cicero (e.g. *On the Orator* 1.52.225-54.233) and Quintilian (*Institutio oratoria*, preface to Book 5), were obliged to take into account deep-seated suspicions of its legitimacy.[26] The most extensive, if also the most ambivalent, attack on pity that survives from antiquity is Seneca's treatise *On Clemency*, where the Stoic philosopher and imperial counsellor denounces it as a vice as opposed to the virtue of clemency. We shall examine this tension further in the next chapter but one.

2

Pity versus Compassion

Let us return once more to Aristotle's definition of pity in the *Rhetoric* (2.8.2), which runs as follows (I have numbered the clauses for convenience of reference): 'Let pity, then, be (1) a kind of pain (2) in the case of an apparent destructive or painful harm (3) of one not deserving to encounter it, (4) which one might expect oneself, or one of one's own, to suffer, (5) and this when it seems near.' In the preceding chapter, we concentrated on the implications of the third point, in which Aristotle stipulates that misfortune, to be pitiable, must not be merited. As Cicero puts it in the *Tusculan Disputations* (4.18): 'pity is distress arising out of the wretchedness of another who is suffering undeservedly [*iniuriâ* = *anaxiôs*]; for no one is moved by pity at the punishment of a parricide or a traitor' (cf. Aristotle *Rhetoric* 1386b26-9). In this chapter, I should like to examine one of the implications of the fourth point in Aristotle's definition, which specifies that, to experience pity, one must oneself be subject to the kind of suffering that afflicts the other, either directly or by virtue of someone who is near or dear to us.

This principle of vulnerability has two consequences, which Aristotle spells out. In the first place, those who have lost everything are incapable of pity, since they do not anticipate that anything worse will befall them: it is not the experience of misfortune that renders us susceptible to pity but rather the prospect of it (for further discussion of this proviso, see Appendix). For the same reason, Aristotle observes, neither are people who believe they are extremely fortunate liable to feel pity; they are disposed rather to be arrogant. From this second conclusion it might appear that the gods should be immune to pity, at least to the extent that one entertains a transcendent conception of divinity (I return to this question in Chapter 4).

To pity someone, then, we must recognize the possibility of suffering a like misfortune without actually being in that condition; we cannot anticipate suffering what we are already suffering. It follows that we do not pity those who are suffering the same thing as we are. When a group of people find themselves in a storm at sea, they each feel fear in their own behalf; this is the kind of shared response that Sally Planalp terms 'emotional coincidence', as remarked in the Introduction. They do not experience pity for one another; as Isocrates writes (4.112 *Panegyricus*): 'on account of the quantity of our own afflictions, we ceased pitying one another; for they did not not allow anyone leisure enough to grieve with [*sunakhthesthai*] someone else', although in prosperity people commiserated (*sumpenthein*) over the least misfortune. The pitier, then, must be in a superior position to the pitied – not superior in the sense of being exempt from the misfortune experienced by the other, but simply in that he or she is not undergoing it at the present moment.

In the *Rhetoric* (2.8, 1386a25-7), Aristotle also affirms that 'people pity those who are similar to themselves, whether in age, character, disposition, rank, family' or the like; the reason is not that likeness enables empathy, but rather, as Aristotle explains, that in such cases we more easily perceive that a comparable misfortune might befall us as well. Similarity between the pitier and the pitied is thus a condition for the vulnerability principle, and likewise presupposes a difference in current fortunes. This same consideration accounts for why Aristotle excludes from the domain of pity those who are intimately connected to us. As he puts it (immediately preceding the reference to similarity), 'people pity their acquaintances [*gnôrimoi*], provided that they are not exceedingly close in kinship; for concerning these they are disposed as they are concerning themselves .... For what is terrible [*deinon*] is different from what is pitiable, and is expulsive of pity' (1386a18-23). Aristotle cites the remark of one Amasis, who did not weep when his son was led out to die but did so in the case of a friend: 'the latter was pitiable, the former terrible', Aristotle comments.[1] We recall that, in his definition of pity, Aristotle specified that the anticipated harm must be such as can befall either oneself or one's own. The afflictions of those nearest to us are perceived as ours rather than another's, and

2. Pity versus Compassion

'people stop pitying when something terrible is happening to them', presumably since misfortune is now present rather than prospective. Pity, then, is excited only at a certain remove; when the connection with the sufferer is too close, we experience the misfortune itself, not the anticipation of it (of course, we may solicit the pity of others for the misfortunes of our kin; cf. Apsines 403 Spengel).

It may seem counterintuitive to place just those closest to ourselves beyond the pale of pity, but the logic is, I think, recognizable to those thinking in English as well. Imagine that sudden tragedy strikes a loved one: it is likely that our reaction will be horror and pain rather than pity, at least in the first instance. Citing Max Scheler, Luc Boltanski (1999: 3) remarks: 'we do not say that a father and mother who weep over the body of their child experience "pity" for him or her precisely because they are themselves also suffering misfortune.' And yet, the categorical exclusion of kin from the sphere of pity is foreign, I think, to the modern idiom. Might it then reflect Aristotle's idea that parents love (*stergein*, used particularly of parental affection) their children because the children are a part of themselves, and children love their parents because they are themselves a part taken from them (*Nicomachean Ethics* 8.12, 1161b17-19; an analogous account holds for other blood relations)?[2] Or is Aristotle's view an accurate reflection of the way Greeks in general understood pity? Broadly speaking, the latter is the case, I believe. But of course, this must be demonstrated. I begin by illustrating how the role of pity in two dramatic works produced within a year of one another seems to hinge on the distinction Aristotle draws between relations among intimates and those among more distant acquaintances, and then examine some further implications of this conception.

The plot of Sophocles' *Philoctetes*, staged in 409 BC, bears a remarkable resemblance to that of Euripides' *Orestes*, which appeared the following year, 408. When the action of Sophocles' play begins, Philoctetes, crippled by the snake-bite that had left him subject to agonizing spasms, has been eking out his life for ten years on the deserted island of Lemnos. In Euripides' tragedy, Orestes too is ill, as a result of the madness induced by the Furies after the murder of his mother. What is more, he is in the process of being tried for matricide in the council of Argos, and if convicted – as indeed proves to be the case – he will be sentenced to death. In both cases, moreover, an outsider intervenes with the promise of succour. For Philoctetes, this takes the form of the arrival of Neoptolemus (Achilles' son), who is in fact in conspiracy with Odysseus to trick the ailing hero into departing for Troy, where his bow is needed for victory; in the end, however, moved by Philoctetes' plight and his own sense of honour, Neoptolemus joins forces with the suffering hero. In Orestes' case, two men arrive on the scene: first, his uncle, Menelaus, and then his cousin and dearest friend, Pylades. Orestes pleads with Menelaus to help him, but Menelaus hesitates to oppose the Argives, despite the veterans he has brought with him from Troy. With Pylades, Orestes is inclined rather to dissuade him from needlessly risking his life without hope of success (764), but Pylades regards Orestes' fortunes as his own, and helps his friend to take over the palace and hold Menelaus' daughter hostage, until the epilogue in which Apollo appears and resolves the conflict (Sophocles' play too concludes with a *deus ex machina*).

Despite the similarity in situation, however, the two tragedies differ profoundly in regard to the role of pity. Pity is at the heart of Neoptolemus' response to Philoctetes' condition.[3] The note is sounded by the chorus when they first come upon Philoctetes' wretched lair: 'I for my part pity him [*oiktirô nin egôge*]: no human being to care for him, with no companion in sight, miserable, forever alone, he is afflicted by a savage disease and wanders at the mercy of every need that arises' (169-75; cf. *epoiktirein*, 318). When Philoctetes sees the strangers, whom he recognizes as Greeks because of their dress, he cries out: 'Pity me [*oiktisantes*], a miserable man, alone, deserted, friendless and abused; speak to me, if you come as friends' (227-9). He recalls how merchants who on rare occasions took refuge on Lemnos were moved to pity (*eleousi*), though they balked at taking him aboard their ships (307-11). Philoctetes falls at the knees of the young man, beseeches him by Zeus, god of suppliants, to rescue him from the island (484-6), and concludes by begging: 'pity me [*m' eleêson*]; observe how all things are ominous, and mortals risk not only faring well but also the reverse' (501-3).

Philoctetes' appeal to human vulnerability is a commonplace, and

2. Pity versus Compassion

Aristotle provides the rationale for it, as we have seen, in his definition of pity. Insofar as Neoptolemus is not immune to the kind of harm that Philoctetes has suffered, he should be susceptible to pity. The chorus adopt a similar view: 'Pity him [*oiktir'*], sire: he has recounted the burden of numerous, unendurable sufferings – may no one of my friends experience the like' (507-9), the implication being that, given the uncertainty of human affairs, they might some day. In torment from his wound, Philoctetes again appeals to Neoptolemus' pity (*oiktire me*, 756); when he recovers consciousness, he remarks with surprise on Neoptolemus' extraordinary capacity for pity (*eleinôs*, 870) in staying by his side. Later, Neoptolemus exclaims: 'A terrible pity [*oiktos deinos*] has overcome me for this man, not just now, but long since.' 'Pity me [*eleêson*], my child, by the gods,' says Philoctetes, 'and do not make a shameful spectacle of yourself before mankind by robbing me' (965-8). Philoctetes demands pity of the gods (*oiktirete*, 1042) – this is unusual in Greek tragedy, as we shall see – and of the chorus of sailors (*epoiktireite*, 1071), whom Neoptolemus instructs, again out of pity (*oiktos*, 1074), to remain with Philoctetes till he and Odysseus can get the ship ready to sail. Pity stirs Neoptolemus even as he carries out Odysseus' plan of winning Philoctetes' confidence by the fiction of a quarrel with Agamemnon and Menelaus (see further Konstan 1998).

The reader may have noticed that I have translated as 'pity' Greek words based on two different roots: *ele-* and *oikt-*. Before proceeding with our comparison between the two tragedies, I should note that Aristotle's term in the *Rhetoric* is *eleos*, and in this he conforms to forensic practice: when orators appeal to the pity of the jurors, they almost invariably employ a form of *eleos*, and appeals for *oiktos* are uncommon in Greek literature generally.[4] True, the noun *oiktos* is often a synonym of *eleos*, as in the instances cited above where the two terms are interchangeable, although it may have a slightly more poetic register; it and related terms such as the adjective *oiktros*, 'pitiable', and the verb *oiktirô*, 'to pity', are relatively infrequent in the orators (only five times each in Lysias and Demosthenes, four in Isocrates, once in Aeschines, absent in Isaeus and Lycurgus; cf. Burkert 1955: 51-5; Sternberg 1998: 15, 53-7, with slightly different figures). Sometimes, however, *oiktos*, which probably derives from the exclamation *oi*, refers to the expression of audible grief or lamentation rather than pity (contra Ničev 1985: 61 and Sternberg 1998: 11-50, who hold that the terms are synonymous). The chorus in Sophocles' *Trachiniae* clearly refer to the sound of wailing when they inquire (863-4): 'Do I hear *oiktos* within the house?' (cf. *Ajax* 892-5; *Oedipus at Colonus* 1636). In Euripides' *Trojan Women* the chorus say to Hecuba (155): 'I heard the laments [*oiktoi*, plural of *oiktos*] that you lamented [verb *oiktizô*]' (cf. Aeschylus *Suppliants* 59, 64). The Greek historian Dionysius of Halicarnassus (first century BC), in his *Roman Antiquities*, describes the reaction to a military defeat (5.44.4): 'There was lamentation [*oiktos*] for the dead and pity [*eleos*] for the survivors';[5] and Appian of Alexandria speaks of a 'pitiable *oiktos*' (*eleeinos oiktos*, *Libyan Wars* 383) arising from the lamentations (*oimôzontôn*) of the Carthaginians when the destruction of their city was decreed.[6] The nuance of the term must be determined from the context, but it is well to remember that *oiktos* carries a penumbra of associations different from those of 'pity' and ought sometimes, perhaps, to be rendered by a portmanteau expression such as 'pity/grief' – Stanford (1983: 24) suggests 'compassionate grief' (compare the discussion of the Ifaluk *fago* in the Introduction).

Returning to Euripides' tragedy, I find it remarkable that Orestes, in contrast to Philoctetes, never utters a single appeal for pity, whether to Menelaus or to Pylades. There is no question but that Orestes and Electra recognize their condition as miserable. Orestes is repeatedly described as 'wretched' (*meleos*, 90, 159, etc.), and Electra exclaims (203-4) that 'the greater part of my life is spent in groans and laments and night-long tears'. When Menelaus arrives on the scene, Orestes immediately grasps his knees in supplication: 'Save me; you have come at the critical moment of my troubles' (382-4). Menelaus concludes the line-for-line exchange with the words, 'O wretched one, you have reached the limit of misfortune' (447). Orestes fires back: 'Give your dear ones who are faring miserably a share in your own well-being. Don't keep what's good for yourself, but partake in our struggles in turn, and pay back your debt of gratitude to my father, as you ought. They are friends in name, not deed, who are not friends in misfortune' (450-5; cf. 665-7).

2. Pity versus Compassion

Later, Orestes will even beseech Menelaus' help in the name of Helen (671; cf. 673, and the chorus' entreaty in 680). He has no hesitation about casting himself as a suppliant before Menelaus – but he does not ask for pity.

Menelaus' response to Orestes is revealing: 'I respect you and wish to struggle together with you in your adversity [*xumponêsai sois kakoisi*]' (682-3). He explains that it is right to help bear (*xunekkomizein*) the distress of kin (684) when this is possible, both by dying oneself and slaying opponents. But he protests that he has not the forces to assist Orestes in this way, and for this reason recommends persuasion and gentle words, to which the people are likely to respond, 'for there is pity [*oiktos*] in them, though there is also mighty passion' (702).

Despite Orestes' angry reaction to what he perceives as Menelaus' cowardice (cf. 719: 'O basest of men, when it comes to avenging your friends'), he too, in his subsequent exchange with Pylades concerning the wisdom of making a personal appearance at the assembly, brings up the possibility of arousing pity in the townsmen of Argos (784), and Pylades agrees that Orestes' noble birth may help him in this regard; emphasizing the contrast with one's former state was, as we have seen, one of the standard tropes in appeals to pity.[7] Pylades' own response to Orestes' ruin, however, is to go down together with him (*sunkataskaptois an hêmas*), on the grounds that 'the things of friends are in common' (735). Correspondingly, he is amazed that Menelaus did not have the heart to partake in the struggles of his nephew.

Neoptolemus and Philoctetes are strangers; the scene on Lemnos is the first meeting between them. Orestes, on the contrary, is nephew to Menelaus and close friend and relation to Pylades. He does not seek pity from his uncle: rather, he asks to be treated as kin. To be sure, Orestes believes that Menelaus is in his debt, because his father, Agamemnon, had ventured everything to bring back Menelaus' wife from Troy, and lost his life as a result. Orestes' present predicament is a consequence of the war fought in Menelaus' behalf, and Menelaus should be prepared to take whatever risks are required to rescue him. The moment that Orestes, reviving from one of his episodes of madness, learns that Menelaus is in Argos, his mind turns to the debt his uncle is under (but note too the reference

55

to family): 'What's that? Has a man who is our kin and who is indebted to our father come as a beacon to our ills?' (243-4; cf. 239). Later he demands: 'Give me nothing of your own, Menelaus, but pay back what you received from my father' (642-3). Philoctetes, of course, is in no position to demand recompense for any prior service to Neoptolemus.

But the favour owed to Agamemnon and his offspring is not Orestes' only, or even his primary, claim on Menelaus. Throughout the play he insists on Menelaus' responsibility to his near and dear ones and reproaches him for his disloyalty to them.[8] We have already cited the passage (454-5) in which Orestes states that unqualified support is owed to friends (and, *a fortiori*, to relatives). In regard to the vengeance he took for his own father's death, Orestes explains to Menelaus that he was not wise, perhaps, but he was 'a true friend to his friends' (424). Pylades, by contrast, is the perfect friend, and willing to participate in all Orestes' sufferings. There is no place for pity here: his view is, as we have seen, that true friends share everything (735), which means that they spontaneously take your side and assume your troubles as their own. Hence Orestes' famous exclamation (804-6): 'This proves the proverb: "Have comrades, not just kin!" For a man, though an outsider, who is conjoined by character is a better friend for a man to have than ten thousand of his own blood.'

Family ties, however close, may fail to inspire the loyalty or identification that they ought. Orestes himself, after all, has slain his mother, however much he may have been, in Aristotle's phrase, a part taken from her. In beseeching Menelaus' assistance, however, Orestes elects to remind him of the claims of kinship rather than ask for pity, as he would a stranger – or the Argive citizens. In the same way, Medea, in Euripides' play, never appeals to her husband Jason for pity, though she begs it of Creon, the king of Corinth, in behalf of her children (344-5), reminding him that he too is a father (and hence vulnerable to a comparable misfortune), and of the Athenian king Aegeus (*oiktiron, oiktiron me*, 711) when he passes through Corinth. Pylades, though more a friend than a close relation (he is Orestes' second cousin), needs no encouragement to take

2. Pity versus Compassion

Orestes' danger as his own and 'to suffer the same things'. Friends may be closer than family.

I have so far ignored the question of desert, but it might occur to the reader that Orestes hesitated to appeal to Menelaus' pity because he was not entirely certain of his own innocence. There is some indication to this effect in the play. In his plea to Menelaus, Orestes concedes: 'Suppose I am in the wrong; I should nevertheless obtain for my distress some unjust act on your part – for in fact my father, Agamemnon, marshalled Greece unjustly when he went against Ilium: he was not at fault himself, but was rather remedying the fault and wrong-doing of your wife' (646-50). This is a debater's point, rather than a sign that Orestes really believes that his case is undeserving of commiseration. But I suggest that Orestes would not have mentioned his possible guilt if his aim had been to excite pity, as opposed to claiming the unconditional support of a close kinsman. We may note that, at the end of *Philoctetes*, when the suffering hero refuses the possibility of being healed if it means helping the Greeks defeat Troy, Neoptolemus reproaches him: 'It is not just to show indulgence [*sungnômên*] to or pity [*epoiktirein*] those who are involved in self-willed harm, like you' (1318-20; cf. Ničev 1985: 61-2).

If the hardships of one's friend are one's own, one suffers them jointly or shares in the struggle to overcome them – we might think of it as a limiting case of 'emotional coincidence'. The community of interests ('all things in common') that ideally obtains among friends and near kin thus obviates the role of pity in such relationships. The language of *Orestes* reflects this principle of mutual participation and cooperation in the use of verbs with the prefix *sun-* (or *syn-*), for example *xumponêsai* (683), 'struggle together' and *xunekkomizein* (685), 'help bear' (*xum-* and *xun-* are an older variant, in Attic Greek, of the more common form of the prefix, *sum-* and *sun-*). Orestes informs Menelaus that Pylades collaborated (*sundrôn*, 406) with him in murdering Clytemnestra (cf. 1535), and Pylades explains that his father, Strophius, has banished him because he undertook the slaying jointly with Orestes (*sunêramên*, 767). When Orestes tries to discourage Pylades from perishing along with him on the grounds that 'you didn't slay your mother', Pylades replies, somewhat illogically: 'I did it together with you, and I ought to suffer the same' (1073-4). Recent editors have softened the incoherence by emending the word 'your' to 'you' (cf. Willink 1986 ad 1073); thus West 1987: 133, adopting 'you', translates: 'you didn't kill a mother, as I did.' Without pressing the point, I should like to think that Euripides meant the slip to suggest the degree of identification between the two friends.

As I remarked briefly in the Introduction, the Greek prefix *sun-* introduces a set of compounds which broadly speaking signify 'suffer together with' someone; examples are *sunalgein*, 'feel pain with', *sullupeisthai* and *sunakhthesthai*, 'feel pain or grieve with', and *sumponein*, 'struggle or toil with'. Some time after the classical period, the noun *sumpatheia* came into use in the sense of the English 'sympathy', which is of course derived from the Greek word (see Burkert 1955: 63-7), although in philosophical and medical contexts it continued to bear the sense of physical interrelatedness, and *sumpatheia* is often found in association with *eleos* or pity, as, for example, in Diodorus Siculus 12.24.5 (first century BC): 'he induced pity and intense sympathy in everyone' (cf. Dionysius of Halicarnassus *Roman Antiquities* 8.42.1). So too, the Latin substantive *compassio* (*com-* is equivalent to *sun-*, *-passio* to *-patheia*) is a late formation, occurring for the first time in the Christian apologist Tertullian (*On Modesty* 3.5, second century AD); the deponent verb *compati*, in turn, appears first in the Latin version of the New Testament (Pétré 1934: 388-9), and both forms are particularly common in later Christian authors (see Chapter 4).

In the part of the *Nicomachean Ethics* dealing with affection or *philia* (Books 8 and 9), Aristotle uses participation in another's grief or pain (*sunalgein*, *sullupeisthai*), along with the sharing of joy or pleasure (*sunkhairein*, *sunhêdesthai*), as a criterion of profound love. For example, he argues that it is impossible to have a great many friends because it is 'difficult to rejoice [*sunkhairein*] and condole [*sunalgein*] properly with many; for one is likely to be feeling pleasure [*sunhêdesthai*] with one and pain [*sunakhthesthai*] with another simultaneously' (1171a6-8). It is worth remarking that there is no term combining the prefix *sun-* with the verb *eleein*, 'to pity' (nor does the simple verb occur in the middle voice).

2. Pity versus Compassion

In the passage where Aristotle considers whether it is reasonable to speak of loving oneself (the idea evidently has a paradoxical ring), he observes that some people define a friend precisely as one who suffers and rejoices (*sunalgein kai sunkhairein*, *Nicomachean Ethics* 9.4, 1166a7-8) with one who is dear or *philos*. Aristotle comments in passing that mothers in particular meet this condition – they are his paradigm of natural and selfless love. Since, as he goes on to say, a person does indeed suffer and feel pleasure above all with himself (9.4, 1166a27), he concludes that one can in fact be one's own friend. These compound terms, then, which signify sharing in the feeling of another, would appear to have particular application to loved ones, even to the point of being used self-referentially. To take an example from tragedy, Theseus, whose friendship for Heracles was legendary, says that he has come 'sharing the pain' of the suffering hero (Euripides *Heracles* 1202).[9] As Ferwerda (1984: 60) rightly observes: 'Should the Greeks wish to give expression to a deeper feeling of sympathy (suffering together), they use the word *sullupeisthai*. This is a privilege reserved for a small circle of intimate friends.'[10] So too in English, it has been suggested that 'Typical attitudes of compassion address those near and dear', and that compassion, as opposed to pity, involves 'a greater commitment to substantial help' (Ben-Ze'ev 2000: 327-8).

Pity has no place in this context. Indeed, Aristotle does not discuss pity anywhere in his treatment of *philia*, since it does not pertain, in his view, to those who are very close, whether friends or kin. For Greek (and Roman) pity, as I have been arguing, involves a distance between the pitier and pitied. To put it aphoristically, pity begins where love leaves off.[11] The compound terms for suffering with another, by contrast, may appear to resemble rather the idea of empathy as enabling one to 'feel the other person's feelings' (Planalp 1999: 64, cited more fully in the Introduction). In a similar vein, Diana Cates observes (1997: 162): 'In my compassion for you, I experience myself as becoming who I am, moment by moment, along a continuum between me at *this* pole and you at *that* pole. I experience myself as me-you.' Adam Smith gave a comparable account of the sensibility of the pitier for the pitied (1976 [orig. 1759]: 9 = I.1.i.2), although this is not Aristotle's sense of *eleos* nor that of any other Greek philosopher: 'By the imagination we place ourselves in his situation, we conceive ourselves enduring all the same torments, we enter as it were into his body, and become in some measure the same person with him, and thence form some idea of his sensations.' But it is well to bear in mind that *sunalgein* and *sullupeisthai*, like their positive counterparts *sunkhairein* and *sunhêdesthai* which signify the sharing of pleasure, refer not to emotions in the first instance but rather to pleasure and pain, which are, in Aristotle's view, sensations and contituent parts of emotion (see Appendix; Halliwell 2001: ch. 2). Not even these compound terms, then, indicate the kind of *emotional* fusion that modern coinages such as empathy imply.

In Greek then, the subject and object of pity do not merge but rather maintain distinct emotions – that of the pitier is precisely pity – and perspectives: the pitier is always to some extent in the situation of an observer rather than a participant in the experience of the other, and views the suffering of the pitied from the outside, as it were. In Euripides' *Trojan Women*, when Hecuba seeks to justify the brutal vengeance she has exacted from Polymestor, who slew her son, she says to Agamemnon: 'Consider all these acts of his as shameful, and have respect for me, pity us – step back like a painter and look at me and observe the evils I endure; I was once a monarch [i.e., like you – the vulnerability argument] but am now your slave' (806-9). So too, in Sophocles' *Ajax* (118-32), Odysseus feels pity (*epoiktirô*) for the raving Ajax as he observes him from a distance, while he himself remains unseen. Odysseus acknowledges their common defencelessness: 'I have regard', he says, 'for my condition no less than his: for I see that we who live are nothing but figments, or a frail shadow.' But his pity is a sign of his detachment from the misfortune of his enemy.

The security enjoyed by the pitier may be interpreted as condescension. In *Prometheus Bound* (attributed to Aeschylus), the chorus of Oceanids express their dismay upon seeing the Titan Prometheus fettered and in anguish: 'He is iron-hearted and made of stone who does not grieve with you [*sunaskhalâi*] at your sufferings, Prometheus. I would have wished not to look upon this, and as I look upon it I feel pain in my bosom.' To this, Prometheus responds

2. Pity versus Compassion

indignantly: 'So then, I am pitiable for my friends to look upon' (242-6; cf. 140). Shortly afterwards, Prometheus blurts out: 'It is easy for one who keeps his feet clear of woe to encourage and advise those who are in trouble' (263-5). So too, when the deity Oceanus appears on the scene, Prometheus at once inquires: 'Have you too come as witness [*epoptês*] to my travails?' (298-9), and later notes that Oceanus himself stands free of blame (330).[12] Prometheus associates pity with the privileged position of the bystander, and is quick to suspect contempt or at least a bemused detachment. Centuries later, Cicero will remark that 'pity itself is pleasurable to those who observe the misfortunes of others while free from pain' (*Letters to his Friends* 5.12.5).[13]

In the previous chapter, we noted that pity might be elicited by the suffering of people who, on a strict reckoning, did not deserve it, despite Aristotle's insistence on the primacy of merit and evaluation. It might also be that on a popular view pity was excited by the misfortunes of loved ones – we do not normally evaluate critically their claim to commiseration – regardless of Aristotle and the evidence of Euripides' *Orestes*: it is in the nature of ideologically loaded concepts such as pity to be multiply determined. Indeed, Kevin Crotty has recently argued that the two fundamental 'aspects of *eleos*' in Homeric epic are 'its affinity with the family and its suppression within warrior society' (1994: 46), which contradicts squarely the Aristotelian claim about the affective space that pity requires. It might be thought, then, that the construction of pity in Homeric epic is different from that of Athenian tragedy and the rhetorical tradition represented by Aristotle. For example, in the sixth book of the *Iliad* Andromache pleads with her husband Hector to take pity on her and adopt a defensive strategy against the Achaeans (Crotty remarks of this passage that '*eleos* has a merging effect', 48). Again, in Book 22, Priam and Hecuba appeal to their son to pity them and retreat to safety behind the city walls rather than confront Achilles in battle. Should not their suffering have produced a sense of horror in Hector rather than pity?

The reason for these exceptions, if such they are, may, however, lie in their particular nature. Andromache, Priam and Hecuba all make a prospective argument for pity. Foreseeing the likelihood of

Hector's death if he engages directly with the Achaeans and above all with Achilles, they paint a vivid picture of the outrages to which they will be exposed when Troy is taken. The image of his wife being led off into slavery or his father's corpse being mutilated by dogs moves Hector deeply, of course. But the catastrophe is still hypothetical; what is more, it presupposes that Hector is already dead, and thus cannot intervene to save them. To share in their suffering and struggle along with them (*sunalgein* and *sunponein*) is denied to him, nor will he be in a position to exact vengeance in their behalf. In appealing to Hector's pity, Andromache, Priam and Hecuba reduce him imaginatively to a helpless, spectral bystander of their fates.[14]

Pity would not be Hector's response if he actually saw his family being harmed, any more than it is Agamemnon's reaction when his brother Menelaus is wounded or Achilles' upon learning of the death of Patroclus. Crotty, arguing that mourning is closely related to pity or rather to self-pity, sees in Achilles' lament for Patroclus (*Iliad* 19.321-5, 334-7) 'the most illuminating parallel' for Hector's (proleptic) grief over Andromache (48). But there is no mention of Achilles' pity; his grief is coupled with an intense desire for revenge.[15] Andromache's appeal to Hector's pity casts him, by contrast, not as an actor but as a mere onlooker of her misfortune – a variation on the connection between pity and spectatorship.

Pity is sometimes expressed for the dead on funerary inscriptions, although it occurs almost exclusively in reference to those who have died prematurely, as in the following epigram from the fourth century BC found in the Attic deme of Rhamnous: 'We must all die, but you have left behind pity for your youth.'[16] So too, the Greek rhetorician Menander (third or fourth century AD) comments on the absurdity of reciting threnodies for the aged (436.23-4 Spengel; translation in Russell and Wilson 1981). The sentiment is thus not for the condition of the dead as such, which might be imagined as miserable enough, but rather for their failure to have completed a life in this world by marrying and having a family: burial (*taphos*) takes the place of the hoped-for wedding (*gamos*).

Death itself, like fate, is pitiless (Lattimore 1962: 186, 242). So too, the dead: Richmond Lattimore (1962: 188) notes an unusual

2. Pity versus Compassion

case in which a father is reproached for dying and taking with him his two children, without pity for their mother left behind (Mendel *BCH* 33 [1909] 312-14, found near Prusa). There is an apparent instance of the pitying dead in a late Hellenistic or Roman inscription found on Rhodes (Maiuri, *Nuova silloge* no. 110), which begins: 'Hail Heraclitus, son of Artemon, full of pity [*eleêmôn*].' Kent Rigsby, who called my attention to this text, was surprised by it: 'In gravestones it is common that Death didn't pity ..., or that the dead person ought to be pitied (usually for a reason – young or young and female), or occasionally that survivors should be pitied. The startling item is a gravestone on Rhodes in which the deceased is described as "merciful"' (personal communication 26 March 1999). In a subsequent letter, however (28 April 1999), Rigsby writes: 'Maiuri could only see traces of the second E [in *eleêmôn*] .... I suspect that what the stone really has is *tlêmôn* [wretched], which is just what we would expect from dozens of funerary monuments' (see now Rigsby 2000).

The immediate response to the loss of a loved one, however, was not pity but grief.[17] The genre of the consolation, which was intended to help the recipient overcome sorrow, took it for granted that time was required. To be sure, Anaxagoras had famously replied to the news that his son had died, 'I knew he was mortal when I fathered him.' Similar is Seneca's advice to someone who has lost his sons (*On Remedies for Chance Events* 13.1): 'you're a fool to weep over the mortality of mortals', a sentiment that Rudolph Kassel (1958: 14) describes as 'shocking to the modern reader'. But the consolation addressed to Apollonius on the death of his child (ascribed to Plutarch), begins: 'For a long while now, Apollonius, I have suffered and condoled with you [*sunalgein, sunakhthesthai*]' (101F). So long as the disease was ravaging the boy, Plutarch says, it would have been inappropriate to encourage the father to bear his lot as a mortal; rather, it was necessary to share Apollonius' emotion (*sumpathein*, 102A).[18] But when time enough has passed, friends should help one overcome grief and vain anguish (102B).[19] So too, Menander, in his rhetorical handbook, recommends that in composing a consolation one begin by dwelling on the grief and only afterwards look to comfort it (413.6, 21-3).[20]

Pity Transformed

The Roman poet Statius composed several poems known as 'epicedia', which were to be pronounced at the funeral itself (such at least is the literary convention). In one, on the death of the foster-child of the addressee (*Silvae* 2.1), Statius recognizes that his task is to compose healing words, but this would be cruel, since Atedius Melior is racked with grief (5-6). Statius thus encourages him to indulge his lamentations and the 'joy of weeping' – work it through, we might say today – until he is ready to heed 'friendly entreaties' (15-16). He himself, Statius says, is equally riven by grief (25, 28-30). Only at the end of his poem does he turn to the consolation proper (208-34).[21] So too, Pliny (*Epistles* 5.16) describes his own pain at the death of his friend Fundanus' daughter, and remarks that although Fundanus is a learned man, all his wisdom is for naught; but this is because the wound is still fresh – with the healing of time, he will be ready to accept words of solace. Saint Jerome (*Epistles* 60.3) remarks disparagingly on the old Roman custom of exciting weeping and groaning in funeral orations, but then, the Christians could point to the resurrection (Scourfield 1993: 23-4), and were inclined to discourage displays of grief on religious grounds: Saint Augustine recommended instead the reading of psalms (*Confessions* 9.12.32; cf. Heene 1988).

The pyschological distance that enables pity for the dead, then, derives principally from the passing of time, which allows the initial grief to subside. References to pity on funerary inscriptions express, I think, the lasting sorrow for an unfulfilled life rather than the immediate anguish (*lupê*, *dolor*) experienced by the mourners, although a gravestone may capture both sentiments simultaneously. Sometimes, indeed, the pity is ascribed to the stone itself, as though to emphasize the enduring nature of the emotion (Peek 174, from Pantikapaion, second to first century BC; cf. 331, where a stele feels pity for a husband and father bereaved of his wife).

Aristotle's claim that we experience pity for acquaintances but not for close kin has a further surprising consequence. For if what impedes pity is, as Aristotle says, that we feel toward kin as we do toward ourselves, then it would seem to follow that neither can one feel pity for oneself.[22] The Greeks, then, at least on the testimony of Aristotle, ought not to have recognized self-pity. Given the amount

2. Pity versus Compassion

of wailing and lamentation recorded in our texts, this seems at the very least paradoxical. But it is true, I believe, of the semantics of Greek (and Roman) pity.

Of course, the Greeks were capable of feeling miserable and saying so, and they might refer to such a state as pitiable. But there exists no special term for self-pity, corresponding, for instance, to the word for self-love, *philautia*, and similar formations (Greek is particularly given to such compounds). Nor do they seem to have employed the most common terms for pity – the verbs *eleein* and *oiktirein* and their cognates – reflexively: that is, they did not normally speak of pitying or having pity for oneself. On rare occasions they did so, but in those cases the circumstances were exceptional, as we shall see, and facilitated what was otherwise an odd locution in classical Greek and Latin.

Let us return for a moment to Aristotle: why should he have believed that we do not pity ourselves and, *a fortiori*, those whom we regard as part of ourselves? What is there about the Greek terms for pity that forbids such an expression? The answer, I think, is that pity or *eleos* presupposes a relationship between two parties, pitier and pitied. But unlike in the case of love, the two parties must find themselves in different circumstances, those of the pitied necessarily being more wretched than those of the one who pities. This distinction is what establishes as well the emotional distance between pitier and pitied: for if the other is so closely bound to us that we experience his or her misfortune as our own, as in the case of close kin, then the dissimilarity in our conditions is abolished. This is the kind of participation in the suffering of the other that Aristotle calls *sunalgein* and *sullupeisthai*, and which may, as we have seen, be used self-referentially, albeit only, perhaps, by a philosopher. We must, then, pity from a distance, as onlookers, if we are to pity at all.

Greek usage in respect to pity may seem less strange if we compare it to an emotion which is subject to a similar kind of semantic constraint in English as well as in Greek and Latin. Neither we nor the ancients speak of envying oneself. To the Greeks and Romans, as we have seen, pity and envy were naturally paired: pity is pain on account of the misfortune of another, envy pain on account of the good fortune of another. One can no more feel pity for one's own afflictions, then, than one can feel envy for one's own successes. Both terms have the same semantic structure.

Aristotle treats envy in the *Rhetoric* next but one after pity; between the two, he analyses *nemesis* or indignation. These terms too, as we have said, are closely related: pity is pain felt at the unmerited misfortune of another, while indignation is pain felt at unmerited good fortune – the accent here is on justice and desert rather than on suffering or prosperity as such. Now, we no more feel pity for our own undeserved failure than we resent our unearned success (or that of our loved ones). Again, the parallelism suggests that Aristotle is being consistent in rejecting the idea of self-pity. It bears repeating that usage in regard to emotional concepts varies across languages. One does not speak of having *pitié* for oneself in French. Nor, as I noted in the Introduction, is 'compassion' normally employed reflexively in English, though it may be in Spanish.

We may turn now to some cases in which people are said to pity themselves in Greek, or at least, as in the following example, a part of themselves. Toward the end of Euripides' *Cyclops*, Odysseus chides the chorus of satyrs for the lame excuses they concoct to avoid helping him blind Polyphemus. The satyrs reply (643-5): 'Because we take pity [*oiktiromen*] on our back and spine and don't wish to be bashed and spit out our teeth, that's cowardice?' The effect here is deliberately comical, I think. To take pity on one's back is like envying one's feet because they are enjoying a new, comfortable pair of shoes. We can say that, but we know that it is a catachresis or misuse of words, designed to raise a laugh, and correspondingly revealing of standard usage.

When Theseus, in Euripides' *Hippolytus*, is on the point of banishing his son under the false belief that he attempted to rape Phaedra, Hippolytus cries out in frustration: 'Alas! If I could only stand opposite and view myself, as I weep for the evils I am suffering'; to which Theseus replies: 'You're far better practised at worshipping yourself than being just and treating your parents reverently' (1078-81). The word pity does not occur explicitly here, but the idea is, I think, that Hippolytus, failing to find on his father's part any charity for his anguish, imagines that he might look as an

2. Pity versus Compassion

outsider upon his own suffering, and grant himself the sympathy that is denied him. Indeed, Theseus, moments later, as he orders Hippolytus to be driven out, declares: 'No pity [*oiktos*] for your exile steals over me' (1089).

The last phrase may seem puzzling in light of Aristotle's dictum that we do not feel pity for close kin, whom we regard as part of ourselves (from this we concluded that neither do we pity ourselves). For Theseus' rejection of pity for his son appears to suggest that it would be the natural sentiment in the circumstances. The answer to the conundrum, I think, is that Theseus means that he does not *even* feel pity for Hippolytus, as a bystander would, much less regard his son's punishment as his own misfortune, in the way that parents normally do. One must take the context into account: Theseus has disowned his son.[23] Later, when he learns that the dying Hippolytus is innocent, his grief is too deep for pity: there are plenty of exclamations of woe (*oimoi, aiai, iô*) and groans, but no mention of *eleos* or *oiktos*.

I take as my third example of self-pity a Latin text rather than a Greek. In the course of his demonstration that the fear of death is groundless, Lucretius argues that even someone who avows that death is final and that there is no afterlife nevertheless imagines, in spite of himself, that he will be conscious of the pyre or of the animals that will lacerate his corpse; as Lucretius puts it: 'he unconsciously makes a part of himself survive' (*sed facit esse sui quiddam super inscius ipse*, 3.878). Under such an illusion, Lucretius continues, 'he pities himself' (*ipse sui miseret*, 3.881);

> for he does not separate himself from that other, nor does he sufficiently distance himself from the body that has been laid out, and he imagines that he is that other one and, as he stands near, invests him with his own sensibility. This is why he is upset that he was created mortal, and he does not see that, in real death, there will be no other self, who might be alive and grieve that he has been snatched from himself and, standing by, suffer for the fact that he himself is lying there and being torn to pieces or incinerated (3.881-7).

The point is that to pity oneself, one must imagine oneself divided in two: one self is in torment, while the other stands by as an observer, itself unharmed. This is a most unusual situation, and Lucretius' bare expression, *ipse sui miseret*, already suggests how anomalous it is. So too, in English, we might say of a person who is daydreaming about a blessed afterlife in Heaven or, perhaps, life on a tropical island: 'he's envying himself', although such a locution is no more customary in our language than pitying oneself is in classical Greek. Max Scheler (1954 [orig. 1923]: 150) writes as though he had this passage in mind: 'if it is said of someone that he "pities himself" or that he "rejoices to find himself so happy today" ..., a closer analysis invariably discloses the presence of an element of phantasy, in which the person concerned regards himself *"as if he were someone else"* and shares his own feelings in this (fictitious) capacity. Thus I can fancy myself in the position of taking part in my own funeral, etc.'

The *Heroïcus*, composed by one of the Philostrati (third century AD), is a dialogue between a Phoenician merchant and a winegrower who is privileged to converse with the deceased hero Protesilaus on his visits to the upper world. When asked about Protesilaus' sentiments concerning his premature death, the winegrower replies: 'He pities his own misfortune [*eleei ... to heautou pathos*]' (12.1), for had he had the chance to fight, he would have proved himself a warrior not inferior to Diomedes, Patroclus and Ajax. This is the reverse of the case imagined by Lucretius: a man who has survived his death here feels pity for the person he once was. What remains constant is that the pitier is divided from the pitied, even though they are, in a certain sense, the same individual. Flavius Philostratus' *Life of Apollonius of Tyana* provides an analogous instance of an Indian youth who, in an earlier incarnation, was Palamedes; having in that identity been duped by Odysseus and ignored by Homer, the boy has rejected philosophy and 'laments his own misfortune' (*olophuretai to heautou pathos*, 3.22) – the misfortune, that is, that he suffered in his previous life (lamentation, however, is distinct from pity).

The Christian theologian Gregory of Nyssa (fourth century) actually enjoins his readers to pity themselves. For we pity others whose

2. Pity versus Compassion

appetites cannot be satisfied, but are insensible of our own misfortunes, like madmen unaware of what they suffer. If they could recognize what they were before and what they have now become, they would never cease from pitying. It thus follows that one who feels sympathy with others should also pity himself (*auton eleein*; *On the Beatitudes* 44.1260.5-24, 37-41; translation in Hall 2000; commentary in Drobner and Viciano 2000).[24] Here too, self-pity requires a certain distance toward oneself. The conundrum, though Gregory does not point it out, is that if we perceived and hence pitied our own servitude to the appetites, we should be cured of them and cease to be pitiable. As in the case of the madman, self-pity installs a rift within the conscious self. Saint Augustine too remonstrates with himself for sympathizing, in his ignorance, with pathetic characters in literature rather than his own fallen condition (*Confessions* 1.13): 'For what is more pitiful than a pitiful man not pitying himself yet weeping at the death of Dido.' The idea becomes a commonplace in Christian writers, but does not, I think, lose its quality of paradox.

In the *Chronicon* of Georgius Monachus of Alexandria, composed in the ninth century AD, George admonishes his reader:

Therefore, take pity on yourself [*eleêson seauton*] and take thought for that final and most terrible day of punishment and the affliction and suffocation and the hour of the rending of the soul and the sentence of God pressing down upon you and the angels hastening and your soul in these circumstances dreadfully distressed and dizzy and terribly afraid, helpless and repenting in vain, when there is no use in it (2.697.1-7).[25]

The Christian conception of pity differed substantially from the classical (as we shall see in Chapter 4), and comparisons are difficult. But it is noteworthy that George's injunction to pity oneself reproduces, in an altered register, the kind of situation that we encountered in Lucretius. George, unlike Lucretius, believes that we do survive our own death, and that one can and should imagine oneself suffering in the afterlife, not merely the flames of the pyre but the fires of eternal damnation. He advises that we conjure up in our mind that wretched creature to come, which, though it is our own self, seems foreign and remote; the pity we experience for it is as though for another.

The above examples lead us to reflect on the logical status of self-pity in English. Aaron Ben-Ze'ev (2000: 343) agrees with Aristotle that 'very close relations may prevent pity' but notes that 'the phenomenon of self-pity ... seems to contradict this suggestion'. His solution is that 'In self-pity we construct the required subject-object distance by detaching ourselves from our actual situation and viewing ourselves as if we were superior to what we actually are' (cf. Ortony, Clore and Collins 1988: 106). Wierzbicka (1999: 101) looks to explain the negative connotation attaching to self-pity: '*Self-pity* may seem to be simply a special case of pity, but in fact it is not quite that: since *pity* involves an implicit comparison between another person and myself, one cannot be the target of one's own pity .... Being a sort of misapplication and distortion of *pity*, *self-pity* has always a pejorative and as it were ironic ring' (cf. Solomon 1993: 299; Stocker 1996: 260-3). But this has not always been the case in English. The *Oxford English Dictionary* (s.v. the substantive 'pity') cites Atterbury's sermon on Luke 10.32, written in 1709: 'Take Pity upon Them, who cannot take Pity upon themselves.'

In the course of his history of Rome's war with Carthage, Polybius (second century BC) pauses to explain that when a city enriches itself at the expense of defeated powers, it arouses envy of itself and also pity for the defeated. But if it plunders to excess, it causes 'onlookers to pity not their neighbours but rather themselves, for they are reminded of their own misfortunes' (9.10.9), and this generates anger which in turn leads to hatred. This is a clear case of pity for oneself, which is produced by assuming the perspective of one's own past (and more fortunate) self in regard to one's present debasement, or, as Ben-Ze'ev puts it, achieving the 'required subject-object distance by detaching ourselves from our actual situation and viewing ourselves as if we were superior to what we actually are'.

But the explicit ascription of self-pity, which is anomalous (I am arguing) in classical Greek, is perhaps facilitated here by the contrast with pity for others. Such binary opposites sometimes allow expressions that are otherwise irregular in ordinary language.

2. Pity versus Compassion

Thus, for example, the verb 'have' in English and in most Indo-European languages, is not strictly speaking transitive, because it is not employed in the passive: we say 'I have this', never 'this is had by me' ('be had' has a different sense in colloquial English, that is, 'be fooled' or 'duped'). So too in Latin: the passive form *habetur* does not occur (except in the sense, 'be deemed' or 'believed'), save for a few instances where it is self-consciously contrasted with the active use. Thus, Seneca (*On Anger* 2.17.1) compares anger to weapons that 'have you, they're not had by you' (*habent, non habentur*; see Ramos Guerreira 1998). In Diodorus Siculus' world history (first century BC), the Syracusan Nicolaus, who lost two sons in the war with Athens, says that he deems their end a happy one, but pities his own life (*ton emautou de bion eleô*, 13.20.2) and regards himself as the most unfortunate of all men. Latent here, I think, is the contrast: I pity not them, but rather myself (cf. also the passages from Gregory of Nyssa and Augustine cited above). We may compare Power's warning to Hephaestus in *Prometheus Bound* (67-8): 'Do you groan for Zeus's enemies? Careful you don't bemoan [or pity: *oiktizein* is more ambiguous than *oiktirein*] yourself someday.'[26] Lysias, in his funeral oration (2.70-1), distinguishes the several sentiments: parents will grieve for the dead, while others will miss them, feel pity for their relatives, and lament (*olophuresthai*) for themselves.

Rendering this contrast explicit in contemporary English may produce the effect of irony that Wierzbicka remarked upon. Thus, Thoreau writes in *Walden* (1997 [orig. 1846-47]: 68-9): 'I was wont to pity the clumsy Irish labourers who cut ice on the pond, in such mean and ragged clothes, while I shivered in my more tidy and somewhat more fashionable garments, till one bitter cold day, one who had slipped into the water came to my house to warm him, and I saw him strip off three pairs of pants and two pairs of stockings ere he got down to the skin .... Then I began to pity myself, and I saw that it would be a greater charity to bestow on me a flannel shirt than a whole slop-shop on him.'

We observed in the previous chapter that Aristotle posits pity and fear as the emotions characteristically produced by tragedy. Some critics have interpreted Aristotle's view as a theory of identification. Thus, Alford (1993: 265) takes pity to refer to 'the felt connection to the suffering of others like oneself' (cf. 266, 271), and endorses Stanford's assertion (1983: 24) that, with *eleos* and *oiktos*, 'there is no question ... of the pitier being separate from another's agony. You respond to it in the depths of your being, as a harp-string responds by sympathetic resonance to a note from another source.' Walton, who cites Alford's paper, concludes (1997: 51): 'The Greek concept seems more like what we would call *empathy* or *sympathy* than *pity*.' But it should now be clear that in employing *eleos* rather than a term such as *sunalgein* to describe the audience's response to tragic drama, Aristotle is rather affirming the distance between the spectators' response and the emotions of the actors on stage (cf. Halliwell 1986: 175 n. 8, 178; on drama and spectatorship, Boltanski 1999: 24-6). The onlooker feels pity not for the tragic figure, but for his or her misfortune. The spectator's position is like Odysseus' relation to Ajax, rather than the community of feeling that obtains between Pylades and Orestes: pity entails the gaze. In brief, the audience feels *for* the characters, not *with* them.[27]

Several centuries later, the Greek historian and critic Dionysius of Halicarnassus observes (*Letter to Pompey Geminus* 3.15) that crucial to any genre of history is the writer's disposition (*diathesis*) toward the events he describes; that of Herodotus (in contrast to Thucydides) 'is proper, participating in the pleasure [*sunêdesthai*] of the good and the pain [*sunalgein*] of the bad.' The idea that an author should immerse himself in his characters was a familiar notion; in Aristophanes' *Thesmophoriazusae*, the tragic poet Agathon enters dressed as a woman because he in the process of writing a woman's part (148-52).[28] A spectator or reader too might be expected to assume the point of view of a character in a narrative and to react accordingly. Plutarch, in his essay *How a Young Man Should Listen to Poetry*, offers advice on how to enjoy poetry without yielding entirely to the passions it inspires. A reader, he says, 'will check himself when he is afraid of Poseidon and trembling lest he split the earth and reveal Hades beneath, he will check himself when he is upset with Apollo in behalf of the greatest of the Achaeans ... and he will cease weeping for the dead Achilles and Agamemnon in Hades .... And if he shares the perturbation [*suntarattesthai*] of their emotions and is overcome as if drugged, he will

2. Pity versus Compassion

not hesitate to say to himself: "Hasten to the light, and learn all this so that you may recount it later to your wife [*Odyssey* 11.223-24]" ' (cf. Schiesaro 1997: 103). One is irritated with Apollo if one assumes Achilles' point of view toward the god, who favours Hector.[29] This is not the same kind of response as pity, which is evoked by the condition, not the attitude or feelings, of the other, although weeping for Achilles in the underworld is perhaps more like the case of pity. Plutarch's remedy for such participation in the other's emotion is, predictably, properly to evaluate the situation and recognize that death is not an evil.

Insofar as pity is an emotion, and not an empathic capacity that allows us to 'detect the internal state of another mammal' (Lewis, Amini and Lannon 2000: 63; quoted more fully in the Introduction), it cannot be reducible to a mere simulacrum of what another person feels: pity for someone who is grieving or frightened is a distinct emotion from grief or fear, whereas to feel the same thing as the other would be to experience the other's fear as fear (cf. Levene 1997: 132: 'with fear, one takes over a character's emotions directly', which in the case of pity would occur only when spectators pity 'a character who is pitying another character'). As an emotion, Greek pity requires a difference in response rather than the identity that Adam Smith described. As Aristotle puts it, 'people pity just those things happening to others that they fear [may happen] to themselves' (*Rhet.* 2.8.13; for a more detailed examination of the connection between fear and pity, see Appendix).

But if pity is normally at one remove from love, mediated as it is by the distance that separates the spectator, or auditor, from the sufferer, it may nevertheless serve as a stage along the way to affection and community of feeling. Something like this occurs, perhaps, to the Oceanids, who elect to abide with Prometheus when Zeus' thunderbolts open the earth beneath them. As Achilles Tatius (second or third century AD) puts it in his novel, *Leucippe and Clitophon* (3.14.3): 'A human being who listens to the sufferings of others is somehow disposed to pity [*sumpathês de pôs eis eleon*] and pity frequently is the patron of affection [*philia*]; for the soul is softened in regard to the pain of the people it has listened to, and sympathizing little by little with the narrative of woe it concentrates

Pity Transformed

pity [*oikton*] into affection [*philia*] and pain into pity.' As a result, Clitophon's interlocutor is moved to help him and to take a personal interest in the plight of his beloved. Pity is not merged, here, with the active participation in another's sorrow that love presupposes, but it may lead to it.

3

Pity and Power

'Before World War II there was virtually no general international law of human rights' (Rodley 1999: 1). There were antecedents, of course: Nigel Rodley notes that there existed, for example, 'rules for the conduct of international warfare to protect non-combatants, especially prisoners of war', and that such rules 'had forerunners in religious principles and practices of antiquity' (2, 3). Jurists in ancient Rome differentiated between just and unjust wars, but that distinction concerned the legitimacy of the conflict, not the fair treatment of those defeated in a war – *ius ad bellum* as opposed to *ius in bello*.[1]

It was only after the atrocities associated with the Second World War, and with the subsequent founding of the international organizations, above all the United Nations, that human rights in wartime were formally established in conventions such as the American Declaration of the Rights and Duties of Man (Organization of American States, 30 April 1948) and the Universal Declaration of Human Rights (adopted by the United Nations General Assembly on 10 December 1948). These conventions were followed by the European Convention on Human Rights (Council of Europe, 4 November 1950), the American Convention on Human Rights (Inter-American Specialized Conference on Human Rights, 22 November 1969), and, more recently, the African Charter on Human and Peoples' Rights (Organization of African Unity, June 1981; see Rodley 1999: 4). International conventions concerning the rights of prisoners within a national state, including covenants prohibiting torture, arbitrary execution (or indeed the death penalty as such), disappearances, corporal punishment and other ill-treatment, are more recent still, beginning with the so-called Declaration on Torture adopted by the United Nations General Assembly on 9 December 1975 (and entering into force on 23 March 1976).[2] Jack Donnelly could write in 1984:

'today there is near universal international agreement, at least in theory, although often not in practice, that certain things simply cannot legitimately be done to human beings' (1984: 404, cited in Keenleyside 1999: 142).

In the absence of legal protocols, and of the establishment of a judicial and executive apparatus (e.g. the International Tribunal in The Hague) to try to enforce them, what could a captured soldier or a defeated population expect or appeal to at the hands of a conquering army? Were there standards of treatment of civilians versus combatants, or a conception of elementary human dignity that was incompatible with practices such as torture, rape and genocide or the outright extermination of enemy populations?[3] In classical antiquity, mass enslavement of entire cities, or of women and children following upon the liquidation of adult males, were foreseeable consequences of defeat in battle, along with brutal tortures and the infliction of other indignities (see Volkmann 1961). W. Kendrick Pritchett concludes a lengthy survey of Greek practices in regard to war captives with the following words (1991: 312): 'Cities were regularly destroyed and the inhabitants killed or sold into slavery. It is only on rare occasions that the victor concerned himself with coming to terms with the vanquished .... I find little trace of any element of compassion or generosity.' Pritchett (219-23) collects fifteen examples of mass suicides in anticipation of defeat – slashing of throats, houses burnt to the ground with families inside – which show that fear of maltreatment by the conqueror was sufficient to produce such scenes of desperate self-immolation, even without the religious conviction that motivated the defenders of Masada. Although Brutus, the assassin of Julius Caesar, had a reputation for mildness or clemency (Appian *Civil War* 4.16.123; Cicero *Letters to his Friends* 427.1 = 11.22, *To Brutus* 24 Shackleton-Bailey, etc.), and indeed took pity (*ôikteirein*) on the citizens of Xanthus for their resolute love of freedom, Appian reports (*Civil War* 4.10.80) that he was unable to prevent them from slaying themselves once the city was taken.[4] Pritchett (1991: 208) quotes W.W. Tarn (1948: 65-6) for the view that 'No public man throughout Greek history is, I think, recorded to have shown pity', and suggests that the ancients, for

3. Pity and Power

their part, 'would have found our society obsessed with pity, fear, and guilt' (312).[5]

Nevertheless, Diodorus Siculus, who composed a universal history in the first century BC, indicates that there were some norms by which combat between states was guided, if not regulated (20.18.2): 'Although all war exceeds what is customary and just among human beings, nevertheless it has certain laws, as it were, of its own [*tinas idious kathaperei nomous*]'; for example, one ought not to break a truce, slay heralds, take vengeance on those who have entrusted themselves to the victor, and the like. Pritchett, who cites this passage (1991: 203), observes that Diodorus says nothing about the treatment of captives, and infers that this was not subject to any recognized constraint. The Greeks and Romans did indeed express outrage at certain especially appalling acts, which they often ascribed to barbarians. Mutilation of the bodies of captives, for instance, was particularly associated with the Persians;[6] so too, the mass violation of women, when it is recorded by our sources, meets with disapproval (Pritchett 1991: 238-41). Livy (1.28) records the punishment meted out to Mettius Fufetius, the leader of the Albans who betrayed the Romans during a battle with the Fidenates: to symbolize his divided loyalties, Tullus Hostilius, the third of Rome's legendary kings, ordered that he be bound to two chariots and torn apart. Livy writes (1.28.11) that 'all the people averted their eyes from so foul a spectacle; this was the first and last instance of that punishment among the Romans, of a sort hardly mindful of the laws of humanity [literally, human laws: *legum humanarum*]; for the rest, they may boast that no other nation has favoured milder penalties'.

Virgil (*Aeneid* 8.485-8) describes a similar revulsion at the punishment devised by the tyrant Mezentius, who killed his enemies by binding them alive to corpses. In Apuleius' comic novel, *Metamorphoses* (or *The Golden Ass*), a bandit proposes executing a captive girl who has attempted to escape on the back of an ass (in fact, the hero of the tale transformed by a magic potion) by sewing her into the carcass of the ass itself and leaving her to rot inside it (6.32). This treatment is intended to be seen as an atrocity, but the traditional punishment for parricide was to sew the offender into a

77

leather sack with a cock, a snake, a monkey and a fox, and toss him into the Tiber, a procedure which had a renewed vogue under the emperor Claudius (Seneca *On Clemency* 1.23.1; Bauman 1996: 71-3; cf. Lintott 1968: 37-9). So too, in the debate on judicial punishments recorded by Aulus Gellius (second century AD) in his *Attic Nights*, the last word is given to the jurist Sextus Caecilius Africanus, who speaks in favour of the severe laws of the Twelve Tables (codified in the fifth century BC) and concludes (20.1.53-4) by defending the quartering of Mettius Fufetius on the grounds that it encouraged keeping one's word.[7] What scope was there for pity?

In the heroic world of Homer's *Iliad*, pity is sometimes begged of a conquering warrior, though it is never granted (cf. Burkert 1955: 71-2; Vickers 1979: 483-8). Alastorides falls at Achilles' knees, pleading that he take pity and spare the life of an age-mate (*homêlikiên*, *Iliad* 20.465); likeness of age was one of Aristotle's conditions of similarity that might remind the pitier of his own vulnerability. Alastorides was a fool, says Homer, since Achilles was not in a sweet mood (467) after the death of Patroclus. So too Lycaon slips beneath Achilles' spear, seizes his knees, and begs as a suppliant for respect (*aidôs*) and pity (21.74-5), reminding Achilles that he ransomed him once before, along with other excuses (90-6). Achilles is again implacable: 'Don't speak to me of ransoms' (99), he begins, and advises Lycaon to have done with lamentation (106): Patroclus, who was a better man, has died, as will Achilles himself. Achilles seems here to adduce the common mortality of mankind as a reason why he is immune to pity rather than susceptible to it. That Achilles, after the loss of Patroclus, is resigned to his own imminent death, however, puts him in the category of those who, as Aristotle says, have lost everything and thus have nothing more to fear.[8] Besides, Achilles is motivated throughout the poem by anger, which, as we have remarked, was the antithesis of pity. Similarly, anger (*ira*) drives pity from the heart of Aeneas when he is on the point of sparing Turnus at the end of the *Aeneid*.[9] The rage that motivates human beings in hand-to-hand combat is in a delicate balance with a humane regard for the defeated enemy, above all after the loss of a friend in battle.[10] Joanna Bourke (1999: 46) quotes an Australian veteran of World War I (Idriess 1942: 82-3) who recalls how, after a bayonet battle

3. Pity and Power

with the Turks, the Australian and New Zealander troops shook the hands of the enemy: 'How many others could do that? Fight all day ... right to the bayonet point, then laugh and spare him in the height of maddened excitement.' Such gallantry coexisted, however, with dreadful atrocities toward defeated soldiers and civilians alike, as Bourke amply demonstrates.

Suppliants do not typically sue for pity, although they may, like Alastorides, Lycaon and Sophocles' Philoctetes.[11] The act of supplication in itself is supposed to be honoured, and the protection of suppliants is one of the special provinces of Zeus: 'Aren't you ashamed, you scoundrel', Philoctetes asks Neoptolemus after he has been robbed of his bow, 'to look upon me, your trophy, a suppliant?' (929-30). When they are in a position to do so, suppliants offer a ransom or reward, and ask for respect rather than plead helplessness. Thus Chryses, in the *Iliad*, offers a huge sum for his daughter, who has been captured and awarded to Agamemnon, and the rest of the Achaeans acknowledge the wisdom of showing *aidôs* or reverence to the priest (1.22-3). Orestes, in Euripides' play, adopts the posture of a suppliant, as we have seen (Chapter 2), but makes no appeal to Menelaus' pity.

In general, great warriors are reluctant to ask for pity – Alastorides and Lycaon are young and inexperienced – except in extreme circumstances: Philoctetes is both old and infirm (he refers to Neoptolemus throughout the play as 'child'). More commonly, pity is sought for the elderly, along with women and children; Turnus characteristically begs Aeneas' pity not for himself, but for his father (*Aeneid* 12.933-4; cf. Latinus' appeal that Turnus pity his own father, 12.43-6).[12] The convention obtains throughout antiquity, and is common in trial speeches as well; thus, the speaker in Lysias 20.35-6 asserts: 'others present their children and plead for them, but we plead for my father here and for ourselves' (other examples have been cited in Chapter 1; cf. Sternberg 1998: 34). Before a democratic jury in Athens, however, the self-abasement (*tapeinôsis*) involved in begging for pity could be strategic. Thus, Demosthenes says of Meidias (21.186): 'I know that he will lament, with his children at his side, and utter many humble words, weeping and making himself as pitiable as possible.'[13]

In 428 BC, shortly after the beginning of the Peloponnesian War, Mytilene, a city on the north Aegean island of Lesbos, revolted against Athenian hegemony and was conquered after a siege in the following year. As punishment, the Athenians voted in the Assembly to kill all the citizens, that is, the adult males, of Mytilene and sell the women and children into slavery – what a standard history of ancient Greece describes as pressing 'the cruel rights of war so far as to decree the extinction of a whole population'.[14] On the subsequent day, the Athenians met again to deliberate over whether to rescind that decision and settle instead for the execution of the leading conspirators, numbering about a thousand. Thucydides records the speeches for and against in this second debate. On the one side, Cleon, a popular politician, argued in favour of the original directive of extermination; his opponent was a certain Diodotus, son of Eucrates, who is otherwise unknown (on his role, see Ostwald 1979).

Cleon begins by accusing the Athenians of naively transferring their day-to-day expectations of one another to the behaviour of their allies: hence they are easily deceived and given to pity (3.37.2). He argues further that delay in executing the original decision is bad policy, since one ought to take vengeance (*timôria*) against those who have wronged one (cf. 3.39.1) while anger is still fresh (3.38.1). Cleon then lists the reasons why the rebellion of the Mytilenaeans was unjustified as well as dangerous, and maintains that pardon or indulgence (*sungnômê*) is properly granted only for involuntary offences; the Mytilenaeans, however, acted in full knowledge (3.40.1). So too, Aristotle affirms (*Nicomachean Ethics* 3.1, 1109b30-2) that praise and blame are given for voluntary actions, whereas those that are involuntary obtain pardon and sometimes even pity.[15]

Cleon then chastises his fellow citizens for their sentimental good nature: 'I, for my part, both earlier and again now oppose altering your decision and erring in the three ways most ruinous to empire: pity [*oiktos*], delight in speeches, and kindness [*epieikeia*]. For it is right to pay back pity [*eleos*] to those who are similar [*homoious*], not toward those who will not feel pity in return [*antoiktiountes*] but are of necessity permanently constituted as our enemies' (3.40.2-3). *Epieikeia*, Cleon says, is best extended to those 'who are intending

3. Pity and Power

to be friendly in the future too' rather than 'to those who are similar [*homoious*] and yet remain no less our enemies' (3.40.3).[16]

In his great commentary on Thucydides, Gomme (1956: 309-10 ad 3.40.3) observed that this is 'an exceptionally restricted field to allow this virtue [i.e. pity], about as different from the Christian concept as can be ....; but pity was not an outstanding Greek virtue'. For the Greeks of classical Athens, however, pity was not a virtue so much as an emotion elicited by the *unmerited* suffering of another.[17] By insisting that Mytilene's rebellion was both deliberate and gratuitous, Cleon is making the case, as one would in a court of law, that the Mytilenaeans have brought disaster upon themselves and hence do not deserve pity when it comes to reckoning the penalty. Cleon assumes that the Athenians are by nature all too given to feeling pity; his concern is to demonstrate that in this instance it is misplaced.

Indeed, a capacity for pity was a point of pride with Athens. Isocrates calls the Athenians 'most given to pity and most gentle' (15.20; cf. Demosthenes 24.171; Plato *Menexenus* 244E; Lysias 12.14). In Menander's *The Man who was Hated* (315-17 Sandbach = 716-18 Arnott), the slave Getas affirms, in what is clearly a reminiscence of Thucydides' Cleon: 'We know it's a Greek custom, and goes on everywhere. But pity's only right if it's reciprocated [*antelein*]' (tr. Arnott 1996: 325); the slave's view is meant to be perceived as unGreek. Centuries later, Libanius, the tutor to Julian the Apostate, will write (*Orations* 19.13): 'The greatest point in which I find that Greeks differ from barbarians is that the latter are nearer to animals in that they disdain pity, while the former are quick to pity and to overcome anger'; in the same vein, the rhetorician Apsines (391 Spengel) will aver: 'Those capable of pity differ from the pitiless in the same degree as human beings differ from beasts.'

Nor is Cleon antagonistic to pity as such. He alleges, rather, that the proper response to behaviour such as that of the Mytilenaeans is not pity but anger or *orgê*. Aristotle defines anger as 'a desire, accompanied by pain, for a perceived revenge on account of a perceived slight on the part of people who are not fit to slight one or one's own' (*Rhetoric* 2.2, 1378a31-3); it is a response to an insult or belittlement, not to harm as such. Had Mytilene been a subject state, Cleon asserts, the revolt would have been understandable, although it might have been equally prejudicial to Athens' rule: a dependent city is naturally ambitious for its freedom. But the Mytilenaeans were, Cleon insinuates, already Athens' equals. Hence their rebellion is a sign of faithlessness and contempt: not just injurious but arrogant and unfair (3.39.2-3); thus, the Athenians are wholly justified in exacting vengeance or punishment – the Greek word *timôria* signifies both ideas – as quickly as possible.[18] In castigating the Athenians for their susceptibility to pity toward their allies, Cleon is not just trying to render them dispassionate reckoners of their own interests; he is rather seeking to substitute anger for *eleos*, as good pleaders did before a jury.

In his reply to Cleon, Diodotus does not attempt to defend the Mytilenaeans' claim to pity. On the contrary, his strategy is to dismiss the issue of justice entirely, and to urge the Athenians to look only to the question of advantage (3.44.1-2). Pritchett (1991: 242) comments that Diodotus disdains an appeal to mercy, and 'deprecates the influence of any compassionate sentiment'. But Diodotus' reasoning deserves closer consideration. The debate in the Assembly is not, Diodotus claims, a trial, in which right and wrong must be determined and blame assigned, but rather a situation in which the only relevant matter is the interests of the Athenians (3.44.4). Both pity and anger are appropriate to a lawcourt, Diodotus implies. As Danielle Allen (1999: 194) observes: 'The Athenians had no doubts about why they punished: it was simply because someone was *angry* at a wrong and wanted to have that anger dealt with.'[19] Cleon's error was to imagine that the debate was about the legitimacy of the Mytilenaeans' mutiny, whereas in fact, Diodotus avers, the question is purely one of expediency. Hence it requires sober calculation, not moral indignation or sympathy.[20]

Almost a century afterwards, Aristotle observed in the *Rhetoric* (1.3, 1358b20-9) that each of the three chief genres of oratory, namely deliberative, forensic and display, had its own proper aim; those who speak about policy should look principally to 'advantage and harm', whereas courtroom pleaders must consider what is just or unjust. Diodotus is an early exponent of this doctrine (cf. Heath 1990), and is at least prepared to acknowledge right and wrong to

3. Pity and Power

the extent of arguing that not all the Mytilenaeans are equally deserving of punishment; but in the course of the Peloponnesian war, as Thucydides recounts it, speakers devote ever less consideration to justice, and correspondingly more to interest or advantage (Pelling, unpublished). This is perhaps as it should be in matters of state. What is remarkable is that Cleon and Diodotus both take it for granted that the emotions – above all pity and anger – are entirely appropriate in judicial contexts. Right and wrong are seen through the lens of the evaluative passions.

No abstract moral principle limited the Athenians' freedom to annihilate a conquered enemy. The vanquished had no rights.[21] If their motives were recognized as just or reasonable, they might earn pity, and if not, anger: this is the application of the *ius ad bellum* (the principles of just war) to the treatment of the conquered – a weak reed on which to depend, since it was the conqueror who judged. Otherwise, the interests of the victor would decide their fate.

Near the end of the Second Punic War (201 BC), when Scipio had already crossed into Africa and Carthage had sued for peace, a Roman supply convoy was driven ashore by a storm and impounded by the Carthaginians. Scipio was infuriated, the Greek historian Polybius relates (15.1.2), by this sign of treachery and disregard for the oaths that the Carthaginians had sworn even more than by the material loss, and sent envoys to demand the restitution of the ships and their cargo. The envoys remind the Carthaginians that they themselves had acknowledged that they would justifiably (*eikotôs*) suffer the worst at the hands of the Romans for having violated the original treaty (15.1.8). Should war again break out, what gods could they appeal to, with what arguments might they petition pity from the conquerors, given their faithlessness and folly? (15.1.13-14) – note the connection between pity and innocence. The Carthaginians dismiss the envoys, and subsequently ambush their ship as it approaches the Roman camp. With this, hostilities are renewed.

In response to this second breach of faith, Scipio decides no longer to accept into his trust (*pistis* here = *fides* in the Roman technical sense of a relationship with a client state) even those cities that voluntarily surrender, but enslaves the populations instead, thereby making apparent the anger (*orgê*) he bears toward the enemy as a result of the Carthaginians' perfidy (15.4.2). He does not, however, mistreat the Carthaginian ambassadors returning from Rome with news of the successful negotiations there, in part for strategic reasons, but also, Polybius tells us, because he looks not to what the Carthaginians deserve but to how Romans should behave (15.4.10). Obedient to this principle, he restrains his wrath (*thumos*).

After the Roman victory in the battle of Zama, which put an end to Hannibal's ambitions and (for the time being) the Carthaginians' fortunes, Scipio set the terms of surrender, reminding the foe that they had no right to resent what they were deprived of, but should rather consider it a miracle if any humanity (*philanthrôpon*) were shown to them, for fortune had, because of their own treachery, stripped them of pity and pardon (15.17.5-6).[22] Because they have acted unjustly, pity is out of the question, and only kindness is left as a motive for sparing them the worst.

In 231 or 230 BC, an Illyrian raiding party put in on the coast of Epirus in northwestern Greece, pillaged a major town with the help of the garrison of Gaulish mercenaries who had been hired to defend it, and defeated the Epirotes in pitched battle. The Epirotes sent ambassadors bearing the olive branch of supplication to the Aetolians and the Achaeans, in order to beg their aid. These federations, in turn, took pity (*kateleêsantes*) on their misfortunes, and marched to the rescue (2.6.1-2), but the Illyrians, having been summoned home by their queen, struck a truce with the Epirotes and prevented the battle. In this pass, the Epirotes took the extraordinary measure of compacting with the Illyrians against the Aetolians and Achaeans, thus showing, Polybius complains (2.6.11), that they were undiscriminating in respect to their benefactors as well as foolish in taking counsel for their own affairs. Here Polybius digresses briefly to reflect on moral principles. When human beings encounter adversity that cannot be anticipated, he writes, the blame lies not with them but with chance and the agents of their misfortune: hence they meet with pity along with understanding (*sungnômê*) and assistance. But if for want of judgment they entangle themselves in calamities, then it is agreed, says Polybius, that the error is theirs (2.7.1-3; cf. 8.36.8). Such was the case of the Epirotes, according to Polybius, who exhibited their stupidity in the

3. Pity and Power

first instance by placing their trust in the Gauls. By implication, the Aetolians and Achaeans were mistaken to have pitied them, and ought to have left them to their fate.

Polybius' most extensive discussion of pity occurs, however, in the context of the Achaean War. Under pressure from the Spartans, the Achaeans summoned Antigonus Doson of Macedon to their assistance; he quickly reduced a series of cities beginning with Tegea, which submitted after a brief siege (2.54.7). Antigonus secured matters there, Polybius tells us (2.54.8), and subsequently besieged Mantinea, which also surrendered; still other towns capitulated voluntarily (2.54.11-13). Polybius says nothing here about the treatment of the captives. As winter approached (the year is 223 BC), the Spartan king Cleomenes III struck back and attacked Megalopolis, penetrating the city by night although the inhabitants put up a heroic resistance. Cleomenes' vengeance was bitter, in part, Polybius says, because he had failed to find a single person willing to betray the city, and he so ravaged it that no one expected that it could ever be resettled (2.55.7-8). At this point, Polybius pauses to explain why he has chosen to follow the account of Aratus for these incidents, rather than that of Phylarchus, whom many find more trustworthy (both were contemporaries of the events described).

According to Polybius, Phylarchus was determined to demonstrate the cruelty of Antigonus and Aratus, the leader of the Achaeans, and for this reason claimed that when Mantinea fell, its inhabitants endured misfortunes so dreadful as to draw the attention and elicit the tears of all other Greeks (2.56.6).[23] With a view, then, to rousing his readers to pity and rendering them sensitive (*sumpatheis*) to his account, he introduced descriptions of women baring their breasts and tearing their hair, and of men and women along with children and the elderly weeping and lamenting indiscriminately as they were led off (2.56.7). Polybius faults Phylarchus for the vivid depiction of horrors throughout his history, and affirms that the proper aim of history, as opposed to tragedy, is not to astound the reader but to stick to the truth, however pedestrian it might be.[24] 'Apart from this,' Polybius adds, 'Phylarchus simply narrates most of his reversals, and provides no reason or character traits; but without these it is impossible to feel pity rationally [*eulogôs*] or be angry responsibly [*kathêkontôs*] at any event' (7.56.13; cf. Dio Cassius 51.15.2, who observes that Antony and Cleopatra 'pitied irrationally [*alogôs*]'). Polybius goes on to explain that it is terrible for free men to be beaten, but if this is punishment for instigating a fight, then we regard it as justified; so too with killing another person, as when we catch a thief or adulterer in the act. The critical distinction in all such cases resides not in the events themselves, but rather in the reasons and characters of the actors.[25]

As David Levene (1997: 134) notes, Polybius, like Aristotle, adopts 'a broadly "cognitivist" approach to emotion', in which an evaluation of motives and context is essential to emotion.[26] In Polybius' account, however, the criterion is prescriptive: neither the actors in the narrative nor the reader *should* be moved by good or bad fortune as such. Polybius then applies his principle to the fate of the Mantineans. When Aratus had conquered the city four years previously, he had treated the inhabitants with exemplary humanity (*philanthrôpia*, 2.57.8); no people had ever encountered kindlier (*eugnômonesterois*) enemies. But when the Mantineans went over to the Spartans, they slit the throats of the Achaeans in their midst, in violation, Polybius says, of what it is customary to grant one's enemies under the laws common to mankind (*tous koinous tôn anthrôpôn nomous*, 2.58.6, cf. *ta koina tôn anthrôpôn dikaia*, 2.58.7).[27] They were thus deserving of any degree of anger (2.58.8), nor could they have paid a suitable penalty (*dikên*).

> Perhaps one might say, yes, they could: if, when they were defeated, they had been sold along with their wives and children; but this is something that even those who have committed no impious act suffer, in accord with the norms of war (*kata tous tou polemou nomous*, 2.58.10). Did not they deserve to endure a more thorough and greater punishment, such that even if they suffered what Phylarchus says they did, it is not pity that should have been showered on them by the Greeks, but rather praise and approval on those who did what they did and punished their impiety? But since nothing worse happened to the Mantineans after their reversal than that their livelihoods were plundered and free men were sold [into

3. Pity and Power

slavery], the writer [i.e. Phylarchus] not only introduced lies for the sake of dramatic effect but in fact implausible lies [sc. and thus not even worthy of a tragedian] (2.58.9-12).

There is more in this vein, including a defence of torture (normally applied only to slaves) as an instrument of just vengeance – nothing, Polybius says, in comparison to what the miscreant deserved, which is to have been dragged round Greece so that his agonies might be universally displayed.

That the Tegeans suffered nothing comparable to what the Mantineans did when they were conquered, Polybius adds, proves that Antigonus' vengeance upon the Mantineans was motivated not by native savagery (*ômotês*) but rather by anger (*orgê*), which was inspired and justified by their prior behavior. Just here, however, there is an odd lapse. According to Polybius, mass enslavement was the norm for vanquished cities; if Antigonus treated the Mantineans better than they deserved by merely enslaving them rather than applying the sterner measures that their conduct justified, how is it that he was motivated, not by pity, but by anger, which ought to have made him more violent toward them? As the opposite of *ômotês* or 'savagery', one would have expected to see a term like gentleness (*praotês*) here – not anger – to account for his punishing the treacherous Mantineans merely in accord with the usual rules of war. Polybius' text betrays a sense that the enslavement of an entire people is in itself an extreme measure prompted by rage – witness Antigonus' milder treatment of Tegea and indeed of Sparta. Bernard Williams (1993: 116) observes that, for the ancient Greeks, 'being captured into slavery was a paradigm of disaster, of which any rational person would complain', and the rhetorician Apsines (third century AD) lists slavery and capture in war along with the death of a wife or child as particularly evocative of pity (396 Spengel).[28] A modern political theorist asks rhetorically: 'Who ... would dream of saying that the inhabitants of a country ravaged by famine have what they deserve?' (Boltanski 1999: 5). Polybius would, if he judged that they deserved it. He denounces Phylarchus precisely for treating dire misery as pitiable in and of itself. But he cannot maintain the pose. Phylarchus' emotional historiography seems to have an ethical content of its own, which disrupts or intrudes upon Polybius' own narrative at this point.[29]

We have observed that Polybius' view of pity is prescriptive: he recognizes that Phylarchus succeeds in arousing pity by what he represents as the mere description of suffering, irrespective of desert – by what Aristotle called the sheer *pathos* of the events (*Poetics* 13, 1453b18) – but he rejects the method as unworthy of an historian. According to Polybius, then, pity is of two kinds: the one evaluative, the other responsive to misfortune as such, or at least misfortune of a certain magnitude (cf. Schrijvers 1978: 485-6; Orelli 1912: 170-5 on 'rationalists' versus 'emotionalists'). Aristotle had called this latter response *to philanthrôpon* (*Poetics* 1453a1-7), the fellow-feeling evoked by a story of a bad man passing from good fortune to ill (see Chapter 1). This and the abstract noun *philanthrôpia* become the terms of art for mildness or humanity, as attested in the history of Polybius himself. *Philanthrôpia*, however, was conceived of as a virtue or disposition rather than an emotion – not the kind of thing to be elicited by vivid rhetorical representation.[30] And yet, neither the distinction between pity and humanity, nor the division of pity itself into a cognitive and an uncritically sentimental emotion, provides firm ground for Polybius' attack on Phylarchus. If we accept the premise that no human being deserves to be enslaved – that, in the words of Jack Donnelly, 'certain things simply cannot legitimately be done to human beings' (1984: 404) – then Phylarchus' sense of pity is just as cognitive or evaluative as Polybius' own. Humanity is just the recognition that some forms of suffering are by their nature pitiable. So Aaron Ben-Ze'ev (2000: 330) adverts to pity's 'underlying assumption ... that no human being deserves to be in such a miserable situation'.

In the year 413 BC, the great armada that Athens had sent to conquer Syracuse and bring the island of Sicily under its control was defeated and most of the army slain; some 7,000 soldiers, however, were captured alive. The campaign had been recounted with chilling detachment by Thucydides, who was a contemporary of the events. In the first century BC, Diodorus of Sicily recapitulated the narrative, and introduced a debate (or reproduced one from his source) in the Syracusan assembly, not recorded by Thucydides, over how to

3. Pity and Power

treat the survivors.[31] On one side, a certain Diocles, said to be the most prestigious of the popular leaders, proposed that the Athenian generals be tortured and killed and the rest of the captives sent to the quarries; in due time, the allies of the Athenians might be sold off, but the Athenians themselves should continue to work in bondage on barley rations, that is, slave fodder. Hermocrates, the aristocratic leader who, in Thucydides' account, did most to rally the Syracusans against the Athenian blockade and frustrate the plans of democratic sympathizers in Syracuse to betray the city, rose to speak against this proposal, but was shouted down by the masses. The people fell silent, however, when a certain Nicolaus, who had lost two sons in the war, mounted the podium, since it was assumed that he would back Diocles' motion (13.19.4-6).

Nicolaus tells the assembly that he has ample reason to hate the Athenians, and if it were just a matter of Athens, he would be harshly disposed. But because the issue is the more general one of pity for the unfortunate and the common interest, and the reputation of the Syracusans before all mankind is at stake, he will speak solely to the question of advantage. The Athenians, Nicolaus continues, have paid the due (*axian*) penalty for their injustice in initiating the war, with their overweening ambitions dashed and themselves crushed by calamities. Knowing this, the Syracusans ought to respect the power of fortune and not do something inhuman (13.21.4). 'Some will say, perhaps, the they have done us wrong, and we are in a position to take vengeance on them' (13.21.5). But punishment has already been inflicted, and the enemy surrendered trusting in the Syracusans' kindness (*eugnômosunê*); it is not right, then, that they give the lie to the Syracusans' *philanthrôpia* (13.21.6). They are now suppliants instead of foe. In turn, the winners should trust less to strength at arms than to decency (*epieikeia*) of character. It was the Medes' savagery (*ômotês*) that cost them their empire, and Cyrus' gentleness (*eugnômosunê*) and mildness (*hêmerotês*) that gained the Persians theirs (13.22.2-3). The Syracusans' own history shows how much better it is to have subjects who suffer with one (*sunalgein*) over reversals and rejoice at one's successes (*hêdesthai*). Let the Syracusans be known for having conquered both in battle and in *philanthrôpia* that city that was first to found an altar to Pity, and dare to show pity to their fiercest enemies (13.22.6-8).[32] In addition, by appearing mild toward those in misfortune, they will obtain the pity of all in the event of some all too human reversal (13.23.3; cf. 27.18.1). The hearts of gentle or civilized people are, Nicolaus affirms, overcome by pity because they recognize the common affection (*koinê homopatheia*) of nature (13.24.2) – an extraordinary expression, perhaps owing something to Stoic thought. The speech, which continues at some length, furnishes almost a complete lexicon of Greek terms for pity, kindness and leniency.

In reply to Nicolaus, Gylippus, the Spartan general who commanded the Syracusan troops, reminds the assembled Syracusans of their losses, and denies that the Athenians deserve any consideration: 'For those who originally established the customary practice in these matters granted pity to the unfortunate but vengeance against those who commit a wrong because of their own wickedness' (13.29.3). The Athenians' own mercilessness is amply revealed in their decision concerning the Mytilenaeans, whom they voted to slaughter when they sought to recover their freedom (13.30.4). Although Gylippus suppresses the subsequent debate in which the Athenians voted to temper the original decree and spare the city save for the most seditious element, the allusion reminds the reader of the model for Diodorus' account of the assembly at Syracuse.[33] And so forth: Gylippus is anything but laconic in his tirade against the enemy. As history had already determined, Gylippus wins the day.[34]

At the beginning of his speech, Nicolaus gestures toward an argument based on self-interest that is reminiscent of Diodotus' strategy, but with a difference: the interest of the Syracusans lies, among other things, in their reputation for humanity and pity. Thus Diodotus' manoeuvre for sidestepping both pity and anger is neatly finessed. But Nicolaus also makes a case for pity or clemency on more universal grounds, by pointing to the changeability of human affairs and the consequent vulnerability of everyone to misfortune. Here again, he undermines Cleon's thesis that some enemies are unalterably hostile and will never repay pity. Nicolaus acknowledges the element of desert, but by insisting that the Athenians have suffered adequately by their defeat, he disables the idea of

3. Pity and Power

exacting revenge above and beyond victory. For Nicolaus, kindness and humanity (*epieikeia, philanthrôpia*) toward others, including enemies, are both useful and natural – the terms are 'a hallmark of Diodoran thought' (Sacks 1990: 43), occurring some 300 times in the text – and even those who have done wrong are deserving of magnanimity.[35] But the equation between charity and pity that runs through the speech indicates that pity too is not so bound to considerations of justice and merit as it was on Polybius' description. The profusion of terms for humaneness blurs the distinction between the sentiment (*pathos*) of pity and a disposition (*hexis*) to gentleness.[36] What Nicolaus falls short of asserting, however, is that certain kinds of treatment – enslavement, mass slaughter – are in their very nature wrong. Pity and humanity are not founded, in antiquity, on a concept of human rights – on things that 'simply cannot legitimately be done to human beings'.[37]

As a Sicilian himself, Diodorus perhaps had a personal interest in representing the Syracusan aristocracy as disposed to mercy, but it corresponds also to the image Diodorus projects of the Romans. Scipio, in the Punic war, is the paradigm example of pity and generosity toward the defeated. 'Bested by pity for the unfortunate' (27.6.2), and moved by the magnitude of his fall and the fragility of human affairs, he releases Syphax, the Numidian king who had gone over to the Carthaginians, from his bonds and gives him his own tent (cf. 27.8.1). But the Romans in general excel in the kindness and pity that prudence itself recommends, given that success and failure are mutable and one may someday be at the mercy of one's enemies (31.3.1-4); it was Julius Caesar's motive, according to Diodorus, for restoring the ruined city of Corinth (32.27.1) – shades of Scipio weeping at the site of Carthage! Might Diodorus have been influenced by the Romans' own concern with clemency, especially in the aftermath of Caesar's dictatorship? In the forties BC, the term *clementia* was often interchangeable, as we shall see, with *misericordia* or 'pity'. The answer depends in part on the degree of originality we allow Diodorus in the composition of speeches, but even those scholars who treat him as a slavish compiler acknowledge that he adapted his sources to his own style and vocabulary. It remains an intriguing question.

Pity Transformed

The Alexandrian historian Appian (second century AD) amplifies Polybius' version of the episode in which the Carthaginians plundered the Roman ships that were driven ashore by a storm by putting into the mouth of Hasdrubal a speech in which he begs Scipio's mercy. Hasdrubal ascribes the blame for the Carthaginians' behaviour to the desperate famine that afflicted them: hence they failed to treat others' goods – which by chance lay before them – as they ought to have (*Libyan Wars* 220): 'But if we nevertheless seem to you to be in the wrong [*adikein*], and not just unfortunate, we agree and on this account too make our plea. For arguments based on justice [*dikaiologia*] are for those who have not erred [*hamartontes*], but for those who have erred there is pleading [*paraklêsis*]. And in this, pity on the part of the fortunate is swifter if they are wary of human circumstances, when they perceive that, because of sudden reversals, those who are pleading now were yesterday in a position to wrong them' (221-2). Hasdrubal describes the former power of the Carthaginians, and urges the Romans 'to do what is worthy of your own magnanimity [*megalophrosunê*] and the Carthaginians' earlier fortune' (224), adding suitable warnings about divine nemesis toward those who ignore the lesson of Carthage's own fate: 'It is in the power of the successful to be humane [*to philanthrôpon*]' (226). Scipio replies that the Carthaginians do not deserve pardon (*sungnômê*), but rather the most extreme kind of punishment (230), and that they may chalk up to gain whatever is granted them (233); but he elects not to follow the harsh example of the Carthaginians themselves, and proceeds to dictate the terms on which the Romans will accept peace and spare the city and its territory. In a subsequent debate in the Senate at Rome, Publius Cornelius, a rival of Scipio's, responds to the arguments of one of Scipio's friends (248) by stating the case for destroying Carthage, rehearsing their crimes and concluding that they deserve neither pity nor restraint (*metriopatheia*), since they have never behaved either gently or moderately toward anyone else (283).

The pedigree of this debate is by now clear, but one point in particular deserves closer attention, and that is Hasdrubal's claim that arguments from justice, or legal arguments (*dikaiologia*), are

3. Pity and Power

for those who have not erred, whereas pleas for pity are for those who have. For Hasdrubal appears to be detaching pity from desert, and arguing precisely for its role in forgiving the guilty, the reverse of the strategy employed in the Athenian forensic tradition (the Socratic view that wrongdoers are pitiable is self-consciously paradoxical; see Chapter 1 note 21). Of course, Hasdrubal is in no position to insist on the Carthaginians' innocence when they have just committed the unpardonable offence of attacking envoys, whose sanctity was one of the few rules recognized in the conduct of war in antiquity. The debate composed by Appian differs from its antecedents, moreover, in that the vanquished are pleading their own case; one would expect that they would argue deviously if it were to their advantage, the more so in that the Carthaginians had a reputation for duplicity among the Romans. Hasdrubal's defence may, then, be a bit of irony on Appian's part, intended to be seen as specious.

Hasdrubal speaks more of error (*hamartanein*) than injustice (*adikein*) in an attempt to minimize the Carthaginians' culpability, but his mention of their remorse or repentance (*metanoia*, *metagignôskomai*, 225) is consistent with his admission of guilt. Here again is a feature that is contrary to the practice of the Athenian logographers, who invariably, in the speeches that survive, take for granted their clients' innocence. I am inclined to see in Hasdrubal's appeal to pity an unusually straightforward expression of the argument from wretchedness as opposed to desert, which is the greater in proportion to the height from which one has fallen. Hasdrubal is, then, affirming the view of pity that both Aristotle and Polybius were at pains to discredit.

At the end of the Third Punic War (146 BC), the Romans took the decision to strip the Carthaginians of their arms and destroy the city. The Carthaginian heralds made a desperate appeal to the pity, moderation (*metriopatheia*) and piety of the Romans (364): even the hard-hearted would recognize the surfeit of their misfortunes. When their petition was refused, they hurled themselves to the ground, covered themselves in dirt, and produced so painful and pitiable a spectacle that the Romans themselves wept, although they knew that this violent response would pass in due time. Even the consuls felt *oiktos* at such a human reversal (384), though they retained

Pity Transformed

their strict demeanour, and as a result they were induced to reconsider the matter in a second debate. The Romans' pity has been aroused by the mere sight of the Carthaginians' suffering, which works on them independently of considerations of desert.

Aristotle's cognitive analysis of the emotions, which today is again common wisdom (see Introduction), subverts the radical distinction between reason and passion, but at the same time opens up a space for another contrast between an authentically evaluative emotion and a defective type that omits the necessary element of judgment or assessment. Polybius exploited this opposition, as we have seen, in his critique of Phylarchus' historiographical style as evocative of raw pity, irrespective of desert. His division, however, may reflect what were in reality not so much two ideas of pity as two different assessments of what counts as pitiable, each of them equally evaluative in nature – if, for example, Phylarchus recognized kinds or degrees of suffering from which pity cannot justifiably be withheld.

And yet, pity does tend to exceed the claims of justice and, like mercy, judge the suffering of another in a generous and humane spirit, irrespective of what a strict reckoning of worth might be thought to warrant: hence its assimilation to *epieikeia* and *philanthrôpia* in Diodorus, for example. Demosthenes, in warning against the appeals of demonstrably guilty men to pity, had already paired *eleos* with *philanthrôpia* (25.76 *Against Aristogeiton 1*; cf. 81, and 82-4 on the necessity of coupling pity with desert). Later, Lactantius will defend pity against the Stoics by just such an identification with *humanitas*, *caritas* and *pietas* (see Chapter 4). But this move, as we shall see, threatens to strip pity of its character as an emotion and convert it into a virtue or duty. In Appian – and, as we shall remark below, in Livy too – there abides a tension between the affect spontaneously elicited by the vivid image of another's affliction and an exacting assessment of desert, always as judged by the victor and with a shifting but uniformly harrowing conception of the rights of conquest. Pity itself tugs in two directions, as though there were an instability at the heart of the concept. Some ancient philosophers, in particular the maverick Stoic Posidonius of Apamea (second/first century BC), who wrote historical as well as philosophical works and

3. Pity and Power

influenced both Diodorus Siculus and Roman historians, seem to have defended a non-cognitive view of the passions, arguing, among other things, from the emotional response to music.[38] Whether in response to such theories, or because they were sensitive to the richness of ordinary usage, Latin writers too, like the Greeks, wavered in the way they represented pity.[39]

The Roman historian Sallust was probably indebted directly to Thucydides' account of the Mytilenaean debate as a model for the paired speeches he assigned to Caesar and Cato in the senatorial discussion of the fate of Catiline (*Conspiracy of Catiline* 51-2).[40] Like Cleon, Cato denounces a misplaced sense of pity for an implacable and irreconcilable enemy (52.26-7), and throws in for good measure a critique of the abuse of language prevalent in his day: 'Somebody here mentions to me gentleness and pity (*mansuetudinem et misericordiam*). We have long since lost the true names for things. Just because giving away other people's goods is called generosity and the temerity to commit crimes is called courage, the republic is now in crisis' (52.11) – the diatribe is clearly based on Thucydides' account of the fatal consequences for the Greeks' moral vocabulary of the Corcyrean revolution and of civil war generally (3.82.4-6). Although Sallust's own judgment of his patron, Caesar, is that he is pre-eminent for gentleness and pity (54.2), a trait for which Rome itself is distinguished (34.1), this is not the basis of Caesar's argument against the execution of the conspirators. Rather, he asks, like Thucydides' Diodotus, that the senators refrain equally from hostility and favour, anger and pity (51.1; cf. 51.4).[41] Caesar seems to be at pains to discount his own reputation for mildness as a motive for sparing the lives of the conspirators (the word 'clemency' does not occur in Sallust's essay), and rests his case primarily on the argument that the contrary tendency – toward rage – should not provoke the Senate to violate the law.

If Sallust evades the issue of pity, Livy's vast canvas of Roman history takes us to the heart of the Roman idea. While Hannibal was occupying much of southern Italy, the Petelini were, Livy reports, the only tribe among the Bruttians who remained loyal to the Romans. Embattled by the Carthaginians and the rest of the Bruttians alike, they sent an embassy to Rome to petition assistance.

Their prayers and tears 'aroused a profound pity in both the senators and the people' (23.20.5) – clearly the conscience of the Romans was touched, since they ought not to be failing a faithful ally; we may compare the Senate's response to the news of the fall of Saguntum to Hannibal: 'pity for allies undeservedly [*indigne*] destroyed' (21.16.2; cf. Silius Italicus 1.690-1, 2.650-7).

Livy is well aware, however, that pity, or *misericordia*, may alter a judgment based on consideration of merit alone. We have already mentioned (Chapter 1) how the people of Tusculum, accused of having supported the Veliterni and Privernates in their offensive against Rome, rent their garments and, with their wives and children, made the rounds of the Roman tribes as they prepared to vote, with the result that 'pity was more effective in securing their pardon than their argument was in exculpating them from the charge' (8.37.10). Though the rest of the thirty-five tribes set aside the rigours of justice, one tribe, the Pollia, with Polybian severity, was in favour of executing the men of fighting age and enslaving the women and children 'in accord with the laws of war [*lege belli*]' (8.37.11). Livy remarks that the memory of this 'savage penalty' (*poena atrox*) endured for centuries afterwards. Soo too, Livy describes how Mandonius was sent by his brother Indibilis, king of the Ilergetes in Spain, during the Second Punic War (206 BC) to petition Scipio's pardon: 'previously, he had trusted in his own cause [*causa*], since he had not yet experienced his [Scipio's] clemency; now, however, he rested none of his hopes in his cause, but all of them in the pity of the victor' (28.34.6; cf. 22.22.20, 36.27.7). So too, 'the Aetolians, who had more hope in the pity of the senate than in their own case [*causa*], acted as suppliants' (37.1.2). The clemency of Rome and the Romans, we are given to understand, was legendary (cf. Livy 3.2.6: Quintus Fabius' response to the Aequi in 466-5 BC). Indeed, the senate of Capua decided to surrender the city to the Romans (211 BC), despite their earlier support of Hannibal, because they were well acquainted with the city's clemency (26.14.1-3).[42] Cicero can exclaim in a rhetorical flourish in one of his earliest speeches (*Against Verres* 2.5.74): *O clementiam populi Romani!*

For the Stoic Seneca, the fact that 'pity looks not to the case [*causa*], but to the condition' (*On Clemency* 2.5.1, cited in Chapter 1)

3. Pity and Power

was sufficient reason to condemn it as a vice, in contrast to the virtue of clemency, which, he affirms, 'accedes to reason'. Tacitus, whether because of Stoicism or his own caustic cynicism, did not regard *misericordia* as a desirable quality in leaders save as a tactic used in combination with severity for pragmatic ends (e.g., *Annals* 14.23.2; cf. 13.35.4; Aubrion 1989: 384). Spontaneous pity he associated rather with the unstable opinion of the mob, which neglects the merits of a case and attends, like Phylarchus in Polybius' estimation, only to the pathos of the event.[43]

In ordinary language, however, as in Livy's account of Mandonius' mission to Scipio cited above, clemency and pity are often all but synonyms. In Catullus' miniature epic (64.137-8), Ariadne reproaches Theseus after he has abandoned her on a deserted island: 'Had you no clemency, that your cruel heart might have pitied me?'; and Cicero pairs the ideas in his essay *On Old Age* 17: 'you were unique for clemency and pity.' Stefan Weinstock (1971: 236) noted that up to the time of Caesar and Cicero, '*clementia* was a rare word; so the suspicion arises', he continues, 'that it was intentionally avoided in Roman politics', though I incline rather to believe that the fault lies with the sparsity of our sources. Be that as it may, the civil wars that racked Rome during the century before the establishment of Augustus' principate provided new scope for displays of kindness or cruelty on the part of the victors not just toward foreign enemies but, for the first time on so massive a scale, toward fellow citizens as well. At this point, the issue of clemency or leniency came into its own. The benchmark of ruthlessness was Lucius Cornelius Sulla, whose proscriptions (the legalized slaughter of individual enemies) earned him a reputation for savage vengeance (Livy *Periochae* 88), but even he could be praised for mildness (Dowling 2000). Diodorus Siculus (fragment 38.16) speaks, for example, of Sulla's *epieikeia* toward L. Cornelius Scipio Asiaticus, *epieikeia* being the conventional Greek translation of *clementia* – thus, Plutarch calls the temple dedicated to Caesar's Clemency the temple of Epieikeia (*Life of Caesar* 57). 'In that harsh and violent victory of Lucius Sulla,' Cicero asks (62 BC), 'who was more gentle [*mitior*], who more disposed to pity [*misericordior*], than Publius Sulla [a relative of Lucius]?' (*For Publius Sulla* 72).

Pity Transformed

Clemency was not radically distinguished from pity even when Julius Caesar elevated it almost to the status of a policy (cf. Pliny *Natural History* 7.92-3). In a famous letter to Oppius Cornelius, preserved in Cicero's correspondence with Atticus (9.7C.6), Caesar explains that, unlike Sulla, he prefers to be as mild as possible toward Pompey: 'this is a new strategy of conquest – to arm ourselves with pity and generosity [*misericordia et liberalitate*].' So too, Cicero (*To Atticus* 9.16) remarks on Caesar's renunciation of *crudelitas*. In his historical writings, Caesar rarely mentions the humaneness for which he was later renowned. Twice, he refers to his *clementia* and *mansuetudo* or gentleness (*Gallic Wars* 2.14.5, 2.31.4; cf. *Civil War* 3.20.2). In the *Gallic Wars* he records how, after a battle in which the people and very name of the Nervii had been brought near to extinction, some elders, who had survived along with women and children, sent delegates to him, announcing their surrender and observing that they were now reduced from sixty thousand men capable of bearing arms to barely five hundred. 'So that he might appear to exercise pity in respect to the wretched and suppliants, Caesar dutifully saved them and ordered them to utilize their own towns and territory, instructing their neighbours to restrain their peoples from insult and injury toward them' (2.28.3). His pity at the prospective slaughter of fellow citizens (1.72.3) induced him, by his own account, to seek a peaceful resolution to hostilities during the civil war (cf. 1.85.3, where Caesar charges the generals, rather than the troops, of his opponents with lack of pity).

It is true, as Weinstock observes, that after the civil war *clementia* appears with particular frequency in Cicero's letters, and it occurs thirteen times, by Weinstock's count, in the so-called Caesarian orations of Cicero, delivered shortly before Caesar's assassination (*For Marcellus* and *For Ligarius*, 46 BC; *For King Deiotarus*, 45 BC). It is found five times, as well, in the continuations of Caesar's *Commentaries* composed by his sympathizers after his death. Weinstock, who sees *clementia* as a new coinage in politics, concludes: 'The innovator then was Cicero, but the first move came from Caesar' (237), citing Caesar's decision to spare the Pompeians at Corfinium (21 February 49; the letter is preserved in Cicero's correspondence with Atticus 9.7C.1). But Caesar there refers not to

3. Pity and Power

clemency but rather to his *misericordia* and *liberalitas*, as opposed to Sulla's *crudelitas*. Cicero himself speaks as much of Caesar's pity as of his clemency (Adam 1970 notes that in Cicero, '*clementia* functions like *misericordia*'), and he varies both with such expressions as *lenitas* ('leniency'), *humanitas, mansuetudo, liberalitas, comitas, modestia, temperantia, magnitudo animi, modus* and *moderatio*, along with verbs for sparing and forgiving (*parcere, ignoscere*).[44] While Caesar's generous policy toward the defeated made a powerful impression on his contemporaries and on posterity, it is fair to say that the terminology to describe it was not yet fixed, and clemency still vied with pity and other locutions.

A number of scholars have supposed that Caesar's clemency was in truth a thinly disguised assertion of his tyrannical authority, deeply resented by aristocrats who in their own estimation were his peers and equals. Thus, Barbara Levick (1975: 126) writes that clemency is the 'virtue of an autocrat, of a Caesar', and adds that by the time of Tiberius 'it was already distasteful to the Romans'; she finds it odd, indeed, that Tiberius should have laid claim to it at all. In a recent book on Lucan (1997), Matthew Leigh argues that *clementia* is represented in his epic poem, *The Civil War*, as 'the stuff of absolute monarchy' (65), and adds 'that the acts of forgiveness and the acts of brutality are two sides of the same absolutist coin' (68).[45] I can find no contemporary evidence, however, that Caesar's clemency was in fact unwelcome, and I believe that it was regarded rather as a wholly positive virtue in a ruler.

True, Cicero distrusted Caesar's indulgence – he speaks of his *insidiosa clementia* (*Letters to Atticus* 8.16.2) – but not because he had misgivings about clemency as such. In the year 50 BC, Cicero expressed his anxiety that Caesar might be found wanting in clemency (*To Atticus* 7.7.7) should he emerge victorious in the struggle with Pompey. What troubled Cicero was rather the suspicion that Caesar's clemency was only a pretence; in another letter (10.4.8), he records Curio's view that 'Caesar himself refrains from being cruel not by character [*voluntate*] or nature, but because he <supposes> that clemency is popular [i.e. finds favour with the popular faction]; if he should lose the favour of the people, he would be cruel'. So too,

Pity Transformed

Livy says (21.48.10) that Hannibal, whose severity was proverbial, sought a reputation for clemency for strategic reasons.

Cicero too prided himself on his clemency or mercy, which he associated with virtues such as justice, restraint (*abstinentia*), integrity, and good faith (*To Atticus* 7.2.7 = 125 Shackleton-Bailey). In his speech in behalf of Roscius of Ameria (144), he lamented the loss of pity and humanity among the Romans – by nature the mildest of people – as a consequence of civil strife. And yet, in the aftermath of the assassination of Julius Caesar, Cicero urged on Brutus a policy of severity rather than clemency toward Caesar's partisans (e.g. *To Brutus* 14.3, 5.2, 6.2 Shackleton-Bailey): 'if we wish to be clement, there will be no end of civil wars.' He had learned a lesson from Caesar's fate.

In the year 27 BC, the Senate honoured Augustus with a shield representing the four cardinal virtues (*Res Gestae* 34); one of these was clemency, and from this time onward, it figured prominently among the traits of emperors (see Fears 1981: 885-90; Seneca *On Clemency* 1.3.2). The inscription announcing the condemnation of Piso speaks of Tiberius' 'clemency and justice' (90-1), and of his pity for Piso's wife Plancina (110-11). Pliny says of Trajan in his panegyric (80.1): 'how mild is his severity in all his judgments, how strict [*non dissoluta*] his clemency!' Even the notorious Caligula got into the act: there was a yearly sacrifice to his clemency (Suetonius *Caligula* 16.4, Cassius Dio 59.16.10). Clemency figures prominently on coins, as well as in the imperial biographical tradition; under the Antonines, it is associated with Pietas, Salus, Aequitas and Tranquillitas (Pera 1980). Inscriptions tell a similar story.[46] Scenes on the columns of Trajan and Marcus Aurelius and on the so-called 'General' sarcophagi (c. 150-80), which show barbarians kneeling in defeat before Roman conquerors, perhaps suggest clemency, although they more likely indicate surrender (*submissio*; cf. Hölscher 1986; Dowling forthcoming: ch. 4). As a subtle emotion, pity is not easily identified by facial expression (cf. Allen 1998: 83-7), and does not seem to have had a specific iconography in antiquity even in Christian images (the imagery associated with the Virgin Mary's pity is much later: Perdrizet 1908).

Why did clemency win out over *misericordia* and other rivals as

3. Pity and Power

the virtue par excellence of emperors? *Humanitas* or *lenitas* might have been candidates, but I suspect that these sounded like recent coinages, whereas *clementia* (despite Weinstock's claim) may have been long naturalized as an abstract term in Latin (on *humanitas*, see Schadewaldt 1973; Braund 1997). As for pity, it is possible that this, rather than clemency, would have sounded a note of contempt for the defeated. Cassius Dio reports (43.10.3) that Cato 'believed Caesar's pity [*eleos*] to be far worse than death'; Dio does not employ the word *epieikeia*, which would have corresponded to the Latin *clementia*. Pity would also have offended the Stoics, of course. Above all, however, pity, unlike clemency, was first and foremost an emotion rather than a virtue, and so less suitable to invoke as an attribute of character.

Clemency was understood to be a disposition – a part of one's constitution or *ingenium*, like its opposite, harshness of temperament.[47] It is frequently coupled with *mansuetudo* or mildness, as well as with *humanitas*: Valerius Maximus devotes a section of his collection of edifying anecdotes to the joint topic *humanitas et clementia*, which he illustrates mostly by behaviour in wartime.[48] As a habitual tendency to respond with moderation to an offence, clemency can serve as the basis for concord within the state: 'by means of clemency the harmony of the orders can be stabilized' (Livy 3.58.4-5: the idea is anachronistically projected back to the early Republic), and the imperial poet Calpurnius Siculus can exclaim (1.59): 'Clemency blasted the mad swords.'

Pity is too ephemeral and variable for such a purpose. Evoked by the immediate image of another's suffering, pity is spontaneous and normally short-lived, and liable to be displaced by contrary passions, such as envy, anger, and fear for oneself that the misfortune of the pitied may prompt: 'when they were reminded, by the deaths of others, what was to be feared in their own behalf, their pity turned to terror and they wept, not for those who had died, but for themselves' (Quintus Curtius 8.11.12; cf. 4.16.12: 'then pity was converted into fear').

The syntax of pity versus clemency makes the difference clear. One may experience another's clemency (*clementia experta*), or entrust oneself to it (*se committere clementiae*); contrariwise, one

Pity Transformed

speaks of exercising clemency (*utor clementia*) or exhibiting it (*ostendere clementiam*). Again, one can have clemency as a trait (*habere clementiam*, Seneca *On Clemency* 1.1.4, 1.2.5), though one does not normally grant, give, or bestow it: clemency is not pardon (*venia*) or acquittal (contra Bauman 1996: 40), although pardon may of course be sought or hoped for from a clement victor (cf. Livy 28.25.13-14; 37.55.1-2). Clemency is rather a disposition to lessen the severity of a penalty or to overlook a personal offence.

The emotion *misericordia*, for its part, is excited or stimulated (*commovetur*, Cicero *On the Orator* 2.195; *movetur*, ibid. 2.211, Livy 3.7.4, 23.20.6); one elicits it (*elicere*, Livy 8.26.2), and can be led to it (*adducitur*, Cicero *On the Orator* 2.190). Pity arises or surges up in us (*orior*, Livy 24.26.15; frequent in Tacitus); one's heart or mind can sink or plummet into it (*[animus] prolapsus in misericordiam*, Livy 30.12.18). Again, one can be turned or diverted (*flecti*) by pity, or coerced to feel it by the tears of others; Ennius describes in Book 5 of his *Annals* (Book 5, fragment 7 Skutsch [p. 85]) how the women of a defeated city 'compelled [*cogebant*] the enemy to pity them by their weeping'.[49] None of these locutions occurs with *clementia*. Metaphors such as these are revealing. Often, they vary over the history of a single word. 'The view of *anger* as something that can be manipulated – "controlled", "vented", "released", left "unresolved", "directed" at this or that target, "stirred up", "repressed", "expressed", "suppressed" and so on ... is entirely modern and goes far beyond the semantic range of Shakespearean *anger*' (Wierzbicka 1999: 31).[50] *Misericordia* too has a history, and among Christian writers it begins increasingly to be treated as a permanent quality of character (see Chapter 4).

It is worth noting that there is no Latin verb 'to be clement' (any more than there is in English), corresponding to *misereri* ('to pity').[51] As an adjective, moreover, *clemens* means 'mild' and can be applied to the weather (as in English), the sea, and other natural phenomena (e.g. Catullus 64.272 of a breeze; Columella *De re rustica* 4.23.1 of the sky); so too, a remark can be 'inclement' (Livy 9.34.24) in the sense of harsh. The adjective *misericors*, were it to occur in such contexts, would suggest personification. Nouns, of course, 'do not always mean the same as the corresponding adjectives', as Anna

3. Pity and Power

Wierzbicka observes (1999: 50), citing the difference between 'happiness' and 'happy', 'pleased' and 'pleasure' (53, 56), or as the associated verbs. The Spanish noun corresponding to the verb *saber* ('know') is not *sabiduria*, which means 'wisdom', but rather *conocimiento*. In Greek, the noun *philos* ('friend') and the verb *philein* ('love') have distinct connotations (Konstan 1997a). Examples can easily be multiplied. As abstract nouns, then, *misericordia* and *clementia* are in fact often interchangeable. But even where they seem to converge, pity often retains a distinct emotional colour through its association with the verbal idea that clemency lacks. A propos Cicero's compliment to Caesar: 'none of your many virtues is more admirable or more welcome than pity' (*For Ligarius* 12.37), which evidently raised some eyebrows in late antiquity, St Augustine (*Against Adimantus* 1.11) sagely observes: 'What then would Cicero reply to these quibblers, except that by the word "pity" he meant "clemency"? For we normally speak, and rightly so, using not only exact terms [*verba propria*] but also neighbouring ones [*vicina*]' (cited in Pétré 1934: 377).

The most extended examination of the relation between pity and clemency that survives from antiquity is Seneca's incomplete treatise, *On Clemency*, addressed to the emperor Nero. Unfortunately it is a puzzling document, due in part to Seneca's ambition to square clemency as an imperial virtue with the traditional Stoic hostility to pity. That the second book, in which Seneca addresses himself to the technical distinction between clemency and pity, terminates after a few paragraphs only adds to the confusion, especially since pity, pardon and forgiveness count as virtues in Book 1 but as vices in Book 2 (Adam 1970: 33-4; cf. 1.1.4, 1.6.2, 1.2.2, etc.). One scholar (Dingel 1989) has suggested that the conflation of pity and clemency in Book 1 represents Nero's understanding of the terms, and indeed Seneca himself does not observe the distinction strictly in his other writings, e.g. *On Benefactions* 6.29.1: 'a nature of its own inclined to *misericordia, humanitas* and *clementia*.'[52]

Without going into detail, let it suffice to point out that of the four elements that Seneca selects as salient to clemency (2.3.1-2), the first is restraint in regard to vengeance – 'it is characteristic of a great spirit to be calm and serene and aloofly to despise insults and offences' (1.5.5) – while the next three deal with leniency in setting or exacting a penalty (*poena*). So interpreted, clemency is not so much pity as mercy, defined as treating 'a person less harshly than, given certain rules, one has a right to treat that person' (Murphy in Murphy and Hampton 1988: 20; cf. Ben-Ze'ev 2000: 335).[53] The younger Pliny, in a letter to Geminus (8.22.1-3), captures it nicely: 'Nothing suits those who require no man's clemency more than leniency [*lenitas*]. I regard that man as best and freest of fault who pardons others as though he himself sinned daily, and abstains from sin as though he pardoned no one.'

A note on *epieikeia*

From Homer on, *epieikeia* means 'good' or 'decent' (D'Agostino 1973: 4), but by the fifth century BC (Herodotus 3.53; Antiphon *Tetralogies* 1.2.13) it appears in contrast with justice and signifies a certain softening of the rigour of the law (D'Agostino 1973: 4, 7), a use testified to in tragedy as well (Sophocles fr. 770 Pearson; Euripides fr. 645).[54] Aristotle lent the idea his own slant by specifying that *epieikeia* in legal contexts compensates for the inevitably general character of the law and adapts it to particular cases (*Nicomachean Ethics* 5.10, *Rhetoric* 1.13, 1.15; discussion in Hamburger 1951: 89-105; D'Agostino 1973: 65-100; Lawless 1991: 82-105; Ben-Ze'ev 2000: 348-52). Though the details of Aristotle's theory are obscure, it has had an enormous influence on the evolution of the juridical concept of equity. *Epieikeia* was not a technical term in the vocabulary of the Athenian orators, however (Lawless 1991: 100, 105-9), and never entered in a significant way into the ancient legal lexicon, always retaining the moral connotations of humaneness or charitability.[55]

4

Divine Pity

Sir Kenneth Dover (1994: 156) has observed that the Greeks in classical antiquity 'did not expect gods to be merciful'. In Christianity, by contrast, no formula is more familiar than the invocation *kurie, eleêson*, 'Lord, have pity', addressed to Jesus, which comes immediately after the introitus in the Catholic mass. The phrase entered early into the liturgy in the Greek east;[1] in the west, however, the Latin form, *Domine miserere*, remained in use until Pope Gregory I introduced it into the daily mass in the seventh century.[2]

One might suppose that the two attitudes toward divine pity simply reflect the wholly different religious outlooks of paganism and Christianity. But Christianity was not merely a foreign tradition grafted onto the alien stock of classical culture. In large measure, it developed within, and continually interacted with, the same Greco-Roman world that was host to polytheism and a wide range of other cults and beliefs. In this chapter, I examine some stages in the evolution of divine pity in the classical world both before and after the reception of Jewish and Christian beliefs under the Roman Empire.

In assessing the nature of these changes, we must of course be attentive to the possibility that the meanings of the terms themselves underwent transformation. Whereas Adam Smith, for example, could use pity in the sense of sympathy, in contemporary English 'pity' may suggest contempt (see Introduction), and has been largely displaced by compassion, which seems less arrogant. The article on 'sympathy' in *Webster's New Dictionary of Synonyms* (1968) informs us that '*compassion* suggests a greater dignity in the object than *pity* often does', though it adds that compassion 'also implies a greater detachment in the subject' – a contrast that already seems counter to current usage. It has been suggested that as *misericordia* acquired the sense of 'charity' or 'charitable works' in Christian writers such as Tertullian, Cyprian, Lactantius and Ambrose, this new meaning began to displace the old sense of 'pity'. Hence Latin Christian writers may have developed the new word *compassio* (first attested in Tertullian), modelled on the Greek *sumpatheia*, precisely to express the sentiment of pity, which now lacked an unambiguous name (see also Chapter 2).[3] So too, *eleomosunê* (a longer form of *eleos*), meaning both pity and an act of charity, first occurs in the Hellenistic period, most conspicuously in the Septuagint or Greek translation of the Hebrew Bible.[4]

Let us return, not for the first time, to Aristotle's definition of *eleos* in his treatise on rhetoric (2.8.2): 'Let pity, then, be a kind of pain in the case of an apparent destructive or painful harm of one not deserving to encounter it, which one might expect onself, or one of one's own, to suffer, and this when it seems near.' Pity is a response to misfortunes to which one believes oneself vulnerable. Aristotle draws, as we have seen, the logical conclusion that both those who have lost everything, and those who consider themselves exceptionally fortunate, are not susceptible to pity, the first because they do not expect that anything worse can befall them, the latter because they tend to consider themselves above misfortune.

In a practical way, Aristotle's dictum rings true. People who are overwhelmed by their own troubles are often less inclined to feel pity for the plight of another: 'You think you have problems ...' is the response they are likely to offer, followed by a list of woes. At the other end of the spectrum, the very successful tend to be dismissive of bad luck in others: 'if you want to borrow money, ask a poor man', the saying goes. But however true it may be of daily life, Aristotle's thesis has alarming consequences if taken as a rigorous account of the capacity to experience pity. For if invulnerability to misfortune abolishes pity, it should follow that pity must be alien to the gods, who are vastly more powerful than human beings and live forever. The more exalted our conception of the gods, the more remote they will be from any compassion for humble mortals. Aristotle's description seems to eliminate the very possibility of divine pity, precisely to the extent that the divine is imagined as transcendent.[5]

4. Divine Pity

We are not, of course, obliged to press Aristotle's remarks so hard: perhaps he was merely summing up popular wisdom, or limiting his discussion to one kind of pity, which is specifically human and does not pertain to the gods. In any case, the reflections of a professional philosopher do not necessarily tell us all there is to know about ordinary attitudes toward the gods. In fact, however, contemporary literature seems also to put in question the gods' capacity for pity, and thus lends support to Aristotle's theorizing.

In the opening scene of Sophocles' *Ajax*, Odysseus cautiously approaches the tent of Ajax, who has slaughtered a herd of sheep in a crazy attempt to assassinate the Greek generals at Troy because they denied him the prize of Achilles' armour after Achilles' death. Behind and above Odysseus stands Athena. Athena explains that it was she who rendered Ajax mad, and proclaims to Odysseus: 'I shall reveal to you this visible sickness of his .... Keep up your confidence, and do not consider the man to be a misfortune [i.e. to yourself]. For I shall prevent the twisted beams of his eyes from seeing your face' (66, 68-70). Odysseus reacts with alarm:

Od.: What are you doing, Athena? Don't call him out.
Ath.: Take it in silence and don't convict yourself of cowardice
 .... What can happen? Wasn't he but a man?
Od.: And an enemy of mine, and still is.
Ath.: Isn't the sweetest laughter to laugh at enemies?
Od.: I'm satisfied that he remain inside (74-80).

Athena invites Odysseus to enjoy the total defeat of his enemy, but Odysseus hesitates. After she has summoned Ajax out of doors despite Odysseus' qualms, and made a public spectacle of him, Athena addresses Odysseus once more:

Ath.: Do you see, Odysseus, how great is the power of the gods? Who ever had more foresight than this man ...?
Od.: No one I know. Nevertheless, I pity him in his misfortune [*epoiktirô de nin dustênon*], though he is my foe, because he has been yoked by evil ruin. And in this I have regard for my

Pity Transformed

condition no less than his: for I see that we who live are nothing but figments, or a frail shadow.

Ath.: Since you see this, never utter a proud word against the gods, nor puff yourself up for the power of your hand or deep wealth. A day topples and restores again all human affairs (118-32).

Athena and Odysseus agree that Ajax had been a good man, before he became enraged over the award of Achilles' arms to Odysseus rather than to himself. Both his murderous fury, and the god-inspired madness that causes him to mistake sheep for men, are treated as a misfortune. Odysseus pities Ajax because he recognizes that he too is vulnerable to such a calamity (see Chapter 2, Appendix). As a goddess, however, Athena is not afraid. Hence, she gloats over Ajax in perfect security, though she warns Odysseus that such a response is dangerous for mere mortals.

Sophocles' *Women of Trachis* tells how Hercules, the son of Zeus, died because of a poisoned garment sent him by his wife, who believed she was anointing it rather with a love potion, so as to win back Hercules' affection for her. Racked with pain, his flesh eaten to the bone, Hercules obliges his son, Hyllus, to prepare and light the pyre that will end his life. As servants carry out Hercules' corpse at the end of the play, Hyllus chants: 'show me great fellow-feeling [*sungnômosunê*] for these things, since you see the great unfeelingness [*agnômosunê*] of the gods for the deeds that have been done – gods who, though they begot us and are called our fathers, behold such sufferings. No one sees what is to come, but what is present now is pitiful [*oiktra*] to us, but shameful for them [i.e. the gods], and hardest to him, of all men, who has endured this ruin' (1265-74). Once more, the gods are shown to be aloof from human troubles that inspire pity in mortal men.

At the beginning of Euripides' *Trojan Women*, Troy is in flames, and the surviving women are being parcelled out as slaves to the Greek leaders. Enter Athena, who requests Poseidon's assistance in behalf of Troy. Poseidon: 'Have you, then, abandoned your former enmity and arrived at pity [*oiktos*] now for the city ablaze with fire?' (59-60). She has not. Rather, she is now reconciled with the Trojans

4. Divine Pity

because the Greeks have desecrated her temple, and she wishes, with Poseidon's help, to punish them on their sea-voyage home. 'Why do you leap this way from one mood to another, and hate and love to excess whom you may?' (67-8), Poseidon asks.

In Euripides' *Electra* (671-3), Orestes and Electra beg Zeus for pity (the verb, as usual in this context, is *oiktirein*), but in the finale Castor (twin brother of Pollux) loftily pronounces that what Electra has endured is not pitiable (1311-13). However, upon seeing her and Orestes exchange a final embrace, he weakens and exclaims (1329-30): 'Even I and Uranus' brood have pity [*oiktos*] for suffering mortals.' The word 'even' (*kai*) is telling. Admetus beseeches his dying wife to ask pity of the gods (Euripides *Alcestis* 251), but she ignores the suggestion, and Oedipus, in Sophocles' last tragedy, *Oedipus at Colonus*, asks pity of the Furies and the city of Athens (106-10: *oiktirate*), but his daughter Ismene cannot imagine how the gods will take pity on his misfortunes (383-844).[6]

It might be said that tragedy by its nature raises the question of human suffering in a cold, indifferent universe, and is thus the wrong genre in which to look for divine compassion. In Homeric epic, indeed, there are several scenes in which the gods are described as feeling pity.[7] For example, in the nineteenth book of the *Iliad*, when Achilles, in mourning for the death of his friend, Patroclus, refuses food or drink, Zeus takes pity on him (19.340) and sends Athena to fill his veins with nectar and ambrosia. But then, Homer's gods know what it is to lose a dear one.[8] Shortly before, when Patroclus was still on the rampage, he squared off against the Lycian hero Sarpedon, who was Zeus' own son. Upon seeing them, and knowing that Patroclus was fated to be victorious, Zeus was moved to pity (16.431), and toyed for a moment with rescuing Sarpedon, in spite of destiny; he desists, but weeps tears of blood for him. For all his power, this Zeus is not so remote as to be untouched by grief. So too, in the final book of the *Iliad*, Apollo and the other gods (or some of them, at least) experience pity at the sight of Hector's corpse (24.19, 23), which Achilles, in revenge for the slaying of Patroclus, has dishonoured by dragging it behind his chariot; Apollo complains that Achilles has eradicated all pity (24.44). Unlike Athena in Sophocles'

Ajax, Homer's Apollo is touched by mortal misery, and can even reproach a human being for want of sympathy.

Divine pity, however, is not a quality on which human beings can safely rely.[9] In general, characters in Homer do not ask the gods for pity, and when they do, it is always with the recognition that the result of such a petition is at best doubtful.[10] In the sixth book of the *Iliad*, when the Trojans are hard pressed by Diomedes and the Greeks, the prophet Helenus advises Hector to return to the city and ask his mother, the queen Hecuba, to bring a royal robe to the temple of Athena and promise to dedicate twelve oxen, 'if she might pity the town and the wives of the Trojans and their innocent children' (6.94-5).[11] That uncertain 'if' in the prayer formula is justified, since Athena will in fact refuse Hecuba's petition (6.311).[12]

The same conditional expression occurs again in the last book of the epic, when Priam, as he sets out to ransom the body of Hector from Achilles, consents to ask Zeus for a sign: 'for it is good', he says, 'to lift one's hands to Zeus, if he might pity' (24.301). In his prayer, he begs Zeus to grant that he may reach Achilles' tent 'as a friend or one who is pitiable' (24.309). This time, Zeus will indeed show pity toward the aged king.

The pity of the gods, then, is not something one takes for granted. Even in regard to the return of Hector's body to his parents, there is a dissenting voice on Olympus. Hera, Zeus' wife, defends Achilles' right to abuse Hector's corpse on the grounds that Achilles is the son of a goddess, the sea nymph Thetis, whereas Hector nursed at the bosom of a mere mortal (24.58-9); they do not, therefore, deserve the same consideration. Hera's logic is worth a moment's attention: if Achilles, because of his superior status, does not owe pity to the body of Hector, neither do the gods themselves, and for the same reason. It is as though she were anticipating the view of Aristotle and Athenian tragedy, in which the gods are aloof to human suffering because it is beneath them (cf. Burkert 1955: 83, 85). Apollo himself, shortly before his speech in behalf of Hector's cadaver, begs off from a confrontation with his uncle, Poseidon, on the grounds that it is foolish for gods to fight in behalf of mortals, who are born and perish like leaves on a tree (21.462-7; cf. 8.427-30).

Divine pity in the *Odyssey*, though infrequently mentioned,

4. Divine Pity

seems more central to the narrative, for the poem begins (1.19-20) with a scene in which the gods, apart from Poseidon, take pity on the suffering hero; so too, a dream informs Penelope that Athena pities her (4.828). Odysseus prays to a river when he arrives, half drowned, at the coast of Scheria, home of the Phaeacians (5.445-50): 'Hear me, lord, whoever you are ...; any man who comes as a wanderer is to be respected by gods and mortals, as I come now to your stream and your knees, having suffered much. So pity me, lord [*all' eleair', anax*], for I claim to be a suppliant'; but rivers and river gods are nearer to mortals, and Odysseus appeals in similar terms to the pity of the young Phaeacian princess, Nausicaa (6.175: *alla, anass', eleaire*).[13]

The Homeric world is highly stratified, with kings and princes ruling over common people and the gods mightier than everyone. Nevertheless, pity for lesser beings is at least a possibility.[14] Greek tragedy is the great product of the Athenian democracy, yet it is just here that the gods are typically represented as being indifferent to human sorrow and invulnerable to pity, if not always to other passions. Was there was something in the egalitarian ideology of Athens that widened the gulf between human and divine? We may recall that Aristotle restricts pity to those who are similar (*homoios*) to ourselves. In Thucydides' account of the Mytilenaean debate, Cleon supports the extermination decree with the argument that 'it is right to render pity to those who are similar' (3.40.3; cited more fully in Chapter 3). Citizens in Sparta, who were known as 'the peers' (*homoioi*), practised systematic violence against the helots or serfs whom they tyrannized. And while it was usual for Athenians in court to appeal to the pity of the jurors, who were their fellow citizens (Chapter 1), this sentiment does not appear to have been extended to slaves, who were routinely offered up for torture in order to give evidence. Fred Alford observes (1993a: 290) that 'Democratic judgment depends on pity ... because it depends on identification with others.' But not all others: 'Those who regard pity in itself as a positive emotion restrict its application in principle to members of their own class' (Ferwerda 1984: 64; cf. Solomon 1993: 207, cited in the Introduction). Perhaps the lesson of tragedy is that the gods too care chiefly for their own. When Nicias sought to encourage the

111

Athenian troops in Sicily on the point of defeat, the best he could do was to assure them rather pathetically that they were more deserving of the gods' pity than of their envy (Thucydides 7.77.4).

Apart from the gods' invulnerability to human misfortune, there is a second reason why they might have been considered undisposed to feel pity. As Aristotle stipulated at the beginning of his definition of this passion: 'Let pity be a kind of pain ....' Are the gods, then, subject to psychological suffering? Thinkers like Plato and Aristotle, who entertained a less anthropomorphic idea of divinity than the one we encounter in Homer and the poets, were inclined to think not, though Plato might, in an allegorical mood, speak of the gods as taking pity (*oiktirantes*, *eleountes*) on mankind by granting them holidays or providing them with the blessing of music (*Laws* 653d1-3, 665a3-6); in the *Republic* (611), however, Plato affirms that the immortal soul is purely mental, and in a letter (*Epistles* 3.315c), which if not from Plato's own hand was composed by a disciple after his death, it is asserted that 'the divine rests beyond pleasure and pain'. Consistency required that gods not suffer from the distress associated with an emotion like pity; indeed, Aristotle left them no greater scope of activity than pure contemplation (*Nicomachean Ethics* 10.8, 1178b8-23).

This problem was not specific to the pagan tradition. The Latin word that corresponds to the Greek *eleos* is *misericordia*. Ancient etymologists derived the term from the elements *miseria*, or 'misery', and *cor*, meaning 'heart'; *misericordia* was thus a feeling that results when we take to heart the suffering of others. St Augustine, for example, writes (*Against Adimantus* 11, p. 137.8): '*misericordia* is so called because the misery of others makes our heart miserable.'[15] So too, the sixth-century etymologist Isidore of Seville (*Origins* 10.164) says that 'the word "merciful" (*misericors*) has acquired its name from sharing in the misery of another', but he adds that this view is not universally accepted: 'For there is pity in God,' he explains, 'without there being any *miseria* in his heart.'

We shall return to the question of how Christian thinkers reconciled the emotion of pity with God's transcendence. But first, we may consider how, in the period following the death of Aristotle, the philosophical schools drove still deeper the wedge between divinity

4. Divine Pity

and human feelings like pity. The Epicureans argued that any concern for human beings must necessarily disturb the complete tranquillity that they ascribed to the gods; their gods, accordingly, took no notice at all of human affairs. The Stoics, in turn, believed that any kind of emotion or *pathos* was incompatible with the perfect wisdom of the sage; the ideal state was what they called 'apathy', or freedom from passion. The Stoicizing orator Dio Chrysostom proclaims that 'one who has sense should not feel grief about anything, and for the future be free .... For nothing is in itself terrible, but rather becomes such by opinion and our own weakness' (*Oration* 16.4, 'On Grief'); and the ex-slave philosopher Epictetus declares: 'I secretly laugh at those who pity me' (*Discourses* 4.6.22; cf. 4.1.4-5; Erskine 1997: 43-4). The Stoics produced long lists of the passions, arranged under four generic headings: pleasure, pain, desire and fear. Pity fell under the category of pain, just as it did for Aristotle. The Stoic wise man, who understood the rational harmony of the cosmos and the place that everything, including apparent suffering or evil, had in it, was immune to sorrow. Nor was there room for pity, correspondingly, in the Stoic conception of the divine. A similar view is found in the neo-Platonist Plotinus.[16] A Hellenistic poet could apostrophize a cicada: 'emotionless [*apathês*], bloodless – you are practically like a god!' (*Carmina Anacreontea* 34 West; cf. Furley 2000: 15), and Plutarch quotes Homer against himself in order to prove that his gods were beyond mortal cares (*How a Young Man Should Listen to Poetry* 20E, citing *Iliad* 24.525-6; also 6.138 and *Odyssey* 6.46).

The Stoics also emphasized yet a third problem connected with pity that Aristotle recognized (see *Rhetoric* 1.1, discussed in Chapter 1) but did not dwell upon: the ostensible incompatibility between pity and justice, particularly in legal or administrative contexts.[17] In deciding on guilt or innocence, the Stoics maintained, one should look exclusively to the facts of the case, and not be distracted by emotions such as pity, which caused one to deviate from what strict justice required. Pity, then, was not only irrational and painful: it also had negative social consequences. How could one ascribe so corrupting a passion to the immortal gods?

The conquests of Alexander the Great reduced the political scope of action of the relatively small city-states, and ushered in an age of great kingdoms, like that of the Ptolemies in Egypt, which were governed by Greek ruling castes and warred among themselves until Rome succeeded in incorporating them into its own Empire. Democracy of a kind continued to exist in the city-states, or at least some of them, such as Rhodes, but political power now resided largely in the palace rather than the assembly, and kings and queens were honoured as gods. Royal comportment was then what it is now – not always the most elevated – but the ideal of a fair and dispassionate ruler, governing his people according to the strict application of the law rather than the whims of sympathy, was endorsed by political philosophers,[18] and there are indications that people dwelling under the Ptolemies and elsewhere in the Hellenistic world were appreciative of the rule of law. Petitions to officials preserved on papyrus, for example, normally conclude with a reference to the 'anticipated justice the petitioner will receive' (White 1972: xii), along with a formula indicating that the petitioner is worthy to have the injustice redressed (*axiô* or a similar expression).[19] Appeals to pity, however, apparently do not occur in these documents before the second century AD. One early example is a papyrus from the Fayum dated to about 140 AD, in which the petitioner addresses the magistrate as 'Lord', calls upon him as his saviour, and beseeches his pity.[20] The vocative 'Lord' is not unusual in itself, nor are references to 'saviour', 'benefactor' (*euergetês*), or the like. Petitioners may also mention the humanity (*philanthrôpia*) of the official concerned. But the reference to pity is exceptional.[21]

The great historian Mikhail Rostovtzeff (1928: 154) observed that under the Ptolemies 'one can feel a true sympathy for the country torn by civil wars and groaning under abuses', whereas with the Roman governors, 'the voice of sympathy is dumb'. In reply, H.I. Bell noted that the Romans tended rather to think of the Egyptians as inhumane (*apanthrôpos*, once *ananthrôpos*), and that they themselves regarded *philanthrôpia* or *humanitas* – 'humanity', roughly – 'as an ideal to be aimed at'.[22] Bell's view was taken up by R.L.B. Morris who, on the basis of petitions recovered from the papyrus dump in the Egyptian town of Oxyrhynchus (in the Fayum),[23] concluded that in the first century AD citizens still believed that they

4. Divine Pity

possessed rights to which the Roman government was responsive. Petitions for the redress of wrongs in this period, Morris remarks, 'are not against the government, but are against officials of government' (366-7). In the second century AD, however, there are signs of a marked deterioration of confidence, and indications that people 'felt themselves to be oppressed by government' (368-9). One noteworthy feature in petitions of this era is 'an appeal to pity – an aspect that is totally uncharacteristic of first-century petitions' (369). Morris suggests that this change in style reflects harsher economic conditions and a loss of faith in government; in place of the rights which a citizen of the first century felt he could rely upon, there is the 'rather pathetic plea that the government take pity and grant some kind of relief' (370).

There is some evidence for appeals to imperial pity at an earlier date. A Messenian inscription of the year 14 AD (*Supplementum Epigraphicum Graecum* = *SEG* 41 1991: #328) addresses the emperor as 'sole ruler' (*autokrator*, v. 39) and concludes (in the surviving portion): 'and [the embassy] beseeches that we may find some pity' (*kai hiketeusousan hopôs tukhômes eleou tinos*, v. 41), evidently alluding to some quarrel or other between the Messenians and Spartans. Nero, in his speech granting Greeks freedom and exemption from taxes in 67 AD, specifically excludes pity as a motive – which may indicate that it typically was one (*SIG* 3rd ed. #814 = H. Dessau, ed., *Inscriptiones Latinae Selectae* 1892-1916: #8794). But such instances remain rare.

We seem to have wandered from our theme of divine pity, but kings and emperors, as we have said, were worshipped as divinities.[24] If people appealed to them for justice rather than pity, might they have been similarly disposed in regard to their gods? Indeed, they seem to have been. Let me take a single example from Greek drama – in this case, not a tragedy but rather a satyr play, the mythological burlesque that capped the set of three tragedies each tragedian produced. In Euripides' *Cyclops*, a comic version of the famous story related in the *Odyssey*, Odysseus is about to be herded into Polyphemus' cave, where the monster is preparing to make a meal of the hero and his men. Odysseus apostrophizes the gods: 'O Athena, mistress, goddess born of Zeus, help me now: for I've arrived

Pity Transformed

at greater struggles than Troy and the very depths of danger. And you, who have your brilliant throne among the stars, Zeus of Guests, behold these things: for if you do not see them, then vainly are you deemed a god, o Zeus, although you're nothing' (350-5). Odysseus does not beg the gods for pity; he demands justice, and if it is not forthcoming, this is sufficient reason to withdraw his faith in them.[25] So too, when he is at the point of blinding the Cyclops, he appeals to Hephaestus and Sleep for help: 'After their noble struggle at Troy, do not destroy Odysseus and his crew at the hands of a man who cares nothing for gods or mortals. Else one must believe that chance is god, and what the gods do less than chance' (603-7; cf. Pulleyn 1997: 201). True, this is a comic play, but one can easily cite parallels from literature of the highest seriousness, for example, Virgil's *Aeneid* (4.206-18; for prayer and justice generally, see Pulleyn 1997: 106-202). Henk Versnel (1991: 68) observes that 'The person in antiquity who had suffered an injustice and had gone to the authorities in vain, – if indeed he had bothered to go at all – had in fact only *one* authority at his disposal: he could lodge his complaint with the god(s).' But in Versnel's exhaustive catalogue of such 'justice' prayers, there is none that invokes pity.[26]

Inscriptions seem to tell a similar story. The large tomes of the collection *Inscriptiones Graecae* and other inventories yield meagre results when it comes to pity, and almost all of these are Christian. A typical example of the latter derives from Egypt and is dated to the fourth or fifth century AD (*SEG* 31 1984: #1562); it begins (vv. 1-4): 'Pity me, Lord, in accord with your great pity and the abundance of your mercies.' There are, however, some non-Christian instances. An inscribed gem from Ptolemais in Palestine (*SEG* 31 1984: #1420), dated to the second or third century AD, shows the word *ele   os* on top, a tree in the middle, and the word *kuri   ou* on the bottom, thus reading, 'pity of the lord' (the spaces within the words are part of the design). The original editor of the gem (Rahmani 1981) remarked that *eleos* 'does appear as an epithet of pagan deities of the period in question', though he added that this may be due to Jewish influence: the olive tree in Jewish legend and later was identified with the Tree of Life. There is also a play on words between *eleos*, 'pity', and *elaia* or *elaion*, 'olive tree'.

116

4. Divine Pity

Another example comes from Aizanoi in Phrygia and is dated to the third century AD (*SEG* 40 1993: #1188); this is a dedication to Theos Hypsistos, or 'Highest God', by one Aurelius Asclepiades, in thanks for relief from his sufferings on which the god took pity. Thomas Drew-Bear and Christian Naour (1990: 2039-40), who refound the inscription, comment: 'one will note the use of the verb ["pitied"], which was going to acquire so great an importance in Christian terminology, in our dedication offered to a divinity with monotheistic traits.'[27] References, then, to divine pity in pagan inscriptions are rare, and, what is more, begin to appear at more or less the same time that appeals to the pity of the emperor and other officials turn up in legal petitions, that is, in the second and third centuries AD. Interestingly, Dio Cassius (79.20.1-2) records that the Roman populace, contemptuous of the election of Macrinus as Augustus and his son Diadumenianus as Caesar in 217 AD, declared themselves the only people without a king, and called upon Zeus to pity them as a father: 'for he [i.e. Zeus or Jupiter] is the Augustus of the Romans.'

There is evidence of a comparable development in literary sources as well. In the Hellenistic period, the heroine, Pamphila, of the comedy by Menander called *The Arbitrants*, who had been raped prior to her marriage and now finds herself rejected by her husband (he will turn out to have been the rapist, thus providing the play with what counted, in those days, as a happy ending), exclaims at one point (855): 'Which of the gods might pity me in my wretchedness?' A little later (873-4), the courtesan Habrotonon assures Pamphila: 'O lucky woman, one of the gods has pitied all of you.' The latter formula – 'the god X pitied ...' – is archaic (*Hymn to Aphrodite* 210; *Hymn to Dionysus* 53; cf. Burkert 1955: 76), and is imitated, for example, by the Hellenistic poet Callimachus (*Hymns* 5.95), when he describes the grief of Teiresias' mother when her son is blinded upon seeing Athena naked at her bath: 'the goddess pitied her companion' – though she is herself a nymph. So too the historian Diodorus Siculus (18.25.2) describes the unexpected rescue of Craterus and his men, pinned down in winter by the Aetolians: 'one of the gods pitied their steadfastness [*eupsukhia*].'

Direct appeals to the pity of the gods are much less common, however.[28] The phrase *kurie, eleêson me*, 'Lord, pity me', appears for the first time, I believe, in the Greek translation of the Hebrew Bible, more specifically, the Psalms (70; cf. ps. 40 (41).5.11; Kunz 1961). In Matthew 20.30-1, it is found in the form, 'Lord, pity us' (*kurie, eleêson hêmas*). In a couple of pagan texts of the Christian era, the formula is addressed to a human being by a slave or other dependent individual.[29] However, in the novel by Xenophon of Ephesus, datable perhaps as early as the first century AD or even the first century BC, the heroine, Anthia, prays to the Egyptian god Apis for news about her husband, Habrocomes, with the words (5.4.10.1-5): 'O kindest of gods, you who pity all strangers, pity me too in my misfortune.'[30] And in the romance composed by Achilles Tatius, dating to the second century AD, the hero, Clitopho, after barely surviving a shipwreck, exclaims (3.5.4): 'Pity me, Lord Poseidon [*despota Poseidon*].' It is worth noting that in the immensely popular romance based on the life of Alexander, which circulated in various redactions during the Roman Empire, the word 'pitying' (*eleêmôn*) occurs over sixty times, far exceeding its frequency in any other ancient Greek text (save for the voluminous writings of John Chrysostom). Finally, in the last book of Apuleius' novel, commonly known as *The Golden Ass* (second century AD), Lucius, who has spent the better part of the story in the form of a donkey thanks to his fatal passion for magic, prays for salvation to the Egyptian goddess Isis. The goddess duly responds to his lamentations, and declares: 'I am here, having taken pity on your misfortunes; I am here, kindly and propitious' (11.3).

What is the reason for this apparently new disposition to invoke, or expect, divine pity? Is this too a response to the increasing unreliability of imperial justice and the sense of living under distant and arbitrary rulers (cf. Morris 1981: 368-70), projected onto the divine plane?[31] Yet appeals to pity could as well bespeak intimacy with the gods as alienation from them, or at least a belief in their concern.[32] Are we perceiving here the effects, then, of a rehabilitation of the notion of pity, restored to dignity after the rude dismissal it received at the hands of the Stoics and other exponents of severe rationalism? Perhaps some capacity for emotion was again coming to be seen as a necessary and indeed desirable element in a ruler,

4. Divine Pity

whether earthly or celestial. There is a 'politics of pity', in Hannah Arendt's phrase, as well as a 'politics of justice' (Boltanski 1999: 3-5; Arendt 1990: 59-114). We have seen that, from the time of Augustus onwards, clemency was almost invariably listed among the virtues of a Roman emperor, and the Stoic philosopher Seneca, who was tutor to Nero, was hard pressed, despite his dialectical cleverness, to draw a distinction between *misericordia*, which he continued to regard as a vice, and *clementia*, which he sought to elevate to the status of a virtue.[33] Although the emperor Marcus Aurelius (mid-second century AD), as a Stoic, disavows pity in his private memoirs, and maintains that things seem pitiable (*eleeina*) only because of our ignorance of good and bad (*Meditations* 2.13.1; cf. 9.12.1), he nevertheless allows in one place (7.26.1) that if you understand what someone who has harmed you takes to be good and bad, you will pity him and not be shocked or angry. This lapse or exception suggests that pity may have been seen as a virtue or benign emotion in pagan intellectual and court circles of the time.[34] A similar view that people may be pitied for their ignorance is cited by Clement of Alexandria (second-third century AD) in his *Stromateis* 7.11.62, and becomes a theme in Christian treatments of pity.

A third reason for the currency of pity in political and religious contexts in the first century AD and afterwards might, however, be the spread of Christian ideas of divinity. In a brilliant but controversial book, Glenn Bowersock (1994) has argued that the Greek and Roman novels were directly indebted to the Gospel narrative, beginning in the reign of Nero in the mid-first century AD. If true, this might account for the features we noted in the romances by Xenophon of Ephesus, Achilles Tatius and Apuleius. What of the official petitions, or the rare inscriptions mentioned earlier? Do these too betray the growing influence of Christian views of pity, and their gradual permeation of Greco-Roman culture? Given the lacunose state of the evidence, it is impossible to decide the matter with confidence. It is certain, however, that the translation of the Hebrew Bible into Greek, probably in the third century BC, associated God with the quality of pity – *eleos* and its derivatives, including the new-fangled term *eleêmosunê* – to an extent unknown in pagan cult.[35]

The Jewish God was deeply compassionate (although when angry, he could also be merciless).[36] Of the two words commonly translated as *eleos* in Greek and *misericordia* in Latin, one of them, *hesed*, refers, according to Francis I. Andersen, to 'a generous and beneficial action .... It is associated ... with such words as "compassion" and "grace".'[37] The Septuagint was thus 'close to the mark', Andersen concludes, 'when it used *eleos* (mercy) as its preferred translation of *hesed*' (82).[38] The other word, *rahamim* and related terms from the stem *raham*, seems to be related to a root meaning womb, and suggests a kind of parental bond or love.[39] It is noteworthy that the sentiment is invariably felt by someone in a superior position toward one in an inferior position: thus, it describes God's attitude to mankind, but never the reverse (Stoebe 1971: 764). The New Testament emphasis on God's pity, and on the obligation to perform works of charity (*eleêmosunê*) toward one's fellow human beings, has its roots firmly in the Hebrew Bible's conception of a merciful Deity (see Pétré 1934: 379-80).

But the identification of pity with loving compassion put a strain on the associations attaching to the terms *eleos* and *misericordia*, to which Jews and Christians writing in Greek or Latin were necessarily sensitive. The Greek theologian Gregory of Nyssa, for example (fourth century), feels called upon to argue syllogistically in behalf of human pity (*On the Beatitudes* 44.1249.23-6): 'If God is called merciful (*eleêmôn*) in the inspired Scripture, and what is truly blessed is godliness, then the consequent proposition [*nooumenon*] is obvious, that even if one who is a human being is merciful, he is worthy of divine blessedness.' I conclude this chapter, then, with a brief look at how two such individuals addressed the problems they inherited from pagan conceptions of pity.

In his treatise *On the Virtues*, Philo of Alexandria, a Hellenized Jew whose life spanned the era of Christ's birth and death, paused to consider the prohibition, repeated three times in the Pentateuch, against boiling a lamb in its mother's milk (Exodus 23.19, 34.26; Deuteronomy 14.20). 'If someone thinks it right to boil meat in milk, let him boil it without savagery and impiety. There are thousands of herds of animals, that are milked everywhere, every day by cowherds, goatherds, and shepherds, and their largest source of income

4. Divine Pity

as they raise their cattle is milk .... Thus, since there is an unlimited supply, anyone who boils the flesh of lambs or kids or some other animal in the milk of its mother betrays a cruel depravity of character, which has amputated that passion that is most related and akin to the rational soul, namely pity' (144). Pity remains, for Philo, an emotion, but one that has a place of privilege in relation to reason (cf. *Abraham* 256-7 on Abraham's grief as moderated by reason; Sorabji 2000: 345).

The Christian Lactantius, however, in his *Institutiones Divinae*, composed in the first decade of the fourth century, and the epitome of this text that he prepared some years afterwards,[40] confronted head on the deprecatory attitude toward pity grounded in Stoic theory but pervasive throughout the pagan intellectual tradition.[41] Lactantius attacks the problem on several fronts. To begin with (the order of topics here is my own), Lactantius reconsiders the role of the emotions generally in human life. Three passions (*adfectus*), he says, constitute the primary vices in human souls: anger, greed, and lust (*ira, avaritia, libido*: *Epitome* 56.1 ≈ *Institutiones Divinae* 6.19.14). The Stoics, he observes, believe in extirpating (*amputandos*) these emotions, while Aristotle argues that they should be controlled (*temperandos*).[42] Neither is right, however: for if they are planted in us by nature and have a purpose (*rationem*), they cannot be wholly eliminated; nor can they be moderated, since they must be either bad or good – but if bad, then they are wholly to be avoided, and if good, they ought to be enjoyed entire (56.2 ≈ 6.6.1-11). In fact, Lactantius concludes, in themselves the emotions are natural and good; their value depends on how they are used: if for good ends, then they are virtues (*virtutes*), if for bad, vices (56.3-4).[43] Thus, he explains, anger is good when used to limit sin (56.4), as is lust or sexual desire (*libido*) when it motivates procreation, though it is bad when it leads to adultery (56.6).[44] The idea of choice in the application of the passions, we may note, itself tends to subvert the root sense of *passio* in Latin and *pathos* in Greek, which suggest a passive response to events or impressions. It may be with such a revisionist intention that Gregory of Nyssa formally defines pity as 'a *voluntary* [*hekousios*] pain that arises at the misfortunes of others' (*On the Beatitudes* 44.1252.28-30).

Pity Transformed

If the passions, properly employed, are virtues, then we are halfway to redeeming the worth of pity. The next step is to identify pity's function. To this end, Lactantius offers an anthropological account of the origins of human society. Laws, he says, were originally introduced to control wrongdoing, but the result was merely that people took to committing crimes in secret; hence there was still more dissension and war (*Epitome* 54). As Lactantius puts it, 'the laws could punish crimes, but could not fortify conscience' (*Epitome* 54.8). 'When human affairs were in this condition,' Lactantius continues, 'God took pity on us and revealed himself to us and showed us how we might learn, in him, religion, faith, chastity and pity' (*Epitome* 55.1 ≈ *Institutiones Divinae* 5.7.1; cf. 6.10.2). God gave us the emotion of pity, Lactantius says, 'so that we might chalk up the entire protection of our lives to mutual protection' (*Epitome* 60.2); for we are social creatures, and, as opposed to other species, we are weak by nature. Gregory of Nyssa (*On the Beatitudes* 44.1252.5-14) too explains Christ's words, 'Blessed are those who pity, for they shall be pitied' (Matthew 5:7 in the Sermon on the Mount), as a summons to human beings to mutual affection and sympathy (*to sumpathes*), since the distribution of goods in life is unequal and unfair (*anômalon*), though he does not offer a historical account like that of Lactantius.

If we seek a pagan source for Lactantius' picture of human evolution, the nearest parallel is to be found, I think, in a rather surprising text: the fifteenth satire of Juvenal. According to Juvenal, 'Nature, who gave us tears, declares that she gave to the human race the gentlest hearts. This is the finest part of our sensibility [*haec nostri pars optima sensus*]. That is what bids us weep at the case that a friend is pleading, and the wretched attire [*squalor*] of the defendant' (132-5).[45] Juvenal adds that 'it is by the order of nature that we groan [*naturae imperio gemimus*] when the funeral of a marriageable maiden occurs or an infant is buried in the earth, too small for the flame of a pyre. For what good man ... deems anyone's misfortunes alien to himself?' (138-42). In the beginning, Juvenal explains, the common creator bestowed upon human beings a soul or disposition (*animus*), 'so that mutual affection would bid us seek and grant help' (149-50); thanks to this faculty, people left the forests and assembled in communities, built houses, waged

4. Divine Pity

wars, defended their towns with gates and towers. 'But now', Juvenal concludes in the pessimistic vein of a Rousseau, 'there is greater harmony among snakes' (159).

Juvenal appears to have lost the thread of his argument. He began by describing how the capacity to weep at another's misfortune is the basis of all human solidarity, but he ends by ascribing to this same sentiment the origin of war: a sensitivity to the suffering of others turns out to be restricted, at best, to the misfortunes of our fellow citizens.[46] It is not surprising that several scholars have read the entire satire as a parody or spoof.[47]

But Juvenal's treatment of sympathy in the development of civilization agrees well with Epicurean anthropology as presented in the fifth book of Lucretius' *De rerum natura*.[48] Lucretius explains that, in the beginning, the human race was hardier than now: people 'dwelt in woods and mountain caves and forests .... Nor could they have the common good in view ....' This pre-social stage corresponds to the period in Juvenal's account when human beings still dwelt in the forests. Later, however, 'the human race first began to soften .... Sex sapped their strength, and children by their charm easily broke their parents' stern demeanour. Then too neighbours began to form friendships [*amicities*], eager not to harm one another and not to be harmed; and they gained protection for children and for the female sex, when with babyish noises and gestures they indicated that it is right for everyone to pity the weak.'[49] But this harmonious epoch gave way in turn to new forms of competition and conflict, just as it did in Juvenal and (at an earlier stage) in Lactantius, and mankind has now reached the point at which more people die as a result of murder than did through attacks of violent animals at the dawn of history.[50]

Like the Stoics and pagan thinkers generally, Lactantius insists that the chief human virtue is justice;[51] but pity, he argues (*Institutiones Divinae* 6.10.2), is inseparable from justice.[52] The first duty of justice is to be united with God, the second to be united with man: Lactantius calls the one *religio* (perhaps alluding to the root idea of 'binding' in *lig-*, as in 'ligation'), the other *misericordia* or *humanitas*, which he describes as the highest bond (*summum vinculum*) between human beings.[53]

By equating pity with *humanitas*, Lactantius has brought it

123

within the sphere of humane and just rulership that the Greeks called *philanthrôpia*.[54] We have seen that this equation was already gaining ground in the time of Julius Caesar and his contemporary, the Greek historian Diodorus Siculus. By a similar process of semantic slippage, Lactantius goes on to identify *humanitas* with love (*caritas*) and reverence (*pietas*),[55] thus including in its embrace even the humblest and least deserving. For in truth, as Tertullian observes in his treatise on the Lord's prayer (7), only the Lord is without fault, and we petition him for mercy and forgiveness despite, or indeed just because of, our sinful state.[56]

Lactantius, then, reaffirms the value of the passions as potential virtues, provided they are exercised properly. He goes on to adapt an Epicurean theory of evolution in such a way as to make pity central to human social relations. Finally, he assimilates pity to the virtue of justice and other humane values such as sympathy, charitable love, and piety that include all of mankind in their sphere. Lactantius has thoroughly subverted the classical concept of pity: his *misericordia* is not based on pain or fear; it is not limited to those who are similar to ourselves; it is entirely compatible with justice; and it extends to everyone, for no one is free of error.

Although the pagan Greek and Roman gods might feel pity on occasion, it was not their primary trait, and philosophers never endorsed it as such. In the Jewish and Christian Bibles, however, like the Muslim Scriptures afterwards, compassion was part of the very essence of God. When the Hebrew idea was translated into the Greek *eleos* or the Latin *misericordia*, it generated within the host languages a tension in relation to traditional usages. But the meanings of the Greek and Latin terms were also evolving independently in response to new social conditions and other influences, such as the idea of a merciful Isis in Egyptian religion, and pity was beginning to appear alongside justice in pagan prayers and official petitions. In this flux of meanings, Lactantius' writings are a benchmark in the transvaluation of pity as a passion into the virtue and duty of Christian ethics, which continues to inform the meaning of the term today.

Conclusion

In the opening scene of Euripides' tragedy, *Hecuba*, the queen of Troy is shown reduced to misery, her city in flames and all its men slain, as she waits with the chorus of women to be assigned as a slave to a Greek master. In these straits, she is informed that her daughter Polyxena is to be sacrificed to the ghost of Achilles. When Odysseus enters to lead the girl away, Hecuba tells him: 'It is not right that those in power use their power wrongly, nor that those who are lucky should imagine that they will always fare well; for I too once was what I no longer am' (282-4). We recognize here the appeal to the common vulnerability of human beings. Odysseus replies: 'If you say that you are suffering pitiably, hear this: we have as many wretched old women and men as you, brides stripped of the finest grooms whose bodies this Trojan dust conceals. Endure!' (321-6). Odysseus' sympathy is reserved for his own, and though the actual spectacle of the girl's immolation arouses the pity of the Greek herald Talthybius and even of Neoptolemus, Achilles' son (519-20, 566) – and hence, in the telling, that of the audience as well – we cannot take it for granted that Odysseus' argument met with disapproval among the spectators (see Konstan 1997).

Pity, in classical Greece and Rome, was an emotion that responded to a vivid representation of suffering in others, but was conditioned as well by an evaluation of desert. As queen of an enemy (and 'barbarian') city, which was held responsible for initiating the Trojan War thanks to Paris' rape of Helen, Hecuba might appeal to the pity of the conqueror but could not assume it would be forthcoming, however intense her anguish. Yet a capacity for pity was regarded as necessary to humanity; in this respect, pity always had an ethical dimension. When Patroclus, in Homer's *Iliad*, accuses Achilles of being pitiless (*nêleês*) in disregarding the sufferings of his comrades-in-arms (16.33), he is condemning Achilles' harshness of character, not just a momentary want of feeling; the only other individual so described in the Homeric epics is the half-divine, half-bestial Cyclops Polyphemus (the term is a formulaic epithet for the bronze blade of a spear; cf. Burkert 1955: 73-4, 101-2). So too, Apollo's indignation over Achilles' treatment of Hector's corpse is a moral, not just a psychological judgment (on the meaning of *nêleês*, see Burkert 1955: 26). Graham Zanker (1994: 24-5) captures the complexity of Homeric pity well: 'To pity is a morally right response, and not to pity is wrong ...; the emotional, moral, and honour-related components of pity merge into one another' (cf. Ben-Ze'ev 2000: 346-7). So too at Rome, a character in Ennius' tragedy *Erechtheus* (third/second century BC) declares, 'they have hearts of stone, the multitudes who pity no one' (fr. 140 Jocelyn; cf. Stevens 1941). Aristotle himself had recognized that some emotions, such as envy, are the sign of a base character, while others pertain to good men (*Rhetoric* 8.11, 1388a33-6); pity is clearly among the latter. As Michael Stocker puts it, 'Aristotle thought that to be a good person, one must have the right emotions' (1996: 1; cf. 57).

As might have been expected, ancient pity, like modern, turns out to be a complex and vital concept, available to multiple and sometimes contradictory representations. To some extent, its meaning varies with genre, such as epic poetry, tragedy, forensic speeches, historiography, prayer and panegyric, and different chapters have emphasized one or another of these literary types. Then again, the sense of pity depends on the social context, and I have attempted to explore its contours in the courtroom, in relations among family, friends and strangers, in the treatment of enemies, and in the relations between God (or gods) and mortals, in each case indicating the tensions and possibilities that inform it.

Finally, the idea and expression of pity changed in accord with broad historical and intellectual movements, in the course of which one or another aspect of pity came to the fore while others receded into the background, where they were not extinguished but remained latent. Thus, in Chapter 1, we saw that pity and anger in the courtroom were conceived both as legitimate, indeed mandatory responses to injustice suffered or perpetrated, and as means of

Conclusion

distracting the jury from an impartial attention to the truth, the latter view gaining ground in the Hellenistic period and after but never entirely displacing the former. In Chapter 2 we traced, among other semantic shifts, the strange career of the notion of self-pity in antiquity, which should be incoherent on a strict reading of Aristotle's analysis in the *Rhetoric* but is positively enjoined upon Christians seven centuries later, without entirely losing its paradoxical quality, however, and never acquiring the derogatory sense it has in modern English. In Chapter 3 we examined the tension between pity as an emotion entailing a necessary element of moral judgment or appraisal and a less cognitive conception of pity as a response to suffering irrespective of desert; we looked also at the relationship between pity and moral dispositions such as gentleness or humanity, which seems to have preoccupied historical writers just at the time when clemency was being celebrated as an imperial virtue in Rome. Finally, in Chapter 4 we surveyed the history of divine pity, from its sporadic manisfestations among the gods of archaic Greek epic to its central role in Christian writers, where it acquired the character of a virtue or duty without entirely losing, even then, its traditional status as an emotion – though it seems at last to be doing so in contemporary English usage.

Needless to say, I have been selective – I have not, for example, treated pity in relation to the poor, which became an important aspect of it in the Christian era (cf. Bolkestein 1939; Perkins 1995). Nor have I attempted to reduce ancient pity to a catch-all description that might be valid across its various manifestations. I have tried, rather, to illustrate several aspects of pity in the classical world with a view to identifying how it functioned and was manipulated in different contexts and historical moments, from paganism to emerging Judaeo-Christian attitudes in late Greco-Roman antiquity, without supposing that so supple a concept could ever be captured in a univocal definition. I hope that the investigation has shed some light on the dynamics of this emotion in ancient Greece and Rome and also, in the reflection of that light, on the nature of pity in our own world today.

Appendix

Aristotle on Pity and Pain

Aristotle's analysis of pity in the second book of the *Rhetoric* is part of a more general discussion of the uses of emotion in the art of persuasion. Along with pity, Aristotle includes analyses of passions such as fear and confidence, anger, indignation and love. In this, as we have seen, he conforms to the popular view, although in later, and particularly Christian, usage pity – or the traditional terms for pity – begin to approximate a virtue or duty, as also in modern English, where pity rarely figures in discussions of the emotions. But what was it about pity that made it qualify as an emotion on Aristotle's own criteria? In this Appendix, I offer a close philosophical reading of Aristotle's argument, which has served as the starting point for many of the topics examined in the preceding chapters.

Aristotle's definition of pity in the *Rhetoric* runs: 'Let pity, then, be a kind of pain in the case of an apparent destructive or painful harm of one not deserving to encounter it, which one might expect oneself, or one of one's own, to suffer, and this when it seems near.' Why 'apparent' (*phainomenos*)? The word is sometimes taken in the sense of 'manifest', that is, 'substantial' or 'appreciable'. There is some justification for this latter interpretation in Aristotle's discussion of other emotions, such as anger, which is a response to a manifest (*phainomenos*) slight (*Rhetoric* 1378a30-1378b2).[1] In the present context, however, it perhaps means simply that the harm to another must be perceived by an onlooker. It is possible, however, that Aristotle means that the harm must actually appear harmful. In this case, the reference may be either to the one who suffers – he must perceive that what is happening to him is bad – or to the pitier, in the sense that, whatever view the sufferer holds, we pity him only if his misfortune seems such to us.

To illustrate the first case, we might feel pity for someone in a state of anxiety, even if she were mistaken about the seeming threat. As for the second, the death of a person's relative might seem pitiable to an observer, even though it was not so to the one who is pitied (she knew that her relative was planning to murder her). Saint Gregory of Nyssa will argue (*On the Beatitudes* 44.1228.44-52) that people immersed in bodily pleasures are pitiable, even though they perceive no pain; for irrational animals enjoy their lives, after a fashion, with no awareness of their misfortune, though nothing is more pitiable than to be deprived of reason. Perhaps this is why

Appendix: Aristotle on Pity and Pain

Aristotle specifies that the harm to the pitied is either destructive (*phthartikos*) or painful: the former covers the case of unperceived, and hence painless, harm.

Whatever the precise sense of 'apparent' (or 'perceived') here, however, Aristotle clearly takes it for granted that we know what it means for another to be suffering misfortune, even if we may be mistaken about the cause of it. He is not, in other words, raising an epistemological question about our capacity to recognize another's pain. This will become important later on.

Let us return, then, to Aristotle's definition. Pity is 'a kind of pain'. Since pity is said to be aroused by a painful experience in another, the one who experiences pity is to this extent in a similar condition to that of the one who is pitied. But only to this extent: as we shall see, a stronger equivalence between the state of the pitier and that of the pitied is excluded by Aristotle's theory.

Why does Aristotle describe pity as a kind of pain? The answer lies in Aristotle's definition of the emotions: 'the emotions are all those things on account of which people change and differ in regard to their judgments, and upon which attend pain and pleasure, for example anger, pity, fear, and all other such things and their opposites.' This description is especially relevant to the court-room situation, in which the object in arousing emotion is to influence the opinions of the jurors.[2] We may note, moreover, that pain and pleasure themselves do not count as emotions for Aristotle; rather, they are sensations or *aistheseis*. In the *Rhetoric* (1370a27-34), Aristotle writes: 'since pleasure resides in the perceiving of some affect [*pathos*], and an image [*phantasia*] is a weak perception, some image of what one remembers or hopes for always accompanies the act of remembering or hoping. And if this is so, then it is clear that pleasures also occur when people are remembering or hoping, since perception does. Thus it is necessary that all pleasant things are either present in perception, or have occurred in the case of remembering, or are going to occur in the case of hoping.' So too, we may conclude, the pain involved in fear is a weak perception (in the form of an expectation) of actual pain.[3] Since pleasure and pain are necessary constituents of emotions, Aristotle divides all emotions into two classes: those attended by pain, in which are included pity, fear and such, and their opposites, which are accompanied by pleasure.[4]

So much for the pain entailed in pity, at least for now; we shall return to it when we ask what it is about pity that makes it painful to the one who experiences it. The second and third components of Aristotle's definition may be taken together: they tell us that the pain arises at a perceived harm or pain in another, and one which, moreover, the person does not deserve to experience. The emphasis on the evaluative dimension of pity shows that pity is distinct from an instinctive reaction to suffering, irrespective of desert. We have seen (Chapter 3) that Aristotle in fact acknowledges such an uncritical response, but assigns it a different name, namely fellow-feeling (*to philanthrôpon*), which may be elicited at the sight of a thoroughly bad person brought to ruin (*Poetics* 13, 1453a2-6).[5]

The last two points in Aristotle's definition of pity are again closely connected: pity is aroused, he says, in response to the kind of suffering which the pitier might expect to suffer himself, and the misfortune that arouses pity must seem imminent. As we have seen, it is a commonplace in literature of the fifth and fourth centuries that people feel pity when they themselves are vulnerable to a comparable misfortune (e.g., Odysseus' sentiment as he gazes upon the mad Ajax in Sophocles' *Ajax*, cited in Chapters 2 and 4; cf. Sophocles *Philoctetes* 501-3; Euripides *Trojan Women* 808-9; Lysias 1.1). As usual, however, Aristotle appropriates conventional wisdom to his own, more technical treatment of the subject. This will become apparent when we take up the connection between pity and fear, which figures crucially in his analysis.

Although Aristotle covers, in the course of his discussion of pity, all the elements that enter into his definition, he does not organize his treatment around the parts of the definition itself. As a result, certain important questions raised by the definition are not answered explicitly, and must be inferred from what Aristotle says about pity and other emotions, above all fear. Aristotle's arrangement of the argument follows rather his division of topics relating to the arousal of emotion in general: 'concerning each [of the emotions], one must make a threefold division, by which I mean, for instance in the case of anger, how people are disposed when they are angry, with whom they tend to be angry, and over what kinds of things' (2.1, 1378a23-5). So too with pity, Aristotle says (just before giving his definition): 'let us now discuss what kinds of things are pitiable, whom people pity, and how they themselves [i.e., the pitiers] are disposed' (2.7, 1385b11-12).

Aristotle begins with the last of these topics: the state in which people must find themselves in order to be liable to pity. In fact, the last two elements in the definition addressed this matter: the misfortune experienced by the other must be one 'which one might expect onself, or one of one's own, to suffer, and this when it seems near'. Here Aristotle specifies that those who have lost everything are incapable of pity, since they do not anticipate that anything worse will befall them, and, for the same reason, neither are people who believe they are extremely fortunate liable to feel pity. Those who have suffered previously and recovered, the elderly (thanks to their wisdom and experience), those who are weak or cowardly, and educated people, because they are rational, are most susceptible to pity.[6] So too, those who have parents, children or wives tend to feel pity, because they render a man more vulnerable insofar as they are, as it were, extensions of onself and are potentially exposed to misfortune.

We should be clear that Aristotle is not concerned to argue that a person must have knowledge of misfortune in order to understand a comparable

Appendix: Aristotle on Pity and Pain

catastrophe that has befallen another. Those who have suffered extreme disaster are as incapable of pity as those who believe they are secure against misfortune. In the case of the latter, it is not a cognitive deficit that handicaps them in regard to pity, but rather a confidence in the continuation of their good luck: they know perfectly well what calamity is – they simply do not expect that it will happen to them. If educated and elderly people are prone to pity, it is, again, not because they are better at imagining what another person is feeling in misfortune, but rather because they are more aware of human vulnerability in general, and so can better calculate their own susceptibility to harm than can the very young or people with little knowledge of the world. Aristotle is not making a claim about the pitier's capacity to experience the same grief or pain as the pitied, in the sense of sympathetic identification. The question remains, however: why should the knowledge that we are at risk augment our disposition to feel pity?

Pity is in principle a relationship between people who are in different states: the pitier is better off, the pitied worse.[7] The effect of education or of the experience that comes with age is that, in calculating accurately the probability of finding themselves in the observed situation of the one who is pitied, such individuals are more subject to fear. So too, the weak and cowardly respond with pity to another's anguish because they believe and fear that they are likely to suffer something similar – not because they are good at imagining the quality of the other's pain. Aristotle, as I have said, takes it for granted that we know what it is for another person to experience pain. He does not attempt here to explain how we know this, by appealing, for example, to a theory of sympathy like that of Adam Smith, David Hume, or Arthur Schopenhauer, according to which we actually feel, at least to some degree, just what the pitied person is experiencing.[8] Nor does Aristotle invoke the notion of comparison, by which we imagine what we would feel like were we in the position of the other (cf. Scheler 1954 [orig. 1923]: 39-41). Aristotle simply requires that we believe that we may suffer a misfortune like that now being experienced by the pitied. This belief, which is the sole reason why our prior experience of suffering is relevant, is the source of our fear.[9] As Aristotle puts it in his summary of the kinds of things that cause pity: 'people pity all those things happening in the case of others that they fear [happening] in their own case' (2.8, 1386a28-9).

Aristotle's discussion of emotions that block a disposition to pity (immediately following on the preceding passage) offers a further indication of the close connection between pity and fear. He says that people who are in a martial mood, for example those possessed by anger or by a sense of high confidence (*tharros*) which Aristotle later describes as the opposite of fear (*phobos*), are unlikely to feel pity, because these states are heedless of what is to come. Again, those who are in an arrogant frame of mind are also unreasoning in respect to persuasion (the text here is problematic). Most susceptible to pity are those in a middling state, who are neither free of fear nor exceedingly fearful. People who are numb with terror are not disposed to feel pity, because they are caught up in their own emotion. They will feel just fear, instead of pity. Aristotle sums the matter up by saying that the right disposition for pity is found either in those who recall similar things (i.e. misfortunes) having happened to them or theirs, or have some expectation that such things may happen to them. Those who are at present suffering misfortune are not disposed to pity, presumably because one cannot fear what one is at the moment experiencing (one can, of course, fear its continuation or intensification; compare Plato's treatment of desire at *Symposium* 200a5-d7). But again, why must one fear to feel pity? Is it that fear, in combination with an evaluative response to pitiable circumstances, is just what constitutes pity? Why, then, is fear not part of the definition?

Having examined the disposition of the pitier, Aristotle turns next to the topic of things that are by nature pitiable. Aristotle says that what these are is evident from the definition: grievous and painful things that are deadly or destructive are pitiable, such as death, bodily torment, old age, disease and starvation, as well as fortuitous evils such as deprivation of friends or relatives, disgrace, mutilation, and so forth. The first category consists of direct harm to the individual, while the second involves the element of chance: friendlessness that resulted from a nasty temperament would not be deemed pitiable, nor would merited disgrace or disfigurement (e.g. as a consequence of cowardice in battle). Aristotle also includes here sudden and unexpected reversals, which were a standard part of the rhetorical tradition concerning pity.

Third and finally, Aristotle takes up the kinds of people who evoke pity. He specifies that we pity people we know, provided that they are not very close kin, since in that case we feel about them as we do about ourselves (he cites here the case of Amasis, discussed in Chapter 2). A consequence of this qualification, as we have noted, is that pity is not directly proportional to intimacy, but requires a certain distance: hence Aristotle does not discuss pity in connection with *philia*. Aristotle adds that people pity those who are similar to themselves in age, habits, character, rank and birth, since in all these cases it seems as though the same things could happen to themselves: in this context, Aristotle again adverts to the connection between pity and fear for oneself.

Aristotle concludes this section by noting that remote events do not tend to evoke pity, and that to render themselves more pitiable speakers should make their misfortune seem vivid by the use of gestures, attire, tone of voice and delivery. Above all, it is pitiable when morally serious people are in difficult straits, so that one must strive to make the catastrophe (*pathos*) seem both undeserved and immediate (literally, 'apparent to the eyes').[10] Here, Aristotle returns to one of the essential components of his definition of pity, namely that the suffering of the other must be undeserved. Like its

Appendix: Aristotle on Pity and Pain

contrary, indignation, pity is characteristic of good people, for one should, Aristotle says, suffer together with (*sunakhthesthai*) and pity those who are doing badly through no fault of their own, and resent those who are faring well contrary to what they deserve.

The notion of sharing in the pain of another introduces a new idea, on which Aristotle does not expand. The term belongs to the class of emotions that begin with the prefix *sun-*, and indicate feeling together with another (see Chapter 2). Aristotle may be thinking here of the special case of feelings we entertain for those who are particularly intimate, for example, Amasis' grief for his son; in such cases, as we have argued, one participates in the pain of the other as distinct from feeling pity. We may compare what Aristotle says in the *Rhetoric* on the subject of love or *philia*: 'Let loving be a wish that someone have what he supposes to be good things, for that person's sake rather than for one's own, and to effect these things as much as one can; a friend [in particular] is one who loves and is loved in return .... These things being supposed, it is necessary that a friend is one who is pleased along with [the other] for good things and feels distress along with [the other] for painful things for no other reason but on account of that person himself' (2.4, 1380b35-81a5). In this definition, we may note that love involves a desire, that is, the wish to effect good things for one's friend; in this, it resembles the definition Aristotle provides of anger as 'a desire for revenge accompanied by pain' etc. (*Rhetoric* 1378a30-b2). We shall return to the question of whether pity too entails a kind of desire. Second, love is altruistic by definition (see Konstan 2000). Finally, friends rejoice together and feel pain together over the same things for one another's sake; this last condition excludes the idea that they just happen to feel the same way for independent reasons (e.g. both lament the loss of a mutual friend).[11]

It is now time to draw some conclusions about the role of fear in Aristotle's analysis of pity. To begin with, we may look briefly at Aristotle's treatment of fear itself (cf. van der Ben 1976: 5-6). As with pity, Aristotle first mentions the three factors that one must take into account in order to rouse fear in one's audience: the kinds of things people fear, the kinds of people who feel fear, and how such people are disposed (*Rhetoric* 1382a20-6). Then follows the definition: 'let fear be a kind of pain or disturbance deriving from an impression of a future evil that is destructive or painful; for not all evils are feared, for example that one will be unjust or slow, but as many as are productive of great pain or destruction, and these if they are not distant but rather seem near so as to impend. For things that are remote are not greatly feared.' The resemblances between this definition and that of pity are obvious. Like pity, fear is a kind of pain, although it is further qualified as a perturbation, perhaps to distinguish it from the pain entailed in actual rather than anticipated suffering. This proviso may not have seemed necessary in the case of pity. Second, fear, like pity, involves a perceived evil that is destructive or painful. Finally, again like pity, fear

Pity Transformed

involves an evil that is imminent rather than remote: Aristotle goes on to say that we do not normally fear death, because we do not regard it as imminent.

On the other hand, two components specific to the definition of pity do not occur in that of fear. There is no mention of desert: one fears an evil that threatens one irrespective of whether it is deserved or not.[12] Moreover, in place of the expectation that one might suffer an evil comparable to that which is perceived as occurring to another, fear arises from a direct image or impression (*phantasia*) of a painful thing. While Aristotle does not say so explicitly, it is reasonable to suppose that such an impression is in itself painful (recall that a *phantasia* is a weak perception).[13] So too, in the case of pity, it is the expectation of harm to oneself – just the part of the definition that imports the element of fear – that explains why the emotion of pity is a kind of pain. To put it differently: the fear for oneself that accompanies the perception of another's (undeserved) misfortune is what makes pity painful, and therefore, on Aristotle's definition, qualifies it for being an emotion.[14]

Before considering the implications of the role of fear in Aristotle's analysis of pity, we may note a few further points of contact between the two passions. First, Aristotle writes: 'if fear is accompanied by a certain expectation that one will suffer a destructive experience, it is obvious that no one fears among those who believe that there is nothing they can suffer' (*Rhetoric* 2.5, 1382b29-1383a6); hence, neither those who enjoy great good fortune nor those who believe they have already suffered the worst are disposed to fear. These are, of course, exactly the terms in which Aristotle discusses the disposition to feel pity, which in this respect is clearly parasitical upon fear. So too, in his treatment of the things that are feared, Aristotle concludes (1382b24-9): 'in a word, those things are feared which, in the case of others, are pitiable when they occur or are imminent.' Finally, Aristotle suggests that in order to dispose an audience to be fearful, one should remark that greater people than they have suffered catastrophes, and so they ought to regard themselves as vulnerable (1383a8-12). Just as with pity, the jurors' fear is aroused by a description of the misfortunes of others. This is why there is a danger that an orator who seeks to induce pity may, by too vivid a description of the sufferings endured by another, arouse fear instead.

I have been arguing that the function of fear, that is, an expectation that one may oneself be vulnerable to misfortune, in the definition of pity is just to account for the element of pain, by virtue of which pity counts as an emotion. The expectation or impression (*prosdokia, phantasia*) of imminent harm is a weak perception (*aisthêsis*) of pain – itself painful, but in a lesser degree than an immediate and present experience. Fear is not invoked to explain how one understands or identifies with the painful experience of another, nor to account for why one might be motivated to assist another in

Appendix: Aristotle on Pity and Pain

misfortune. Aristotle's view of human nature is not egoistic in the modern sense, according to which a person is capable of knowing only his own pleasure and pain, and must infer from this what another's suffering must be like;[15] nor does Aristotle believe that one will act only to reduce one's own discomfort and maximize one's one pleasure, so that any service performed for another must be explained by way of selfish motives (this is clear from his discussion of love, and also of *kharis* or benevolence). Thus, Aristotle does not invoke the fear that another's suffering generates in us in order to explain why we are moved to help a person in distress.

Suppose we were to eliminate the element of fear from Aristotle's definition of pity; we should also, on the account offered above, be deleting the accompanying pain. What remains is our response to a perceived, undeserved misfortune experienced by another, independent of any reflections on our own vulnerability to harm. A good person, in such circumstances, will undoubtedly be disposed to be generous. Such a disposition, however, is not a consequence of emotion but rather of a virtuous character. Of course, it involves perception and judgment, but without the pain that results from fear for oneself. In a word, it is a dispassionate response.

We may compare the way in which Aristotle describes courage in the *Nicomachean Ethics* (1117a5-15): 'when human beings are angry, they feel pain, and when they avenge themselves, they feel pleasure; but those who fight for such reasons are warlike, yes, but they are not courageous: for they do so not for the sake of what is good or in the manner dictated by reason, but rather out of emotion.' Similarly, those buoyed by high hopes are not so much courageous as bold (*tharraleoi*) – recall that *tharros* is the emotion that is opposite to *phobos* in the *Rhetoric*. Courage, unlike anger or confidence, on Aristotle's view, is not an emotion, and does not involve attendant pain or pleasure in its definition. It may certainly be a basis for action, however, in accord with reason and an assessment of what is good or noble. Similarly, a person who judges that another's misfortune is undeserved might be moved to act out of reason and a sense of what is right, without the stimulus of pain or pleasure that is associated with passion – for example, the discomfort induced by the fear for oneself that accompanies pity.

This line of reasoning may also explain why Aristotle does not include desire (*orexis*) in the definition of pity. The wish to assist a person who has suffered unmerited misfortune derives from the judgment that it is undeserved, not from the pain resulting from the pitier's fear in his or her own behalf (which might equally well induce one to withdraw). Aristotle explains in the *Rhetoric* that of the things we do of our own volition, some result from our character, while others are motivated by desire or *orexis*; a desire, in turn, may be rational, as in a wish for what is good, or irrational, as in the case of anger or appetitive desire (*Rhetoric* 1368b32-1369a7). I would suggest that the desire to help a person for whom we feel pity is rational, and thus not specific to a discussion of pity as a passion. The desire that is associated with fear, for its part, is not in principle other-regarding, and is thus irrelevant to the analysis of pity. This view, incidentally, rescues Aristotle's analysis of tragic pity from the objection raised by St Augustine, who asks (*Confessions* 3.2; trans. Pine-Coffin 1961: 56): 'What sort of pity can we really feel for an imaginary scene on the stage? The audience is not called upon to offer help but only to feel sorrow.' The pain associated with pity is not the source of our impulse to render aid. As a Christian, however, Augustine is quick to deny that even tragic pity is to be banished entirely: he continues to be moved by the plight of those who ignorantly wallow in sin.

In defining the emotions in the *Rhetoric*, Aristotle, it will be recalled, isolated just two features: first, emotions influence judgment; second, they involve pleasure or pain. A juror, say, who recognizes that the suffering of a pleader is undeserved will be disposed to vote in his favour, irrespective of whether he is moved by pity or the pain associated with it. If an element of fear is present, however, thanks, for example, to an exceptionally vivid description of the other's misfortune, the juror's verdict may prove different from that at which he or she would have arrived through a dispassionate consideration of the merits of the case. A fearful response to the other's suffering may condition the rational, character-based desire to help another in distress. Fear, as we have said, does not involve a judgment of desert, but depends solely on a perceived harm. The difficulty with an appeal to the emotion of pity, then, is just that it is a compound of a rational concern for others and a self-regarding passion, with the result that one may be moved, because of fear, to ignore desert, or to suppose that another's misfortune is undeserved just because one fears a comparable harm to oneself. Or, perhaps, the element of pain lends a salutary urgency to dispassionate good will, and motivates a kind of personal interest that is not wholly incompatible with a fair and rational verdict on guilt or innocence.[16] Whichever is the case, Aristotle's analysis of pity is invaluable for an understanding of the intensely felt and morally critical emotion that was *eleos* in Greek.

Notes

Introduction: Pity as an Emotion

1. All translations are my own unless otherwise indicated.
2. Cf. Zanker 1994: 23: 'the history of the meaning of pity in English should caution us not to assume that its modern English usage is necessarily a guide to pity in a foreign work of art like the *Iliad*.'
3. Cf. Elster 1999: 104: 'The emotion of depression does not belong to the conceptual repertoire of the Tahitians [citing Levy 1973; cf. Levy 1984]; similarly, Bernard Williams [1993] has argued that the emotion of guilt did not belong to the repertoire of the ancient Greeks; Patricia Spacks [1995] that the emotion of boredom, conceptualized as an involuntary mental state rather than as a reprehensible sin, did not exist until fairly recently; and C.S. Lewis [1936] that the emotion of romantic love did not arise until the European Middle Ages.' Harré and Finlay-Jones 1986: 221 examine 'accidie ... as an obsolete emotion' which 'may be needed once again'. Heelas 1986 surveys emotion terms and ways of speaking about emotions across several cultures; cf. also Morsbach and Tyler 1986 on the Japanese emotion, *amae*.
4. Shapiro 1993; Stevens 1941: 426 cites Tennyson's 'scornful pity' (*Geraint and Enid* 859); in modern Greek, *oiktos* may mean either 'pity' or 'contempt'. On variation in the use of emotion terms even among specialists, such as psychologists and psychiatrists, see Wallace and Carson 1973.
5. I have mixed items from several different catalogues; see LeDoux 1996: 112-14 for a summary of the various theories; cf. also Hillman 1992: 40-1, and Ortony, Clore and Collins 1988: 27 for a handy chart.
6. Plutchik 1991: 117-18.
7. Descartes, who provides a typology based on six primary emotions, does include pity (1988: 264, article 185): 'Pity is a kind of sadness mixed with love or good will toward those whom we see suffering from some evil of which we consider them undeserving.'
8. Solomon 1993: 15; Oatley 1992: 23.
9. It was just the involuntary character of pity or compassion that inspired Kant's distrust of it (Kant 1959: 16).
10. Lewis, Amini and Lannon 2000: 39. LeDoux 1996: 292 locates the basis for such differentiation in physiology: 'Recent studies show, for exam-

Notes to pages 9-17

ple, that different emotions (anger, fear, disgust, sadness, happiness, surprise) can be distinguished to some extent on the basis of different autonomic nervous system responses.' Contrast Fowler 1997: 17: 'There is no physiological essence of anger.'

11. On cognitive interpretations of the emotions, see LeDoux 1996: 22-72.

12. Fortenbaugh 1975; see also Hinton 1999a: 6, who traces the cognitive approach back to Aristotle; Sorabji 2000: 19-36; for non-cognitive, post-Aristotelian views of the passions in antiquity, Alcinous *Didaskalikos* 23; Plotinus 1.1.5; cf. Nussbaum 1993a: 100-5, 109-21; Sorabji 2000: 121-32; and Chapter 3 below.

13. Gardiner et al. 1937: 54; cf. *Problemata* 28 ('On Fear and Courage') 947b11-949a20; on anger, 889a15-25.

14. Cf. ps.-Aristotle, *Physiognomonica* 806b28-34, Gleason 1995: 29-54 (on the eyes, 32 n. 61, 57); for ps.-Aristotle's description of the type disposed to pity [*eleêmôn*] as 'pale and fatty-eyed' etc., see 808a33-b2.

15. Planalp 1999: 11.

16. LeDoux does not indicate whether information transmitted by the two pathways must coincide in producing an emotion; if one rears back at a snake-like thing but then recognizes either that it is not a snake or that it is a particularly tasty variety, was there fear? Rolls 1999: 6 emphasizes that approach to and avoidance of positive or negative reinforcers typically go on '*after* the object has been identified' (cf. 97, 104). Rolls treats appetites such as hunger and thirst as equivalent to emotions, which he defines as 'states elicited by rewards and punishers' (60; cf. 64); it is crucial to learning and evolution that the response not anticipate the identification of the stimulus; for discussion, cf. responses of various authors in Rolls 2000: 192, 196, 200, 213.

17. Burke 1990: 41.

18. Planalp here follows Wispé 1991.

19. Malebranche 1972: 2.121; cited from the translation by Lennon and Olscamp 1980: 377. For discussion, see James 1997: 118-19, where these passages are quoted.

20. Jacobs 1987: 365; cited in McCoskey 35.

21. See Sophocles' *Women of Trachis* 298-302, where Deianira pities captive women 'who might be daughters of free men'; also 303-6, where she recognizes her own vulnerability to a comparable fate. In Sophocles' *Ajax*, Ajax declares (580) that 'woman is a pity-loving creature [*philoiktiston*]', that is, 'inclined to pity' (the term occurs only here in surviving Greek literature), while in Euripides' *Heracles* 534-7, Megara, about to recite her woes, says: 'the female sex is more pitiful [*oiktron*] than men are' – 'more prone to pitying' seems to be the sense. Vulnerability to emotion was commonly imagined as a feminine characteristic in the classical period; see Stears 1998: 120-1.

22. In neither case must we conclude that the Greeks and Romans experienced pity in a more 'visceral' way than we do (Stanford 1983: 23).

23. For a sensible evaluation of Elias' theories, see Newton 1998; Stearns and Stearns 1986 is an in-depth study of the increasing repression of anger over two centuries of United States history.

24. For the gendered character of expressions of grief in Homeric epic, see Monsacré 1984.

25. Quoted in Comas 1999.

26. On cock-fighting in ancient Greece, see Csapo 1993.

1. Pity and the Law

1. On the authorship, see Heath 1998.

2. The *oiktos*, by contrast, was a lament, that is, a literary genre comparable to tragedy, comedy, and epic, according to Dionysius Thrax's *Art of Grammar* 6.11 (ed. Uhlig 1883).

3. Cf. Moore 1997: §4.04 (commentary on Rule 403): 'Unfair prejudice is caused by evidence that suggests decision on an improper basis, as by arousing horror, sympathy, instinct to punish, or impulses other than the issues in the case.'

4. For a concise review of modern theories of the emotions in relation to legal practice, see Reilly 1997/98. Modern theorists customarily distinguish justice from revenge on the grounds that justice is dispassionate and disinterested, whereas revenge is motivated by anger or resentment; see Allen 2000: 18-24.

5. The view that the emotions interfere with proper reasoning is developed in the *Port Royale Logic*; see the edition of Antoine 1981: 16-18, 261-3; translation in Buroker 1996: 6, 204-5. Cf. also James 1997: 159-63, who notes (160) that the authors of the *Logic* also recognized the need for a love of truth that is itself a form of emotion; also 219: 'For some writers [of the seventeenth century], then, passions are an essential ingredient of reasoning, without which it could neither set sail or make any headway.'

6. Minow 1998: 975, summarizing West 1997: 205-6. A related approach, called 'restorative justice', emphasises face-to-face mediation and reconciliation between victim and offender. In such sessions, feelings of guilt and remorse are commonly elicited in the offender, and these may elicit in turn understanding and forgiveness; see Umbreit et al. 1994; Galaway and Hudson 1996; Wright 1996.

7. Cicero *On Invention* 2.109, *To Atticus* 4.5.2; Appian *Civil War* 3.3.23, 5.1.6; Aesop *Fables* 82; Pétré 1934: 378 with n. 2; Schrijvers 1978: 484-7; Ben-Ze'ev 2000: 329.

8. For a critical appraisal and history of US sentencing guidelines, see Stith and Cabranes 1998.

9. For an argument in favour of extending the jury's responsibility for sentencing, see Lanni 1999: 101-29.

10. For a summary of the history of jury nullification in English and American law, and a comparison with ancient Athenian practice, see Allen 2000: 5-8.

11. Cited from a brief of amici curiae in support of the Ohio Adult Parole Authority, 1996 US Briefs 1769 (October Term, 1997) 21 August 1997, in Ohio Adult Parole Authority et al. v. Eugene Woodard.

12. The phrase is cited from Rhodes 1998: 161; Finley 1977: 11 used it as the subtitle of his introduction, borrowing it in turn from Jones 1962.

13. Cf. Quintilian *Institutio Oratoria* 4.1.28-9; C. Chirius Fortunatianus *Art of Rhetoric* 2.31 = p. 119.31-3 Halm; Martianus Minneus Felix Capella *Art of Rhetoric* 53 = p. 491.18-22 Halm.

14. But see Johnstone 1999: 40-2 for the importance of justice, fairness and respect for the law in Athenian trials. Johnstone argues (47-54) that judicial narratives conform to certain rules which distinguish them from non-legal stories, whether in ancient Athenian or in modern American courtrooms.

15. On the *antitimêsis*, see Harrison 1998: 80-2; Cicero *On the Orator* 1.54.232 notes that in Athenian courts capital crimes (that is, those involving homicide) were just those in which there was no penalty phase.

16. On the cognitive nature of the emotions, see Fortenbaugh 1975; Zierl 1994: 22; in modern treatments, Lyons 1980: 70-91; Gordon 1987; de Sousa 1987; concise summary in Griffiths 1997: 21-43. The best defence of the *argumentum ad misericordiam* with which I am familiar is Brinton 1994; cf. also Brinton 1988, Striker 1996: 297-8; Walton 1997.

17. See Flavius Philostratus' comment on Apollonius of Tyana's apologia before the emperor Domitian (8.6): 'When a wise man pleads in his own defence ..., he requires a different character in comparison to men practised in the courts .... Let pity be gone when he speaks: for what would someone who does not consent to supplicate say in regard to pity?' Philostratus' point is that the sage does not deign to beg for anything, and hence has no need to appeal for pity.

18. Gorgias, in his playful defence of the mythological hero Palamedes (33), eschews an appeal to pity (*oiktos*) before so distinguished an audience as the Greek princes.

19. Barnes inclines to believe (262) that the two chapters were doublets, that is, one was written to replace the other. Kennedy 1991: 28 prefers to 'acknowledge frankly that chapter 1 is inconsistent with what follows' and locates the probable cause in the attempt to address different audiences and the difficulty of reconciling the aims of dialectic with those of rhetoric.

20. On the coherence of Aristotle's account of the emotions in the *Rhetoric*, in particular with respect to Aristotle's remarks in the opening chapter, see Frede 1996: 264-5; Wardy 1996: 115-16 distinguishes between proper and improper appeals to emotion (but note Wardy's doubts at 135-8). Rainolds 1986 [orig. c. 1572]: 125-53 cleverly argues both sides of the question.

21. Plato's statement in the *Laws* (731d) that the unjust person is indeed pitiable (*eleeinos ... ho ge adikos*) depends on his paradoxical doctrine that no one does wrong intentionally. I owe this observation to Peter Woodward.

22. A conundrum: if pity is elicited by unmerited suffering, why does Aristotle affirm in the *Poetics* (1452b34-6) that the spectacle of decent men passing from good fortune to bad is neither frightening nor pitiful, but rather disgusting (*miaron*)? It may be that in real life such events do elicit pity. Poetry, however, represents not what happens but the kind of thing that happens (for this reason it is more philosophical than history). The suggestion that virtuous people *typically* are cast into misfortune produces disgust because it casts doubt on the moral order of the world; see the elegant discussion of tragic pity in Halliwell 2001: ch. 7.

23. Apicella Ricciardelli 1971-72; Carey 1988: 137-9; Zierl 1994: 24, 28, 138; cf. *Poetics* 18, 1456a20-4.

24. Speaking of the modern, aesthetic sense of the word 'pathos', Silk 1987: 86 observes that it 'lacks the moral basis' of pity.

25. Cf. Schrijvers 1978: 485-6; Orelli 1912 distinguishes between 'rationalists' on the question of pity, among whom he includes Aristotle and the Stoics, and 'emotionalists', for example Rousseau and Schopenhauer.

26. Cf. the remarkable discussion of Egyptian justice in Diodorus Siculus, who affirms (on what evidence no one knows) that the Egyptians banned speeches in favour of written pleas in order to guarantee that judges attend only to the truth and not be deceived, seduced or carried away by pity (1.76.1-2); the *Theodosian Code* (9.1.5) ruled that an accusation must be presented in writing to allow time for anger to pass (cit. Harries 1998: 120). Pétré 1934: 378 notes that pity plays no role in Cicero's *On Duties*, which is dedicated to the theme of justice.

2. Pity versus Compassion

1. The story is related in a slightly different form in Herodotus 3.14; cf. Ben-Ze'ev 2000: 342-3 for discussion.

2. In English too we may describe a loved one as part of oneself; cf. Wierzbicka 1999: 67, citing C.S. Lewis 1989: 8 'The beloved is ... part of ourselves.'

3. Cf. Johnson 1980: 1-2, 195-8; Alford 1993: 267-8; Halliwell 2001: ch. 7.

4. I owe this observation to Johannes Haubold; an exception is Gorgias *Palamedes* 33. One may, of course, employ the verb *oiktirein* in beseeching pity.

5. But note 9.64.1, where pity for the dead is paired with weeping for their fate.

6. Cf. Herodian 6.9.3 *oikton kai eleon*; Burkert 1955: 43-5; Bultmann 1964-76 s.v. *oiktirô*. In Demosthenes 1.108, *eleoi* means 'pitiful appeals' and does not refer to audible cries as such (contra Sternberg 1998: 27).

7. Cf. Isocrates 16.48; Apsines (392 Spengel) dubs this argument 'contrary to rank [*axia*]',

8. Cf. 628, 652, 665-8, 718-20, 740, 748, 794, etc.

9. In Sophocles' *Electra* 1199-1202, Orestes is moved to pity for his sister, who at this point still does not know his identity; she exclaims: 'Then you are the only mortal who does so', to which he replies: 'I am the only mortal who feels the pain of your misfortunes.' Electra draws the conclusion: 'Are you then kin to me?' Common feeling suggests the bond of kinship.

10. These compounds are not found in Homeric epic, and Burkert 1955: 57-62 associates with their introduction in fifth-century Greek a progress in human sensibility. The idea, which is indebted to Bruno Snell's theories of moral evolution (Snell 1955), does not lend itself to demonstration (contrast 114-15, where Burkert allows that Homer has the concept, if not the term, for sympathy). So too Schadewaldt 1955 treats *eleos* as a primitive affect (*Elementaraffekt*), distinct from later terms such as *sunakhthesthai* and *sunalgein* which convey a genuine participation in another's suffering. In his reply to Schadewaldt, Pohlenz 1956 observes that *eleos* is always felt for someone and is an irreducibly social sentiment.

11. Pétré 1934: 378-9 notes that Cicero omits any reference to *misericordia* in his treatise, *On Friendship*; I do not agree, however, that the reason is that he did not count pity among the qualities of the *vir bonus*. The solidarity between friends presupposes that they share one another's distress; cf. Ovid *Letters from Pontus* 2.3.63-4: 'You used to swear that whatever pain struck the heart of great Augustus was at once yours as well.'

12. The following line, which seems to say that Oceanus had a hand in the actions for which Prometheus is being punished, is corrupt.

13. Cf. Stevens 1941: 427-9; Mulroy 1973-4 on pity and gloating; Boltanski 1999: 103-9, who speaks of 'sadistic pity'; Montaigne (tr. Screech 1991: 892; cit. Elster 1999a: 16) observes: 'In the midst of compassion we feel deep down some bitter-sweet pricking of malicious pleasure at seeing others suffer.' Such pleasure, however, derives from comparison, for pity in itself, according to Aristotle, is not pleasurable; see Belfiore 1985; Ben-Ze'ev 2000: 336-7.

14. Cf. Tecmessa's appeal to Ajax in Sophocles' *Ajax* 650; also Livy 7.11.6-7, who explains that the sight of their parents, wives and children during the Gauls' siege of Rome 'inflamed the troops with both reverence and pity' – pity at the thought of what might befall them. In Aeschylus' *Libation Bearers*, Electra appeals to her dead father for pity (130; cf. 502). Radford 1995: 74 notes in regard to pity that 'the ontological gap between ourselves and fictional characters precludes our trying to ameliorate their fate'; true, but such a gap is precisely the condition for pity: we pity such characters in the same way that we pity the dead. Ben-Ze'ev 2000: 337 relates pity for the dead to 'the element of helplessness'; cf. Halliwell 2001: ch. 7.

15. Crotty also maintains that 'Meleager was prompted by pity for Cleopatra' (52); however, pity is not mentioned in this episode, and in any case Meleager's feelings are said to be stirred by the disaster that awaits the entire community.

16. *Supplementum Epigraphicum Graecum* 40: 212, revised text in *SEG* 42 1992; cf. J. Bousquet in *Bulletin épigraphique* (supplement to *Revue des Etudes Grecques*) 1994: 35. Note also *SEG* 32 for 1982 (published 1985) 323 from Athens c. AD 120-5; *Greek Anthology* appendix on funerary epigrams 649, and cf. Lattimore 1962: 178, 184-99; Griessmair 1966: 24-9; Schrijvers 1978: 487, 493; on Roman funerary inscriptions indicating grief for the very young, see King 2000.

17. The dying Hercules in Euripides' drama of that name invokes his son's pity as a reason why Hyllus should kill him, that is, to put his father out of his misery (801-2; cf. 1032, 1070); this is clearly a special case. For grief in funerary inscriptions of the so-called consolatory type, see Robert 1968: 410 = 1989: 86 with n. 3; for the connection to literary consolations and rhetorical treatises, Ehrhardt 1994, and on pain, esp. 44, 50; Strubbe 1998, with reference also to consolatory decrees (I owe these references to Marc Kleijwegt).

18. For *sumpatheia* in consolatory grave inscriptions, see Robert 1968: 411-12 = 1989: 87-8.

19. Cf. Plutarch's consolation to his wife on the death of their daughter; Seneca's consolation to Marcia 1.1-7; Aristippus as cited in Aelian *Var. Hist.* 7.3: 'I come not to share in your grief but to stop you from feeling it.'

20. Cf. 2.11, p. 419.6-7, in which close relatives are encouraged to join in the family's mourning; Braund 1997a: 70-1.

21. Cf. *Silvae* 2.6., 3.3, 5.3, and 5.5.56-64, on the death of Statius' own adopted child.

22. On the absence of self-pity in Aristotle, cf. Stocker 1996: 260.

23. Compare Euripides' *Electra* 968-9, where Electra asks her brother Orestes whether, perchance, he is deterred by pity from slaying his mother; cf. also Sophocles *Electra* 1411-12, Euripides *Bacchae* 1120-1, where Pentheus begs pity of his maddened mother who is about to murder him; Demosthenes 24.196, accusing Timocrates for failing to pity his own father, or to see his sufferings as terrible (*deina*).

24. I thank Stuart G. Hall for calling my attention to this text.

25. Georgius Monachus *Chronicon* (ed. de Boor 1904).

26. On *oiktizein* vs. *oiktirein* or *oikteirein*, see Burkert 1955: 31-2. Other examples of pitying oneself: Euripides *Ion* 1276-7 (the text is suspect); Dio

Cassius 51.10.6, where Antony 'pitied Cleopatra, so to speak, more than himself'; Josephus *Jewish Antiquities* 2.26: 'we do not pity [*eleein*] ourselves ... but do pity [*oiktirein*] the old age of our father'; Appian *Roman History: Royal Period* 5.1.8, where the Sabine women beg their fathers to have pity (*oiktos*) on themselves, their sons-in-law, their grandchildren, and their daughters; Josephus *Jewish War* 7.380.

27. Cf. Heath 1987: 15; Zierl 1994: 26; Ben-Ze'ev 2000: 328: 'Pity is more spectator-like than compassion.'

28. Cf. Euripides *Suppliant Women* 180-3; Aristotle *Poetics* 1455a22-33; Horace *Art of Poetry* 101-2; Stanford 1983: 8-9. It was a commonplace of classical rhetoric that a pleader should manifest the symptoms of, and indeed feel, the emotion he wished to communicate to the audience (cf. Cicero *On the Orator* 2.190-6; Quintilian 6.2.34). The reason may be in part to convey the emotion by 'contagion' (Planalp 1999: 62; discussed more fully in the Introduction), but it is also a consequence of the cognitive view of the emotions: if the orator's description of events is such as to rouse the pity or anger of the jury, it ought to evoke a similar response in him, and not feeling it convicts him of producing a deceitful narrative.

29. A reader might presumably adopt Hector's perspective, or even Achilles' and Hector's simultaneously; see Pelling 1997: 16-17; Konstan 1999.

3. Pity and Power

1. The latter was developed in the Middle Ages (Russell 1975). On the different principles that underlie the two issues, see Denyer 2000; I am much indebted to this excellent discussion. For a historical survey, see Weissbrodt 1988; also Best 1983, 1995. Documents are collected in Roberts and Guelff 1982. Augustine, whose views had a profound influence on Christian thought, held that 'The real evils in war are the love of violence, the cruel passion for revenge, the blind hatred of the enemy' etc. (*Against Faustus the Manichaean* 22.74). Burt (1999: 183) understands that 'the rights of noncombatants must be preserved', but Augustine is concerned with moral dispositions, not rights. See also Evagrius (fourth century AD) *Antirrheticus*, '*Orgê* [Anger] #28' on pity for enemies, trans. (from Syriac) O'Laughlin 1990: 259.

2. Rodley 1999: 5; documents collected on 389-471. On the events and developments that motivated declarations on human rights, see also Keenleyside 1999: 138-45. For attitudes toward punishment and torture in late Roman antiquity, see Harries 1999: 118-52, who notes (133) that 'it may be twentieth-century western society which, albeit enlightened in its assertion of the rights of the imprisoned and oppressed, is nevertheless out of step with much of recorded history'.

3. Whether the idea of human rights, as opposed to laws of nature or the universal law of peoples (*ius gentium*), existed in classical antiquity is doubtful; as Wiltshire (1992: 16) pithily puts it, 'the Stoics offer a general guideline about how to decide what to *do* ..., but they say nothing at all about what human beings are *due*.' Bauman 1996: 38 suggests that in the sphere of criminal law, *humanitas* comes close to the modern idea of human rights. Cf. Seneca *On Clemency* 1.18.2: 'although one may do anything to one's slave [*qua* property], there are some things that the common law of humanity [*commune ius animantium*] prohibits in the case of a human being.'

4. On Roman cruelty toward the defeated, cf. Lintott 1968: 42-4. Silius Italicus *Punic War* 2.475-707 vacillates on whether the self-immolation of the Saguntians besieged by Hannibal is an act of madness inspired by the demon Tisiphone or a sign of superhuman steadfastness (*fides*) worthy of immortality in the Elysian Fields (698).

5. Cf. Rostovtzeff (1941: 1458): 'For the Romans, as for the Greeks, the ideas of *humanitas, fides, clementia* remained pure theory so far at least as concerned the practice of war.'

6. Diodorus Siculus 17.69; Quintus Curtius 5.5; Josephus *Jewish War* 4.384; cf. Xenophon *Anabasis* 1.19.13; Pritchett 1991: 207 nn. 305, 304. According to Herodotus (9.78), a certain Lampon of Aegina, thinking to ingratiate himself with the Spartan general Pausanias, advised him to mutilate the corpse of the Persian Mardonius in revenge for the maltreatment of the body of Leonidas after the battle at Thermopylae. Pausanias rejects the suggestion – which Herodotus characterizes as 'a most impious argument' – as being 'more appropriate to barbarians than to Greeks' (9.79).

7. On the amelioration of attitudes toward punishment in Rome, see Cicero *For Rabirius* 10-17, esp. 15: 'My opponent dares to call himself a populist, and me a stranger to your interests, when he has searched out every harsh punishment and account not only within your own memory and that of your fathers but in ancient records and histories of the age of the kings' (cf. Bauman 1996: 13). Blinding inspired particular horror; by contrast, an article in the Visigoth law code drawn up under Chindaswinth (642-53: *Lex Wisigothorum* 2.1.18 MGH LL 1:55) stipulated that if the king out of pity (*pietas*) spared the life of someone who rebelled against him, he was obliged to gouge out his eyes (Bührer-Thierry 1998: 78-9). Augustine had a particular qualm concerning the death penalty because it deprived a sinner of the chance to repent (Harries 147-9).

8. Burkert 1955: 97 speaks of 'a solidarity with death and in death'; for a different analysis, Zanker 1994: 103-6.

9. For Virgil as for Aristotle, anger has positive and negative manifestations; see Wright 1997, esp. 182-4. Boltanski 1999: 57 suggests that pity 'transformed by indignation ... acquires the weapons of *anger*'; in antiquity, however, the ideas of pity and anger are generally treated as mutually exclusive.

Notes to pages 78-83

10. See Shay 1994: 39-68; on pity for fallen comrades, Burkert 1955: 69; cf. also the appeals to Achilles to pity the Achaeans and return to battle, 9.300-2, 496-7, 632, 11.654-65.

11. I cannot agree with Giordano 1999: 62 that 'pity is the central emotion in supplication .... The success of supplication depends almost entirely on the capacity to arouse pity' (cf. 34). Supplication may be reinforced by an appeal to the emotion pity, but as a ritual it lays claim rather to respect for customary practices; for the pattern, see Thornton 1984; 113-42; for the relation between the terms *aidôs* and *eleos*, Burkert 1955: 38, 129. Zanker 1994: 25 (cf. 41) sees pity in the *Iliad* as requiring 'the support of shame and honour constraints'; cf. Burkert 1955: 129.

12. Besides being weak, non-combatants are less responsible for initiating war; Turnus can scarcely pretend to innocence in this regard. For the much discussed question of Aeneas' slaying of Turnus at the end of the *Aeneid*, see especially Schrijvers 1978; Burnell 1987.

13. Demosthenes argues that, if Meidias were violent by nature, he might deserve pity because he would be unable to act otherwise; since his humility in court is just a pose, he deserves rather the hatred of the jurors (this interpretation differs from that of MacDowell 1990: 400 ad loc.). On humility and fearfulness in soliciting pity, cf. Josephus *Jewish Antiquities* 14.172.

14. Bury 1975: 261; Bury observes that this decision 'shows how deep was the feeling of anger against Mytilene'.

15. Hornblower 1991: 430 ad 3.40.1; cf. Antiphon 1.27.

16. On *epieikeia* in Thucydides, see Romilly 1974.

17. Cf. Sternberg 1998: 87-96. Contrast the status of pity and compassion in popular ethics today, e.g. Comte-Sponville 1995: 137-75; Battaglia 1978: 557, s.v. *misericordia*: 'A moral virtue, particularly important in Christian ethics .... Also, the sentiment of compassion'; *Enciclopedia Cattolica*: 1082, s.v.: 'A moral virtue, the active part of justice; it consists in feeling compassion for the unhappiness of another and acting to relieve it.' Descartes 1988: 250 says flatly that 'virtue does not seem to sit as well [*symbolise*] with emotion as much as vice does'.

18. On the double sense of *timôria*, see Allen 2000: 68-72.

19. Modern thinkers, such as Adam Smith, have shared this view; cf. Murphy and Hampton 1988: 2-4.

20. Cf. Carl von Clausewitz 1955 [orig. 1832-4]: 53: 'When civilized peoples refrain from killing their prisoners and from devastating cities and fields, this means that intelligence assumes a larger role in the conduct of war and that it has taught them how to use force in a more efficient manner than by a brutal manifestation of instinct.'

21. On the idea of natural rights in antiquity, see Mitsis 1999, who argues that the Stoics, at least, developed the requisite vocabulary for such a concept, although it played a limited role in their ethical system. Barbalet

1999: 127 defines as human or basic rights those 'which are claimed precisely in the absence of trust, which by their nature can have no necessary support in law' (p. 127), and cites Turner 1993: 506-7 for the importance of sympathy in realizing such rights. But Barbalet notes (p. 129) that sympathy is a weak basis, since it is 'the emotion of the observer, not the violated' and it is 'notoriously unreliable in ensuring the rights of others'.

22. Cf. Xenophon *Cyropaedia* 7.5.73, a fictional romance in which Cyrus tells the Persian troops in the aftermath of a victory: 'It is by virtue of no injustice that you will acquire whatever you do, but rather in virtue of your humanity [*philanthrôpia*] that you will not strip them, should you permit them to retain anything.' On Cyrus' mildness or *praotês*, see *Cyropaedia* 6.1.37.

23. But see Walbank 1957: 260-1 on Polybius 2.56.6: 'The fate of Mantinea caused a sensation throughout Greece; it marked a reversion to a standard of warfare which had been mitigated during the third century ..., and Phylarchus voices contemporary opinion better than P[olybius], who writes from the harder background of the second century, when the fate of Mantinea had become the common lot of captured towns.'

24. Compare Plutarch *On the Glory of the Athenians* 345 E = *FGrHist* (Part 2A) 81 T2 on Phylarchus' style, *hôsper dramatôn hupokritai* ('like actors in tragedy'). In his commentary (Part 2C, p. 134), Jacoby notes that Polybius depended heavily on Phylarchus, despite his negative opinion of his methods, and attributes Polybius' hostility to differences in style or politics between the two historians. Fornara 1983: 120-30 suggests that the Peripatetic historian Duris of Samos (*c*. 300 BC) proposed a theory of history as a genre with its own kind of pleasurable emotion, namely surprise (126); hence the central role of chance in Duris' conception of history, which leads to unforeseeable reversals or *peripeteiai* (127). But chance is also relevant to pity, since suffering that results from accident rather than one's own fault excites pity, and a sense of vulnerability to vicissitude is a necessary element of pity; also surprise is not obviously an Aristotelian emotion. But wonder or amazement (*to thaumazein*) may be; Aristotle *Rhetoric* 1371b4-11 associates wonder with the pleasure derived from *mimêsis*, and says of reversals and narrow escapes from dangers that 'all these things are astonishing [*thaumasta*]'. Conceivably, Duris found inspiration for his conception of history in this passage; Herodotus long before had viewed marvels (*thômata*, in his dialect) as salient to the writing of history.

25. Walbank 1957: 263 on Polybius 2.56.13 remarks that 'P. here implies that both these emotions [i.e. pity and anger] are legitimate for an historian in certain conditions; these were fulfilled when the emotions were harnessed to a didactic purpose'. The point is rather that those who sought to excite pity irrespective of the justice of the case were manipulating their audience rather than rousing the emotion proper to the event.

26. For pity in Polybius and Aristotle, see Ničev 1978.

27. Cf. Walbank 1957: 264 on Polybius 2.58.6, who cites Herodotus 7.136.2 (*ta pantôn anthrôpôn nomima*) on the sanctity of heralds. Far more common, as Walbank shows, was the notion of laws common to the Greeks.

28. Apsines (395 Spengel) also classifies *erôs* along with grief and madness as states that of themselves evoke pity, and the pitiable lover is a staple of erotic poetry; cf. the funeral monument for the freedman Gaius Ateilius Euhodius (*CIL* 1.2.1212 = Dessau 7602 = Warmington vol. 4 p. 28): 'the bones of a good man, full of pity, a lover, and poor'; and the graffito from Pompeii (*CIL* 1.2.2540c; around 90-80 BC): 'pity me, grant me pardon (*veniam*) that I may come (*veniam*) to you.'

29. Polybius' impartiality is not above suspicion: he was a native of Megalopolis and a partisan of Aratus. It is amusing to note that Strabo (*Geography* 8.6.23) accuses Polybius himself of narrating the capture of Corinth 'in a piteous fashion' (*en oiktou merei*).

30. The distinction is not rigid, of course. Apsines (third century AD) begins the long section devoted to pity in his handbook on rhetoric by affirming that the way to arouse this sentiment is to exploit 'the commonplaces concerning *eleos* and *philanthrôpia*' (391 Spengel).

31. Stylianou 1998: 60-1 argues that the speeches are derived from the fourth-century historian Ephorus (who modelled them on the Mytilenaean debate); if so, Diodorus doubtless retouched them stylistically, and may have embellished them in other respects, although he declares himself opposed to the practice of including lengthy speeches in histories (preface to Book 20).

32. The Altar to Pity perhaps goes back to classical times (cf. scholium on Sophocles *Oedipus at Colonus* 260, although Parker 1996: 232 remarks that it 'seems in fact to have been a late creation'), but it gained particular prominence in literary sources from the first century AD onward; if the reference in Diodorus was borrowed from Ephorus, the antiquity of the altar is assured (cf. also Carneades [second century BC] as cited by Sextus Empiricus [second century AD] *Against the Mathematicians* 9.186-8). Cf. Pausanias 1.17.1, Quintilian *Institutio oratoria* 5.11.38, Statius *Thebaid* 12.481-518; Apsines *Rhetoric* p. 391 Spengel; Philostratus *Lives of the Sophists* 2.593.18-22; *Epistulae et Dialexeis* 1.13.1-6; Lucian *Demonax* 57.3-5, *Tim.* 42.10; *Twice Accused* 21.22; for further references to the altar and a survey of the archaeological evidence, see Stafford 2000: 199-225, who allows that the altar may date to the sixth century (35, 221) but doubts that Eleos was ever regarded as a divinity.

33. The demagogue Diocles is the counterpart to Cleon, despite the tradition that the popular faction at Syracuse was sympathetic to Athens; in both debates, the more lenient speaker is represented by an otherwise unknown individual: Diodotus in Thucydides, Nicolaus in Diodorus.

34. When Plutarch, writing roughly a century and half after Diodorus,

composed the biography of Nicias for his parallel lives, he included no debate between Nicolaus and Gylippus; to the contrary, he represents Gylippus as sympathetic to Nicias' plea for pity, in the one passage in which he actually mentions the term *eleos* (*Life of Nicias* 27.5). The notion of pity plays a restricted role in Plutarch's writings generally.

35. Though Polybius uses *epieikeia* rarely (he favours *philanthrôpia* and its cognates), when he does it clearly has the sense of humaneness (5.10.1-2): 'When Philip defeated the Athenians in the battle at Chaeronea, he succeeded not so much by arms as by his personal *epieikeia* and *philanthrôpia*. For by war and arms he conquered and became master only of those who took the field against him, but by his kindness [*eugnômosunê*] and moderation he subdued all the Athenians and their city' (cf. Titus Flamininus' speech in Thessaly, 18.37.7). Polybius, needless to say, associates neither term with pity.

36. So too, Diodorus characterizes Alexander the Great's magnanimity toward the mother of the defeated Persian king, Darius, as the greatest of his deeds, outstripping the conquest of cities (17.38.4-5); for such victories depend largely on chance, but 'pity granted to the fallen on the part of those in power is the result of wisdom [*phronêsis*] alone' (17.38.5.4). At 17.69, Diodorus describes Alexander's intense pity for the captives who had been mutilated by the Persians.

37. For the idea that certain things may be 'absolutely wrong'. see Denyer 1997; cf. Schofield 1999: 141-59 on the absence of 'rights' in antiquity.

38. See Nussbaum 1993a: 109-14; Cooper 1998; Sorabji 2000: 121-32; contra, in part: Gill 1998: 124-30.

39. Compare Fessler 1999: 77 on the Malay concept *malu*, or 'shame', as employed by the inhabitants of Dusun Baguk on Sumatra: 'It appears that there are two facets to *malu*, one premised on failure of some sort, and the other premised on inferiority irrespective of failure or success ...; looking only at behaviour, it is impossible to tell whether an individual feels *malu* because he has failed in a public arena or because he must interact with a superior', a double sense that Fessler suggests also pertains to the Greek idea of shame or *aidôs* (83). Fessler concludes that '*malu* has two logics' and that a single emotional experience 'can be elicited by two different types of situations' (78).

40. See Scanlon 1980: 102-8; Lintott 1968: 47. Some scholars have preferred to see the influence rather of Ephorus, the presumed source for Diodorus' version of the debate in Syracuse over the treatment of the Athenian captives (Scanlon 1980: 102-3 with bibliography).

41. This may correspond to Sallust's own view, to judge from the way Caesar's opening words echo the beginning of Sallust's treatise.

42. Cf. 33.12.8, 37.6.6, 42.38.4, 44.9.20, 44.31.1-2, 45.4.6-7, 45.8.5-6.

43. See *Annals* 12.47.4, 13.15.2, 14.16.4, 15.44.5; *Histories* 1.69, 2.61; cf. Publilius Syrus *Aphorisms* P. 26, B. 34; Aubrion 1989: 386.

44. E.g., *For Marcellus* 1, 9, 12, 16-19; *For Ligarius* 1, 6, 10-16, 37; *For King Deiotarus* 40.

45. Cf. Weinstock 1971: 234-7; Borgo 1985, 1985a; Dyer 1990; Dowling forthcoming; contra Levene 1998: 68-9. Leigh equates pardon in Lucan with clemency, although Seneca insists on 'the clear distinction between *clementia* and *venia*' (Bauman 1996: 78), which is in accord with common usage; cf. Cicero *For Ligarius* 18-19. When Cicero says to Caesar, 'I take refuge in your clemency, I ask pardon for his offence, I beg you to forgive' (*For Ligarius* 30), clemency is not identified with pardon but represents a disposition to overlook offences to oneself. Cf. also Augustus *Res Gestae* 3.14: *veniam petentibus peperci*: 'I spared those who sought pardon.'

46. For later emperors, cf. *CIL* 6.1106 = *ILS* 548, Gallienus as *clementissimus princeps*; *CIL* 13.9001-2, Tacitus as *clementissimus*; *CIL* 2.4102 = *ILS* 599, Carus *clementissimus imperator*; the use of *Clementia vestra* or *tua* as title, *Historia Augusta*: *Aelius* 2.2; *Antoninus Geta* 1.1; *The Two Maximinuses* 1.1; *The Three Gordians* 1.2; Dowling forthcoming.

47. Seneca the Elder *Controversies* 7.1.13 quoting Junius Gallio; for *saevitia* as the opposite of *clementia*, cf. Cicero *Partitiones oratoriae* 11; Quintilian *Major Declamations* 9.1.

48. *Mansuetudo* corresponds to Greek *praotês* (cf. Plutarch *Caesar* 57), which Aristotle (*Nicomachean Ethics* 4.5, 1125b26-9) defines as a mean in respect to anger: the excess is a tendency to anger (*orgilotês*) while the deficiency has no name (what Athenian was too little disposed to anger?). Whereas anger is the *pathos* (1125b30), mildness here is described as a dispositional state or *hexis* (1126b8-10); hence it can be a virtue. Romilly (1974: 100) observes that the term was in vogue in the fourth century BC, and 'will lead to Polybian *philanthropia* and to Roman *clementia*'.

49. In Greek, you may have *eleos* or *oiktos* or lead (*agein, proagein*) someone to it, or it may enter you; cf. Burkert 1955: 35-7; Sternberg 1998: 79-80.

50. For a detailed survey of the imagery of emotion in several languages, see Kövecses 2000; Kövecses suggests (17, 61-86) that force as a metaphor for passion is universal.

51. Neither is there a verbal form of the Greek *epieikeia*.

52. See also Fears 1975: 489. For the relation between *clementia* and *epieikeia*, see Adam 1970: 94-5; D'Agostino 1973: 115; contra Griffin 1976: 160-1. We may note that in the Hellenistic period, the Stoics acknowledged a relationship between *epieikeia* and pity, and scorned both as deviations from the strict application of justice (Diogenes Laertius 7.123; cf. Plutarch *Cato the Younger* 4); see further the 'Note on Epieikeia' at the end of this chapter. For a review of interpretations of *On Clemency*, see Mortureux 1989.

53. Hampton, in the same volume, adds that mercy 'is granted out of pity and compassion for the wrongdoer' (158).

54. Cf. also Gorgias *Funeral Oration* 19; Plato *Laws* 6.757b, e; ps.-Plato *Definitions* 412b. D'Agostino 1973 is useful for its collection of citations; but the general argument that *epieikeia* is related to the spiritual development of classical Athens and a new valorization of the individual (10-11, 16) contributes little, in my view, to an understanding of the concept.

55. Once in the Justinian compilations (*Nov. gr.* 145, praef. 26; cf. Silli 1984: 282-3), where the Latin equivalent is *quies* or 'tranquillity', not *aequitas*, which is commonly rendered as *isotês* or 'equality': 'In truth *epieikeia* does not correspond at all to Roman *aequitas*' (Silli 1984: 282 n.2). By contrast, *dikaiosunê* is found thirty-two times, *isotês* thirty-eight times, and *philanthrôpia* fifty-two times (Silli 1984: 283-4 n. 7).

4. Divine Pity

1. It is preserved also in the Coptic, West Syrian and Ethiopic liturgies.

2. Gelasius I (492-6) had already brought the Greek formula into the *oratio fidelium* or prayer of the faithful; see Dodd 1935: 59-62; Callewaert 1942; Huglo 1958.

3. Pétré 1934: 388-9. So too *pietas* came to acquire the modern sense of 'pity' as opposed to 'piety' in later Latin (the division into two distinct forms is specific to French and English). The earliest example I have found of the Latin term in this sense is Apuleius' *Golden Ass* 6.18 (second century AD), not noticed in the lexica I have consulted.

4. Sternberg 1998: 36-8 argues on the basis of a lexical analysis that, in classical usage, the feeling of pity was distinct from the action it might inspire.

5. Aristotle seems to allow that the gods feel indignation or *nemesis* (*Rhetoric* 2.9, 1386b15-16) which he defines as pain experienced for the undeserved good fortune of another, and hence as pity's contrary (1386b9-12).

6. The chorus in Aeschylus' *Suppliant Women* 209-10 appeals to Zeus for pity (*oiktirein*); cf. 1030-2 (of Artemis). Mortals sometimes invite pity when conversing directly with a divinity, e.g. Clytemnestra of the Furies, who, overcome by sleep, have allowed Orestes to escape (Aeschylus *Eumenides* 121); but then, she herself is a ghost. In Aristophanes *Peace* 400, Trygaeus begs Hermes, 'Pity their plea' (i.e. the chorus'). But this is comedy, where the distance between gods and mortals was reduced, and Hermes has just been labelled 'the most humane [*philanthrôpos*] of divinities', 392-4.

7. Burkert 1955: 67, 81-107 argues that pity in the *Iliad* is especially associated with Zeus, Achilles and Hector.

8. Cf. Burkert 1955: 75: 'Homer's gods belong to the human sphere, of which *eleos* is characteristic.' But Halliwell 2001: ch. 7 relates the pity of the gods to their status as observers of human action, like the audience in the theatre.

9. Ferwerda 1984: 59 notes that 'The gods [in Homeric epic] are also frequently besought to show sympathy, and often they do so. But this is not entirely a matter of course'; cf. *Iliad* 21.273, where Achilles complains to Zeus that no god has taken pity on him; Burkert 1955: 119; also *Odyssey* 20.201-2, in which Philoetius reproves 'father Zeus' for not pitying human beings.

10. It is an epic convention that mortals, as opposed to the inspired poet, know only what transpires on earth, not on Olympus; it is thus useful to distinguish between how human beings pray and what the gods say among themselves.

11. The same formula is repeated twice more, when Hector puts the request to his mother (6.275-6), and when she in turn beseeches Athena (6.309-10).

12. Cf. Burkert 1955: 75-6. Why does Athena refuse? Pulleyn 1997: 205 plausibly explains that the prayer 'ran counter to Athene's plans'.

13. Burkert 1955: 48 suggests that *eleein* in these contexts (as opposed to *oiktirein*) connotes a relation of distance or superiority.

14. A fragment of a poem by the seventh-century BC elegist Callinus (2-2a West), addressed to Zeus (Strabo *Geography* 14.1.4.4-7), reads: 'Pity the Smyrnaeans .... Remember them, if ever [the Smyrnaeans burnt] lovely thighs of cattle for you.'

15. Cited in Maltby 1991: 387, s.v. *misericordia*; cf. Isidore *Orig.* 10.164. The term *miser* itself was explained as a state of loss; according to Isidore of Seville (*Origins* 10.173), 'one is properly called *miser* because he has lost [*amiserit*] all his happiness'. That, of course, is pushing it.

16. E.g. *Enneads* 1.4 (46) 8.3; 2.9 (33) 7.33-9, 9.12-19; 3.2 (47) 44-8, etc.; see Ferwerda 1984: 54-8 for these and other passages; also Emilsson 1998. On the Stoic view of fate as unmoved by appeals to pity, see Seneca *Natural Questions* 2.35.1-2. Virgil ascribes to Juno a fierce capacity for anger (*Aeneid* 1.4, 11, 25-8), but Jupiter, as the supreme god, is represented as dignified and just (despite 12.830-1); see Wright 1997: 174-5; Konstan 1986. The sceptics in this period seem to have entertained a more moderate view on the appropriateness of experiencing emotion; see Bett 1998.

17. An analogous problem is posed with regard to mercy and justice; see Murphy in Murphy and Hampton 1988: 162-86.

18. Both Stoics and Epicureans wrote treatises on the nature of the good king.

19. Cf. White 1972: 28-30, 47. Petitioners also frequently mention the retribution they expect to be visited on a malefactor.

20. Papyrus Fayum 106 = #52 in White's Appendix (discussed on 59-60).

21. By comparison, a petition as late as AD 280 (#65 in White's Appendix = P. Ryl. [papyri in the Rylands Library] 114) by a widow in behalf of herself and children makes no mention of pity. For an appeal to the emperor's pity in an inscription, cf. G. Dittenberger, ed., *Sylloge Inscriptionum Graecarum* = *SIG* 1915-24: 888 (letter to Gordian, 238 AD).

22. Bell 1949: 36. We have seen (Chapter 3) that Diodorus Siculus (first century BC) pairs *eleos* or pity with *philanthrôpia*, e.g. 13.23.3-4, 13.27.1, 13.29.3, 17.38.3; as well as with *sumpatheia*, 12.24.5, 17.57.3-4, 15.6.5, 17.36.1-2, 17.69.2-4, 32.27.1, 34/35.4.2, etc. In the Septuagint, *epieikeia* is associated with pity (of God: Psalms 85.5 *epieikês kai polueleos*; cf. Bar. 2.27; D'Agostino 1973: 142, 146).

23. Morris 1981: 365. Morris 1975: 95-100 provides a complete list of Oxyrhynchus petitions. He concludes (72): 'The most striking difference in these petitions is the confidence displayed in those of the first century and a half of Roman rule and the obvious lack of confidence, both personal and in the government, that begins to be seen in the petitions after about AD 150.' No longer do petitioners insist on their rights; rather, there is now 'a rather pathetic plea that the government take pity and grant some kind of relief' (73; cf. also 128-9, 136-7, 161-3). For justice as the chief virtue of the Roman emperor in the Greek east, see Fears 1981: 937; Robert 1939.

24. For the analogy between royalty and divinity in Hellenistic treatises on kingship, see Fears 1975: 491 with n. 24; Nock 1972: 47; Pleket 1981: 153-4.

25. Dio of Prusa (turn of the second century AD) remarks (21.20) that human beings tend to blame the gods for misfortunes brought on by their own misdeeds, 'and we deny that they are just or humane or that they mostly punish us justly when we have sinned'. The reproach against the gods, albeit unfair, has to do with their want of justice, not of mercy. There is an allusion here to the *Odyssey* 1.32-43; cf. also Solon fr. 11 West.

26. Versnel's 'mercy' or 'merciful' (69 bis, 70, 73) for forms of *hileôs* are better rendered as 'propitious'; cf. *hilaskomai* = 'appease' (75); Graf translates *hilaros* as 'gracious' (1991: 193 bis). Aeneas exclaims to Dido (Vergil *Aeneid* 4.603-5): 'may the gods grant you a worthy reward, if there are divine powers that have regard for those who are dutiful, if there is any justice anywhere and a mind conscious of what is right.' On the gods' respect for duty and piety (*pietas*), cf. *Aeneid* 2. 689-91, Catullus 76.26: 'O gods, grant me this [recovery from love's malady] in return for my piety.' In the same poem (17-20), Catullus prays: 'O gods, if it is yours to pity, or if you have ever brought last-minute aid to anyone at the point of death, look at me in my misery and, if I have led a pure life, rid me of this scourge and plague.' The reference to pity as a characteristic of the gods is striking, and is perhaps motivated by the association between love and illness (the Greek god most closely associated with pity was Asclepius; see n. 27).

27. The editors of *SEG* 40 1993: 378 (H.W. Pleket and R. Stroud) note that 'saved' rather than 'pitied' was 'the usual pagan term'; cf. Kotansky 1991: 120-1. Given the special connection between the god of healing,

Asclepius, and pity, I wonder whether the name of the inscriber, Asclepiades, may have been assumed after his recovery from an illness. Fears 1981: 939 notes that in 224 AD an altar to Eleos was 'to be found in the *temenos* of Asclepius at Epidaurus' along with altars to Dikaiosyne, Homonoia and Pronoia (see *Inscriptiones Graecae* = *IG* 4.1060, 1282, 994, 1318); cf. also *IG* 2 (2nd ed.) 4786, with Stafford 2000: 208.

28. Examples from Homer and Greek tragedy are discussed above, e.g. Sophocles *Philoctetes* 1040-4; cf. Turnus' anxious prayer that Aeneas' spear remain stuck in the stump of the wild olive tree sacred to Faunus (Virgil *Aeneid* 12.777): 'Faunus, I pray, take pity.'

29. See Epictetus *Discourses* 2.7-12; Achilles Tatius 5.17.3; Dionysius of Halicarnassus *Roman Antiquities* 8.40.3.

30. Cf. the appeal to the pity of Isis in the *Life of Aesop* G 5.1-5.

31. Versnel 1991: 80 notes that in prayers for justice, 'the deity is presented as a superior, majestic autocrat to whom human beings in all humility submit their cases'; cf. also 90, 93.

32. Festugière 1976 argues that the practice of accompanying prayers with gifts to the gods expressed a sense of intimacy with the deity rather than fair dealing, but there is no reference to pity in the texts (drawn from Book 6 of the *Greek Anthology*) he discusses.

33. Griffin 1976: 152 n. 1 suggests that Seneca did not complete the treatise because he found the distinction impossible to maintain.

34. The term *epieikeia* does not appear in the *Meditations*, but Marcus does praise mildness (11.18.10); on Marcus' view of 'enlightened emotions', see Engberg-Pedersen 1998.

35. On *eleêmosunê* in the Septuagint, see Lee 1983: 108; in pagan Hellenistic literature, it is found in Callimachus *Hymns* 4.152 and *PCair. Zen.* = Zenon Papyri (*Catalogue général des antiquités égyptiennes du Musée du Caire*) 495.10 (third century BC). Judge 1986: 120-1 n. 21 notes that the term is nevertheless rare afterwards, and its greater currency in the third century AD and later may well be due to Christian influence.

36. Cf. Josephus *Jewish Antiquities* 6.138 of the extermination of the Amalekites; on God's pity, 1.304; 4.239, 269; 10.202.

37. Andersen 1986: 44; Andersen examines the more than 250 appearances of the term in the Hebrew Bible; cf. also Ferwerda 1984: 65.

38. Andersen's view of the meaning of the Hebrew term is not uncontroversial. Sakenfeld 1978: 149-50 argues that divine *hesed* represents a radical extension of its use in human contexts: 'By a stretching of the secular usage for delivering and protective action and concern to embrace even forgiveness, the term came to express the uniqueness of God's *hesed*.' Sakenfeld notes, however, that *eleos* in the Septuagint means 'mercy or sympathy', and that this sense becomes 'dominant in the intertestamental period' (15).

Notes to pages 120-123

39. Cf. the Arabic *rahim*, 'uterus', 'womb', and hence 'relationship', 'kinship'; *rahma* = 'pity', 'compassion'; Cowan 1976 s.vv.

40. For the *Epitome*, see Heck and Wlosok 1994.

41. *Epitome* 33.6-8 ≈ *Institutiones Divinae* 3.23.8-10; cf. 6.10.2-4, 11-12; he also criticizes the Stoic view that all sins are equal (*Epitome* 33.9-10).

42. Both positions had Christian defenders: for elimination of emotions, Origen and Clement (*Stromateis* 6.9), and, after Lactantius, Evagrius and, on the Latin side, Cassian; for moderation, Augustine and Jerome (both later than Lactantius); see Sorabji 2000: 386-99.

43. Cf. Descartes 1988: 277 art. 211: 'we see that they [the emotions] are all good by nature, and we have nothing to avoid but their misuse or their excess.' On Aristotelian moderation of the emotions, see Sorabji 2000: 194-97.

44. Gardiner, Metcalf, and Beebe-Center 1937: 92 note that Tertullian 'protests against the invariable attribution of the irascible and concupiscible faculties to the irrational nature on the ground that our Lord possessed both and that righteous anger belongs to God' (*On the Soul* 16); so too Lactantius identified certain emotions, including anger and pity, as belonging to God (*On the Anger of God* 15.8-12; discussion in Kendeffy 2000). Some Christian thinkers, above all Origen, denied that mentions in the Gospels (e.g. Matthew 26: 37) of Christ's sadness or grief refer to full-blown emotions; cf. Origen *Commentary on Matthew* 26: 36-9; Sorabji 2000: 348-9. Jerome, however, insisted that Christ was truly sad because he had taken on full humanity (*Commentary on Matthew* 26: 37; Sorabji 2000: 352-5, who exhibits both thinkers' debt to Stoic categories). Lactantius' positive view of *libido* is remarkable; contrast Augustine's view that it is a consequence of original sin (e.g. *The City of God* 14.16-24); for further passages and discussion, see Sorabji 2000: 400-13.

45. It was the practice for the accused to go about in an 'unkempt and dishevelled condition in order to arouse sympathy' (Bauman 1996: 15, citing Suetonius *Life of Augustus* 32.22); cf. Lintott 1968: 16-20.

46. Indeed, his theme in this satire is the hatred between communities, which he illustrates by a case of cannibalism alleged to have occurred in Egypt.

47. See Fredericks 1976; Singleton 1983; McKim 1986; Anderson 1987.

48. For the influence of Lucretius on Lactantius, see Brandt's (1890) apparatus criticus (*'auctores'*) at *Institutiones Divinae* 6.10.13-17.

49. Lucretius 5.955, 958, 1014, 1017-23, trans. Long and Sedley 1987: 127.

50. There is even Epicurean precedent, I believe, for Lactantius' idea that laws and punishments caused violence to increase in early communities; see Konstan 1973: 52-8.

51. *Iustitia*: cf., e.g., *Epitome* 50.5, 51, etc.; *Institutiones Divinae* 6 passim. Cf. also Ambrose *On the Psalms* 118, esp. 8.22: 'pity indeed is a part of justice.'

52. The tension between God's justice and his mercy or pity persists as a theme in Christian theology; thus St Anselm (twelfth century) explains (*Proslogion* 10) that God punishes sinners because they deserve it, but pardons them because he is merciful in himself, and not, Anselm adds, on the basis of emotion.

53. Cf. Plato *Gorgias* 507a-b, where Socrates says that a man who is temperate (*sôphrôn*) does what is right in regard to gods and men, in the one case what is holy, in the other what is just.

54. In the ensuing discussion (6.11.1 ff), Lactantius mainly speaks of *humanitas*, but he later reverts to *misericordia*. Although *humanitas* could signify gentility and a high-class education, like the Greek *paideia* (so Aulus Gellius [second century AD], *Attic Nights* 13.17), Lactantius employs it in an inclusive sense, as encompassing 'the entire race of human beings' (*omne hominum genus*, St Jerome *Letters* 55.3.4). See Braund 1997; also Beckmann 1952; Sider 1971. For the role of Cicero in elaborating the broader or anthropological sense, see Michel 1984.

55. See Colot 1994.

56. See Lactantius *Institutiones Divinae* 6.13.5: 'no one is without fault', and cf. Cyprian's treatise, *De opere et eleemosynis* 5, one of the sources for Lactantius' treatment of pity; also St Ambrose, *On Repentance* 1.1-5, for God's pity toward sinners, in response to the sterner doctrine of the Novatians. The idea that we have all erred is familiar from Seneca, e.g. *On Clemency* 1.1.9; 1.6.3: *peccavimus omnes*; *On Anger* 2.28.1-3.

Appendix

1. Roberts 1984: 2195 renders the phrase, 'a conspicuous revenge for a conspicuous slight'; cf. Grimaldi 1988: 21 ad 1378a31.3, who takes *phainomenon* to mean 'manifest' or 'public'.

2. On the meaning of *krisis* or 'judgment', see *Nicomachean Ethics* = *NE* 1126b3-4, 1109b20-3, 1118a27-9; cf. also 1119b23-5, 1159a23-4; for the connection with justice, 1134a31-2, 1143a19-24. On how emotions may influence judgments, see Leighton 1982: 145-54; Jason T. Ramsay and Marc D. Lewis in Rolls 2000: 216: 'Whereas traditional appraisal theories favour a lock-step sequence from cognitive appraisal to emotion, a new generation of models allows emotions both to cause and result from appraisal.'

3. There is an apparent inconsistency between Aristotle's account of pleasure in *NE* 10.3, 4-7 (1174ff), where it is denied that pleasure is a motion on the grounds that it is instantaneous, and *Rhetoric* 1.11, 1369b33, where pleasure is described as a 'kind of motion of the soul'; but since Aristotle adds 'and a sudden and perceptible *katastasis*', it is evidently an 'all-at-once' motion and hence not subject to the critique developed in *NE*.

Notes to pages 129-134

4. Some emotions, in Aristotle's account, are compounded of pleasure and pain. Frede 1996 sees here the influence of Plato's account in the *Philebus*, whereas Striker 1996: 291-4 suggests that Aristotle is moving toward a dichotomized classification of emotions in terms of pleasure versus pain. Aspasius, in his commentary (second century AD) on the *Nicomachean Ethics* (pp. 42.27-47.2 Heylbut), affirms that the emotions are grouped generically according to *hêdonê* and *lupê*; contra Sorabji 1999, who sees desire or appetite (at least) as essential to the Aristotelian classification. Note that Aristotle treats pity and indignation as opposites, although both are painful emotions.

5. In the *Poetics*, Aristotle transfers the role of similarity from pity to fear; for possible reasons why, see Konstan 1999. For the interpretation of *to philanthrôpon*, see Chapter 2.

6. In Euripides *Electra* 294-6, Orestes declares: 'There is no pity [*oiktos*] in ignorance [*amathia*], but only in wise men'; cf. Euripides fr. 407 Nauck: 'It is uneducated [*amousia*] not to shed a tear for things that are pitiable.'

7. Wierzbicka 1999: 100 remarks that pity 'involves comparing our own lot with that of other people'.

8. Cf. Smith 1976 [orig. 1759]: 9 = I.1.i.2, quoted in Chapter 2; Schopenhauer 1995 [orig. 1840]: 143-4, quoted in the Introduction.

9. Wisse 1989: 292-4 contrasts Aristotle's treatment of pity in the *Rhetoric* and Cicero's in *On the Orator* (2.211; cf. *On Invention* 1.108); Cicero, Wisse suggests, puts a new emphasis on the personal experience of the pitier as a factor that enables pity. In the words of Antonius, a character in Cicero's dialogue, 'Pity is aroused when he who listens can be brought to refer to his own circumstances [*ad suas res revocat*] – the bitter things that he has endured or fears – that which he is lamenting in the case of the other, so that he may, while contemplating the other, frequently turn back to himself [*ad se ipsum revertatur*].'

10. For the rhetorical tradition concerning vivid representation or *enargeia* (Latin *evidentia*) see Webb 1997; it has a special connection with the arousal of pity and indignation (Webb 1997a: 120-1).

11. Cf. Planalp 1999: 61 on 'emotional coincidence', discussed in the Introduction.

12. When we speak of a cognitive view of the emotions, it is important to distinguish the different senses in which the term is used. Cognition may imply moral evaluation, as in the case of pity, where desert enters into the definition; it may also refer to a judgment concerning possible harm or benefit, as in the case of fear, where desert plays no role (Ben-Ze'ev 2000: 52 observes that we do not fear motorcycles unless we have 'some knowledge about the dangers of motorcycles'. Again, some investigators (e.g. Rolls 1999: 6, discussed in Chapter 1) use 'cognitive' in relation to perception, which is a complex process that goes on in the cerebral cortex. Aspasius, an ancient commentator on Aristotle (second century AD), criticizes the peripatetic philosopher Andronicus' view that 'an emotion arises on account of a supposition of good or bad things', countering that 'certain emotions are generated simply by impressions [*phantasiai*]', and hence in advance of any supposition; this is particularly evident in the case of desires, he says, as for something beautiful (*Commentary on Nicomachean Ethics*, pp. 44-5 Heylbut).

13. Cf. Thomas Hobbes' definition of memory as 'decaying sense'.

14. It is worth noting that the fear aroused by tragedy is the indirect fear deriving from the recognition that one is liable to the kind of misfortune that afflicts another, rather than a direct fear of impending harm. Tragic fear is thus twofold: on the one hand, it is a component of the pity elicited by undeserved suffering; on the other hand, it is an independent emotion based simply on a sense of vulnerability. As we have seen, direct fear, when it is intense, is incompatible with pity (for a different view, see Halliwell 1995: 92).

15. Contrast Schopenhauer 1995 [orig. 1840]: 132, quoted in the Introduction.

16. On the emotions as a positive factor in judgment, see Brinton 1988, 1994; Striker 1996: 297-8; Walton 1997, cited also in Chapter 1 n. 14.

Bibliography

Adam, Traute. 1970. *Clementia Principis: Der Einfluss hellenistischer Fürstenspiegel auf den Versuch einer rechtlichen Fundierung des Principats durch Seneca.* Stuttgart: Ernst Klett Verlag = Kieler Historische Studien 11.
Alford, C. Fred. 1993. 'Greek Tragedy and Civilization: The Cultivation of Pity.' *Political Research Quarterly* 46: 259-80.
—— 1993a. 'Reply to Joel Schwartz.' *Political Research Quarterly* 46: 289-90.
Allen, Christopher. 1998. 'Painting the Passions: The *Passions de l'Âme* as a Basis for Pictorial Expression.' In Stephen Gaukroger, ed., *The Soft Underbelly of Reason: The Passions in the Seventeenth Century* (London: Routledge) 79-111.
Allen, Danielle. 1999. 'Democratic Dis-Ease: Of Anger and the Troubling Nature of Punishment.' In Susan A. Bandes, ed., *The Passions of Law* (New York: New York University Press) 191-214.
—— 2000. *The World of Prometheus: The Politics of Punishing in Democratic Athens.* Princeton: Princeton University Press.
Andersen, Francis I. 1986. 'Yahweh, the Kind and Sensitive God.' In O'Brien and Peterson 1986: 41-87.
Anderson, William S. 1987. 'Juvenal Satire 15: Cannibals and Culture.' *Ramus* 16: 203-14.
Antoine, Arnauld. 1981. *La Logique ou l'art de penser*, ed. Pierre Clair and François Girbal. 2nd ed. Paris: Presses Universitaires de France.
Apicella Ricciardelli, Gabriella. 1971-72. 'Il *philanthrôpon* nella *Poetica* di Aristotele.' *Helikon* 11-12: 389-96.
Árdal, Páll S. 1966. *Passion and Value in Hume's Treatise.* Edinburgh: University of Edinburgh Press.
Arendt, Hannah. 1990 [orig. 1965]. *On Revolution.* Harmondsworth: Penguin Books.
Armon-Jones, Claire. 1986. 'The Social Functions of Emotions.' In Harré 1986: 57-82.
Arnott, W.G., ed. and tr. 1996. *Menander*, vol. 2. Cambridge MA: Harvard University Press.
Aubrion, Étienne. 1989. 'Tacite et la *misericordia.*' *Latomus* 48: 383-91.
Averill, J.R. 1982. *Anger and Aggression: An Essay on Emotion.* New York: Springer.
Barbalet, J.M. 1998. *Emotion, Social Theory, and Social Structure: A Macrosociological Approach.* Cambridge: Cambridge University Press.
Barnes, Jonathan, ed., 1984. *The Complete Works of Aristotle*, vol. 2. Princeton: Princeton University Press.

Bibliography

───── 1995. 'Rhetoric and Poetics.' In Jonathan Barnes, ed., *The Cambridge Companion to Aristotle* (Cambridge: Cambridge University Press) 259-85.
Battaglia, Salvatore, ed., 1978. *Grande Dizionario della lingua italiana*, vol. 10. Turin: Unione Tipografico-Editrice.
Bauman, Richard A. 1996. *Crime and Punishment in Ancient Rome.* London: Routledge.
Beckmann, F. 1952. *Humanitas: Ursprung und Idee.* Münster: Aschendorff.
Belfiore, Elizabeth. 1985. 'Pleasure, Tragedy and Aristotelian Psychology.' *Classical Quarterly* 35: 349-61.
Bell, H.I. 1949. '*Philanthrôpia* in the Papyri of the Roman Period.' In *Hommages à Joseph Bidez et à Franz Cumont* (Brussels: Collection Latomus #2) 31-7.
Ben-Ze'ev, Aaron. 2000. *The Subtlety of Emotions.* Cambridge MA: MIT Press.
Best, Geoffrey. 1983 [orig. 1980]. *Humanity in Warfare: The Modern History of the International Law of Armed Conflict.* London: Methuen.
───── 1995. *War and Law Since 1945.* Oxford: Clarendon Press.
Bett, Richard. 1998. 'The Sceptics and the Emotions.' In Sihvola and Engberg-Pedersen 1998: 197-218.
Bodei, Remo. 1991. *Geometria delle passioni. Paura, speranza, felicità: filosofia e uso politico.* Milan: Feltrinelli.
Bolkestein, Hendrik. 1939. *Wohltätigkeit und Armenpflege im vorchristlichen Altertum: Ein Beitrag zum Problem Moral und Gesellschaft.* Utrecht: A. Oosthoek Verlag.
Boltanski, Luc. 1999 [orig. 1993]. *Distant Suffering: Morality, Media and Politics*, translated by Granham Burchell. Cambridge: Cambridge University Press.
Borgo, Antonella. 1985. 'Clementia: Studio di un campo semantico.' *Vichiana* 14: 25-73.
───── 1985a. 'Questioni ideologiche e lessico politico nel *De clementia* di Seneca.' *Vichiana* 14: 179-297.
Bourke, Joanna. 1999. *An Intimate History of Killing: Face-to-Face Killing in Twentieth-Century Warfare.* London: Granta Books.
Bowersock, Glenn W. 1994. *Fiction as History: Nero to Julian.* Berkeley: University of California Press.
Brandt, Samuel, ed., 1890. *L. Caeli Firmiani Lactantii opera omnia.* Vienna: Corpus Scriptorum Ecclesiasticorum Latinorum vol. 19.
Braund, Susanna Morton. 1997. 'Roman Assimilations of the Other: *Humanitas* at Rome.' *Acta Classica* 40: 15-32
Braund, Susanna Morton. 1997a. 'A Passion Unconsoled? Grief and Anger in Juvenal "Satire" 13.' In Braund and Gill 1997: 68-88.
───── and Christopher Gill, eds, 1997. *The Passions in Roman Thought and Literature.* Cambridge: Cambridge University Press.
Brennan, William. 1988. 'Reason, Passion, and "The Progress of the Law".' *Cardozo Law Review* 10: 3-23.
Brinton, Alan. 1988. 'Pathos and the "Appeal to Emotion": An Aristotelian Analysis.' *History of Philosophy Quarterly* 5: 207-19.
───── 1994. 'A Plea for the *Argumentum ad Misericordiam*.' *Philosophia* 23: 25-44.
Bührer-Thierry, Geneviève. 1998. ' "Just Anger" or "Vengeful Anger"? The Punishment of Blinding in the Early Medieval West.' In Rosenwein 1998: 75-91.
Bultmann, Rudolf. 1964-76. '*oiktirô* (including *oiktirmos, oiktirmôn*).' In Geoffrey W. Bromley, trans., *Theological Dictionary of the New Testament* [orig.

Bibliography

German ed. Gerhard Kittel and Gerhard Friedrich, 1954], 10 vols. (Grand Rapids, MI: Eerdmans).
Burgess, Francis. 1936. 'The Discovery of Pity.' *Quarterly Review* 267: 281-93.
Burke, Edmund. 1990. *A Philosophical Enquiry into the Origin of our Ideas of the Sublime and the Beautiful*. Oxford: Oxford University Press.
Burkert, Walter. 1955. *Zum altgriechischen Mitleidsbegriff*. Erlangen: Inaugural-Dissertation, Friedrich-Alexander-Universität.
Burnell, Peter. 1987. 'The Death of Turnus and Roman Morality.' *Greece and Rome* 34: 186-200.
Buroker, Jill Vance, trans., 1996. *Logic or the Art of Thinking*. Cambridge: Cambridge University Press.
Burt, Donald X. 1999. *Friendship and Society: An Introduction to Augustine's Practical Philosophy*. Grand Rapids, MI: W.B. Eerdmans.
Bury, J.B. 1975. *A History of Greece to the Death of Alexander the Great*, 4th ed., rev. by Russell Meiggs. London: Macmillan.
Cairns, Douglas. 1999. 'Representations of Remorse and Reparation in Classical Greece.' In Murray Cox, ed., *Remorse and Reparation* (London: Jessica Kingsley Publishers) 171-8.
Callewaert, C. 1942. 'Les étapes de l'histoire du Kyrie.' *Revue de l'Histoire d'Eglise* 38: 20-45.
Carey, Christopher. 1988. ' "Philanthropy" in Aristotle's *Poetics*.' *Eranos* 86: 131-9.
Cates, Diana Fritz. 1997. *Choosing to Feel: Virtue, Friendship, and Compassion for Friends*. Notre Dame: University of Notre Dame Press.
Clausewitz, Carl von. 1955. *De la guerre*. Paris: Minuit.
Colot, Blandine. 1994. '*Humanitas* et ses synonymes chez Lactance.' In Claude Moussy, ed., *Les problèmes de la synonymie en Latin: Colloque du Centre Alfred Ernout de Paris IV, 3 et 4 juin 1992* (Paris: Presses de l'Université de Paris-Sorbonne = Lingua Latina 2) 101-21.
Comas, J. 1999. 'Un oficial serbio denuncia que en la provincia sólo queda una etnia.' *El País* 24 (15 June): 4.
Comte-Sponville, André. 1995. *Petite traité des grandes vertus*. Paris: Presses Universitaires de France.
Cooper, John M. 1998. 'Poseidonius on Emotions.' In Sihvola and Engberg-Pedersen 1998: 71-111.
Cowan, J.M., ed., 1976. *An Arabic-English Dictionary*, based on the Hans Wehr *Dictionary of Modern Written Arabic*, 3rd ed. Ithaca, NY: Spoken Language Services, Inc.
Crossley, David J. and Peter A. Wilson. 1979. *How to Argue: An Introduction to Logical Thinking*. New York: Random House.
Crotty, Kevin. 1994. *The Poetics of Supplication: Homer's* Iliad *and* Odyssey. Ithaca, NY: Cornell University Press.
Csapo, Eric. 1993. 'Deep Ambivalence: Notes on a Greek Cockfight.' *Phoenix* 47: 1-28, 115-24.
D'Agostino, Francesco. 1973. *Epieikeia: il tema dell'equità nell'antichità greca*. Milan: A. Giuffré.
Damasio, Antonio R. 1994. *Descartes' Error: Emotion, Reason, and the Human Brain*. New York: Avon Books.
Darwin, Charles. 1965 [orig. 1872]. *The Expression of the Emotions in Man and Animals*. Chicago: University of Chicago Press.
de Boor, C. 1904. *Georgius Monachus Chronicon Books 1-4*, 2 vols. Leipzig: Teubner.

Bibliography

Denham, Susanne A. 1998. *Emotional Development in Young Children*. New York: Guilford Press.

Denyer, Nicholas. 1997. 'Is Anything Absolutely Wrong?' In David S. Oderberg and Jacqueline A. Laing, eds., *Human Lives: Critical Essays on Consequentialist Bioethics* (Basingstoke: Macmillan Press) 39-57.

—— 2000. 'Just War.' In Roger Teichmann, ed., *Logic, Cause and Action* (Cambridge: Cambridge University Press and London: Royal Institute of Philosophy = *Philosophy* Supplement 46) 137-51.

Descartes, René. 1988. *Les Passions de l'âme: Précédé de La Pathéthique cartésienne par Jean-Maurice Monnoyer*. Paris: Gallimard.

de Sousa, Ronald. 1987. *The Rationality of Emotion*. Cambridge MA: MIT Press.

Dingel, Joachim. 1989. 'Misericordia Neronis: Zur Einheit von Senecas "De clementia".' *Rheinisches Museum* 132: 166-75.

Dodd, C.H. 1935. *The Bible and the Greeks*. London: Hodder and Stoughton.

Donnelly, Jack. 1984. 'Cultural Relativism and Universal Human Rights.' *Human Rights Quarterly* 6: 400-19.

Dover, Sir Kenneth. 1994 (orig. 1974). *Greek Popular Morality in the Time of Plato and Aristotle*. Indianapolis: Hackett Publishing Co.

Dowling, Melissa Barden. 2000. 'The Clemency of Sulla.' *Historia* 49: 303-40.

—— Forthcoming. *Begging Pardon: Clemency and Cruelty in the Roman World*. Ann Arbor: University of Michigan Press.

Dreitzel, H.P. 1981. 'The Socialization of Nature: Western Attitudes towards Body and Emotions.' In Paul Heelas and Andrew Lock, eds., *Indigenous Psychologies: The Anthropology of the Self*. London and New York: Academic Press, 205-23.

Drew-Bear, Thomas and Christian Naour, eds., 1990. 'Divinités de Phrygie.' In W. Haase, ed., *Aufstieg und Niedergang der Römischen Welt* 2.18.3: 1907-2044.

Drobner, Hubertus R. and Albert Viciano, eds., 2000. *Gregory of Nyssa: Homilies on the Beatitudes. An English Version with Commentary and Supporting Studies. Proceedings of the Eighth International Colloquium on Gregory of Nyssa (Paderborn, 14-18 September 1998)*. Leiden: Brill.

Duncan-Jones, Katherine, ed., 1985. *Sir Philip Sidney: The Old Arcadia*. Oxford: Oxford University Press.

Dyer, R.R. 1990. 'Rhetoric and Intention in Cicero's Pro Marcello.' *Journal of Roman Studies* 80: 17-30.

Ehrhardt, Norbert. 1994. 'Tod, Trost und Trauer. Zur Funktion griechischer Trostbeschlüsse und Ehrendekrete post mortem.' *Laverna* 5: 38-55.

Eisenberg, Theodore, Stephen P. Garvey, and Martin T. Wells. 1998 (September). 'But Was He Sorry? The Role of Remorse in Capital Sentencing.' *Cornell Law Review* 83: 1599-637.

Ekman, Paul, ed., 1982. *Emotions in the Human Face*, 2nd ed. Cambridge: Cambridge University Press and Paris: Editions de la Maison des Sciences de l'Homme.

Elias, Norbert. 1983. *The Court Society*. Oxford: Blackwell.

—— 1994 [orig. 1978, 1982]. *The Civilizing Process*, vols. 1 and 2. Oxford: Blackwell.

Elster, Jon. 1999. *Strong Feelings: Emotion, Addiction, and Human Behavior*. Cambridge MA: MIT Press.

—— 1999a. *Alchemies of the Mind: Rationality and the Emotions*. Cambridge: Cambridge University Press.

Bibliography

Emilson, Eyjólfur Kjalar. 1998. 'Plotinus on the Emotions.' In Sihvola and Engberg-Pedersen 1998: 339-63.
Enciclopedia Cattolica. 1952. Vatican: Ente per l'Enciclopedia Cattolica e per il Libro Cattolico; 'misericordia', cols. 1082-3.
Engberg-Pedersen, Troels. 1998. 'Marcus Aurelius on Emotions.' In Sihvola and Engberg-Pedersen 1998: 305-37.
Erskine, Andrew. 1997. 'Cicero and the Expression of Grief.' In Braund and Gill 1997: 36-47.
Faraone, Christopher A. and Dirk Obbink, eds., 1991. *Magika Hiera: Ancient Greek Magic and Religion.* New York: Oxford University Press.
Fears, J. Rufus. 1975. 'Nero as the Vicegerent of the Gods in Seneca's *De clementia.' Hermes* 103: 486-96.
―――― 1981. 'The Cult of Virtues and Roman Imperial Ideology.' In W. Haase, ed., *Aufstieg und Niedergang der Römischen Welt* 2.17.2 (Berlin: De Gruyter) 827-948.
Ferwerda, R. 1984. 'Pity in the Life and Thought of Plotinus.' In David T. Runia, ed., *Plotinus amid Gnostics and Christians: Papers Presented at the Plotinus Symposium held at the Free University, Amsterdam on 25 January 1984* (Amsterdam: VU Uitgeverij) 53-72.
Fessler, Daniel M.T. 1999. 'Toward an Understanding of the Universality of Second Order Emotions.' In Hinton 1999: 75-116.
Festugière, A-J. 1976. '*Anth'hôn*: La formule "en échange de quoi" dans la prière grecque hellénistique.' *Revue des Sciences Philosophiques et Théologiques* 60: 389-418.
Finley, Moses I. 1977. *Aspects of Antiquity: Discoveries and Controversies*, 2nd ed. Harmondsworth: Penguin.
Fornara, Charles William. 1983. *The Nature of History in Ancient Greece and Rome.* Berkeley: University of California Press.
Fortenbaugh, William W. 1975. *Aristotle on Emotion.* London: Duckworth.
Fowler, D.P. 1997. 'Epicurean Anger.' In Braund and Gill 1997: 16-35.
Frede, Dorothea. 1996. 'Mixed Feelings in Aristotle's *Rhetoric*.' In Amélie Oksenberg Rorty, ed., *Essays on Aristotle's Rhetoric* (Berkeley: University of California Press) 258-85.
Frijda, Nico H. 1986. *The Emotions.* Cambridge: Cambridge University Press.
Fredericks, Sigmund C. 1976. 'Juvenal's Fifteenth Satire.' *Illinois Classical Studies* 1: 174-89.
Furley, William D. 2000. ' "Fearless, Bloodless ... Like the Gods": Sappho 31 and the Rhetoric of "Godlike".' *Classical Quarterly* 50: 7-15.
Galaway, Burt and Joe Hudson, eds., 1996. *Restorative Justice: International Perspectives.* Monsey NY: Criminal Justice Press.
Gardiner, H.M., Ruth Clark Metcalf, and John G. Beebe-Center. 1937. *Feeling and Emotion: A History of Theories.* New York: American Book Co.
Garland, Robert. 1995. *The Eye of the Beholder: Deformity and Disability in the Graeco-Roman World.* London: Duckworth.
Geertz, Hildred. 1959. 'The Vocabulary of Emotion: A Study of Javanese Socialization Processes.' *Psychiatry* 22: 225-37.
Gergen, Kenneth J. 1985. 'Social Constructionist Inquiry: Context and Implications.' In Kenneth J. Gergen and Keith E. Davis, eds., *The Social Construction of the Person* (New York: Springer-Verlag) 3-18.
Gill, Christopher. 1998. 'Did Galen Understand Platonic and Stoic Thinking on Emotions?' In Sihvola and Engberg-Pedersen 1998: 113-48.

Bibliography

Giordano, Manuela. 1999. *La supplica: rituale, istituzione sociale e tema epico in omero*. Naples: *AION* = Annali dell'Istituto Universitario Orientale di Napoli, Quaderni 3.

Gleason, Maud W. 1995. *Making Men: Sophists and Self-Presentation in Ancient Rome*. Princeton: Princeton University Press.

Gomme, A.W. 1956. *A Historical Commentary on Thucydides*, vol. 2. Oxford: Clarendon Press.

Gordon, Robert M. 1987. *The Structure of Emotions: Investigations in Cognitive Philosophy*. Cambridge: Cambridge University Press.

Graf, Fritz. 1991. 'Prayer in Magic and Religious Ritual.' In Faraone and Obbink 1991: 188-213.

Grastyán, Endre. 1986. 'Emotion' s.v. 'Human Emotion and Motivation'. In *The New Encyclopaedia Britannica*, 15th ed., vol. 18 (London: Encyclopaedia Britannica) 347-65.

Griessmair, Ewald. 1966. *Das Motiv der Mors immatura in den griechischen metrischen Grabinschriften*. Innsbruck: Universitätsverlag Wagner, 1966 = Commentationes Aenipontanae 17.

Griffin, Miriam T. 1976. *Seneca: A Philosopher in Politics*. Oxford: Oxford University Press.

Griffiths, Paul E. 1997. *What Emotions Really Are: The Problem of Psychological Categories*. Chicago: University of Chicago Press.

Grimaldi, William M.A. 1988. *Aristotle Rhetoric II: A Commentary*. New York: Fordham University Press.

Hall, Stuart George, trans., 2000. *Gregory of Nyssa: On the Beatitudes*. In Drobner and Viciano 2000: 23-90.

Halliwell, Stephen. 1986. *Aristotle's Poetics*. London: Duckworth.

―――― 1995. 'Tragedy, Reason and Pity: A Reply to Jonathan Lear.' In Robert Heinaman, ed., *Aristotle and Moral Reason* (London: UCL Press) 85-95.

―――― 2001. *The Aesthetics of Mimesis: Ancient Texts and Modern Problems*. Princeton: Princeton University Press.

Halm, Carolus, ed., 1863. *Rhetores latini minores*. Leipzig: Teubner.

Hamburger, Max. 1951. *Morals and Law: The Growth of Aristotle's Legal Theory*. New Haven: Yale University Press.

Harré, Rom, ed., 1986. *The Social Construction of Emotions*. Oxford: Basil Blackwell.

Harré, Rom. 1986a. 'An Outline of the Social Constructionist Viewpoint.' In Harré ed. 1986: 2-14.

―――― and Robert Finlay-Jones. 1986. 'Emotion Talk across Times.' In Harré 1986: 220-33.

Harries, Jill. 1999. *Law and Empire in Late Antiquity*. Cambridge: Cambridge University Press.

Harrison, A.R.W. 1998 [orig. 1971]. *The Law of Athens*, 2nd ed., edited by D.M. MacDowell, vol. 2. London: Duckworth.

Heath, Malcolm. 1987. *The Poetics of Greek Tragedy*. London: Duckworth.

―――― 1990. 'Justice in Thucydides' Athenian Speeches.' *Historia* 39: 385-400.

―――― 1998. 'Apsines and Pseudo-Apsines.' *American Journal of Philology* 119: 89-111.

Heck, Eberhard and Antonie Wlosok. 1994. *L. Caeli Firmiani Lactantii epitome divinarum institutionum*. Stuttgart and Leipzig: Teubner.

Heelas, Paul. 1986. 'Emotion Talk across Cultures.' In Harré 1986: 234-66.

Bibliography

Heene, Katrien. 1988. 'La manifestation sociale de l'expérience du chagrin: le témoignage de la poésie épigraphique latine.' *Epigraphica* 50: 163-77.

Henderson, Lynne. 1998 (spring). 'Criminal Law Symposium Commentary: Co-opting Compassion: The Federal Victim's Rights Amendment.' *St Thomas Law Review* 10: 579-606.

Hillman, James. 1992 [orig. 1960]. *Emotion: A Comprehensive Phenomenology of Theories and their Meanings for Therapy*. Evanston, IL: Northwestern University Press.

Hinton, Alexander Laban, ed., 1999. *Biocultural Approaches to the Emotions*. Cambridge: Cambridge University Press.

――― 1999a. 'Introduction: Developing a Biocultural Approach to the Emotions.' In Hinton 1999: 1-37.

――― 1999b. 'Outline of a Bioculturally Based, "Processual" Approach to the Emotions.' In Hinton 1999: 299-328.

Hirschman, Albert O. 1977. *The Passions and the Interests: Political Arguments for Capitalism before its Triumph*. Princeton: Princeton University Press.

Hochschild, Arlie Russell. 1975. 'The Sociology of Feeling and Emotion: Selected Possibilities.' In Marcia Millman and Rosabeth Moss Kanter, eds., *Another Voice: Feminist Perspectives on Social Life and Social Science* (Garden City NY: Anchor Doubleday) 280-307.

Hoffman, Martin L. 1978. 'Toward a Theory of Empathic Arousal and Development.' In Michael Lewis and Leonard A. Rosenblum, eds., *The Development of Affect* (New York: Plenum Press) 227-56.

Hölscher, Tonio. 1986. 'Clementia.' In *Lexicon Iconographicum Mythologiae Classicae*, ed. Hans Christoph Ackermann and Jean-Robert Gisler (Zurich: Artemis) 3.1: 295-9.

Hornblower, Simon. 1997 [orig. 1991]. *A Commentary on Thucydides*, vol. 1, reprinted with additions. Oxford: Clarendon Press.

Huglo, H. 1958. 'Origine et diffusion des Kyrie.' *Revue Grégorienne* 37: 85-87.

Hume, David. 1906 [orig. 1739-40]. *A Treatise of Human Nature*, ed. L.A. Selby-Bigge. Oxford: Oxford University Press.

Idriess, Ion Llewellyn. 1942. *Lurking Death*. Sydney: Angus and Robertson.

Inwood, Brad. 1993. 'Seneca and Psychological Dualism.' In Jacques Brunschwig and Martha C. Nussbaum, eds., *Passions and Perceptions: Studies in the Hellenistic Philosophy of Mind* (Cambridge: Cambridge University Press and Paris: Editions de la Maison des Sciences de l'Homme) 150-83.

Jacobs, Harriet. 1987. *Incidents in the Life of a Slave Girl: Written by Herself*, ed. L. Maria Child; introduction by Jean Fagan Yellin. Cambridge, MA: Harvard University Press.

James, Susan. 1997. *Passion and Action: The Emotions in Seventeenth-Century Philosophy*. Oxford: Clarendon Press.

James, William. 1884. 'What is an Emotion?' *Mind* 9: 188-205.

Johnson, James Franklin. 1980. *Compassion in Sophocles' Philoctetes: A Comparative Study*. Austin: Diss. University of Texas.

Johnstone, Steven. 1999. *Disputes and Democracy: The Consequence of Litigation in Ancient Athens*. Austin: University of Texas Press.

Jones, John. 1962. *On Aristotle and Greek Tragedy*. New York: Oxford University Press.

Judge, Edwin. 1986. 'Mercy in Late Antiquity.' In O'Brien and Peterson 1986: 107-21.

Bibliography

Kant, Immanuel. 1959 [orig. 1785]. *Foundations of the Metaphysics of Morals*, trans. Lewis White Beck. Indianapolis: Bobbs-Merrill.

Kassel, Rudolf. 1958. *Untersuchungen zur griechischen und römischen Konsolationsliteratur*. Munich: C.H. Beck'sche Verlagsbuchhandlung = *Zetemata* 18.

Keenleyside, Terence A. 1999. 'The Western Approach to Human Rights in Foreign Policy with Special Reference to Canada.' In Hasan Ashraful, ed., *Human Rights in Contemporary Times: Issues and Answers*. San Francisco: Austin and Winfield, 135-70.

Kendeffy, Gábor. 2000. 'Lactantius on the Passions.' *Acta Classica Universitatis Scientiarum Debreceniensis* 26: 113-29.

Kennedy, George A., trans. and ed., 1991. *Aristotle on Rhetoric: A Theory of Civic Discourse*. New York: Oxford University Press.

Kirchmeier, Jeffrey L. 1998. 'Aggravating and Mitigating Factors: The Paradox of Today's Arbitrary and Mandatory Capital Punishment Scheme.' *William and Mary Bill of Rights Journal* 6: 345-459.

King, Margaret. 2000. 'Commemoration of Infants on Roman Funerary Inscriptions.' In G.J. Oliver, ed., *The Epigraphy of Death: Studies in the History and Society of Greece and Rome* (Liverpool: Liverpool University Press) 117-54.

Konstan, David. 1973. *Some Aspects of Epicurean Psychology*. Leiden: E.J. Brill.

――― 1981 'Venus's Enigmatic Smile.' *Vergilius* 32: 18-25.

――― 1997. Review of Judith Mossman, *Wild Justice: A Study of Euripides' Hecuba*. *International Journal of the Classical Tradition* 4: 115-18.

――― 1997a. *Friendship in the Classical World*. Cambridge: Cambridge University Press.

――― 1998. 'Philoctetes' Pity: Comment on Julius M.E. Moravcsik, "Values and Friendship in the *Philoctetes*".' *Proceedings of the Boston Area Colloquium on Ancient Philosophy* 13: 276-82.

――― 1999. 'The Tragic Emotions.' In Luis R. Gámez, ed., *Tragedy's Insights: Identity, Polity, Theodicy* (West Cornwall, CT: Locust Hill Press, 1999) 1-21 = *Comparative Drama* 33: 1-21.

――― 1999a. 'Pity and Self-Pity.' *Electronic Antiquity* 5.2. Available on the web at http://scholar.lib.vt. edu/ejournals/ElAnt.

――― 2000. 'Altruism.' *Transactions of the American Philological Association* 130: 1-17.

――― 2000a. 'Pity and Two Tragedies.' In Ekkehard Stärk and Gregor Vogt-Spira, eds., *Dramatische Wäldchen: Festschrift für Eckard Lefèvre zum 65. Geburtstag* (Hildesheim: Olms = *Spudasmata* 80) 47-57.

――― 2000b. 'Pity and the Law in Greek Theory and Practice.' *Dike: Rivista di Storia del Diritto Greco ed Ellenistico* 3: 1-21.

――― 2000c. 'Las emociones trágicas.' In Ana María González de Tobia, ed., *Actas del Congreso: Una nueva visión de la cultura griega antigua en el fin del milenio* (La Plata: Editorial de la Universidad Nacional de La Plata) 125-43.

――― 2000d. 'La pitié comme émotion chez Aristote.' *Revue des Etudes Grecques* 113: 617-31.

――― 2001. 'La misericordia divina.' *Phaos: Revista de Estudos Clássicos* 1: 115-28.

――― 2001a. 'Pity and the Historians.' *Histos* 5 at http:// www.dur.ac.uk/Classics/histos/index.html.

Kotansky, Roy. 1991. 'Incantations and Prayers for Salvation on Inscribed Greek Amulets.' In Faraone and Obbink 1991: 107-37.

Bibliography

Kövecses, Zoltán. 2000. *Metaphor and Emotion: Language, Culture, and Body in Human Feeling*. Cambridge: Cambridge University Press and Paris: Editions de la Maison des Sciences de l'Homme.

Kunz, L. 1961. 'Kyrie eleison.' In Michael Buchberger et al., *Lexicon für Theologie und Kirche*, 2nd. ed, vol. 6 (Freiburg; Verlag Herder) coll. 705-6.

Lanni, Adriaan. 1999. 'Jury Sentencing in Noncapital Cases: An Idea Whose Time Has Come (Again)?' *Yale Law Journal* 109: 101-29.

Lattimore, Richmond. 1962. *Themes in Greek and Latin Epitaphs*. Urbana: University of Illinois Press.

Lawless, John Martin. 1991. *Law, Argument and Equity in the Speeches of Isaeus*. Providence, RI: Dissertation Brown University.

Lazarus, Richard S. 1991. 'Cognition and Motivation.' *American Psychologist* 46: 352-67.

——, Allen D. Kanner, and Susan Folkman. 1980. 'Emotions: A Cognitive-Phenomenological Analysis.' In Robert Plutchik and Henry Kellerman, eds., *Emotion: Theory, Research, and Experience*, vol. 1: Theories of Emotion (New York: Academic Press) 189-217.

LeDoux, Joseph. 1996. *The Emotional Brain: The Mysterious Underpinnings of Emotional Life*. New York: Simon and Schuster.

Lee, J.A.L. 1983. *A Lexical Study of the Septuagint Version of the Pentateuch*. Chico, CA: Scholars Press = Society of Biblical Literature Septuagint and Cognate Studies Series 14.

Leigh, Matthew. 1997. *Lucan: Spectacle and Engagement*. Oxford: Clarendon Press.

Leighton, Stephen R. 1982. 'Aristotle and the Emotions.' *Phronesis* 27: 144-74.

Levene, D.S. 1997. 'Pity, Fear and the Historical Audience: Tacitus on the Fall of Vitellius.' In Braund and Gill 1997: 128-49.

—— 1998. 'God and Man in the Classical Panegyric.' *Proceedings of the Cambridge Philological Society*. 44: 66-103.

Levick, B.M. 1975. 'Mercy and Moderation on the Coinage of Tiberius.' In Barbara Levick, ed., *The Ancient Historian and his Materials: Essays in Honour of C.E. Stevens* (Farnborough, Hants.: Gregg) 123-37.

Levy, Robert I. 1973. *Tahitians: Mind and Experience in the Society Islands*. Chicago: University of Chicago Press, 1973.

—— 1984. 'Emotion, Knowing, and Culture.' In Shweder and LeVine 1984: 214-37.

Lewis, C.S. 1936. *The Allegory of Love*. Oxford: Oxford University Press.

—— 1989. *A Grief Observed*, Foreword by Madeleine L'Engle. San Francisco: Harper and Row.

Lewis, Thomas, Fari Amini, and Richard Lannon. 2000. *A General Theory of Love*. New York: Random House.

Lintott, Andrew W. 1968. *Violence in Republican Rome*. Oxford: Clarendon Press.

Long, Anthony A. and David Sedley, eds. and trans. 1987. *The Hellenistic Philosophers*, vol. 1. Cambridge: Cambridge University Press.

Lutz, Catherine A. 1988. *Unnatural Emotions: Everyday Sentiments on a Micronesian Atoll and their Challenge to Western Theory*. Chicago: University of Chicago Press.

Lyons, William. 1980. *Emotion*. Cambridge: Cambridge University Press.

MacDowell, Douglas M., ed., 1990. *Demosthenes: Against Meidias (Oration 21)*. Oxford: Clarendon Press.

Bibliography

Malebranche, Nicolas. 1972 [orig. 1674-5]. *De la recherche de la vérité*, ed. Geneviève Rodis-Lewis. In *Oeuvres complètes*, ed. A. Robinet, 2nd ed., 3 vols. Paris: J. Vrin.

────── 1980. *The Search after Truth and Elucidations of the Search After Truth*, trans. Thomas M. Lennon and Paul J. Olscamp. Columbus, OH: Ohio State University Press.

Maltby, Robert. 1991. *A Lexicon of Ancient Latin Etymologies*. Leeds: Francis Cairns.

McCoskey, Denise Eileen. 1998. ' "I, Whom She Detested So Bitterly": Slavery and the Violent Division of Women in Aeschylus' *Oresteia*.' In Sheila Murnaghan and Sandra R. Joshel, eds., *Differential Equations: Women and Slaves in Greco-Roman Culture* (London: Routledge) 35-55.

McKim, Richard. 1986. 'Philosophers and Cannibals: Juvenal's Fifteenth Satire.' *Phoenix* 40: 58-71.

McNeal, Keith E. 1999. 'Affecting Experience: Toward a Biocultural Model of Human Emotion.' In Hinton ed. 1999: 215-55.

Michel, Alain. 1984. 'Humanisme et anthropologie chez Cicéron.' *Revue des Etudes Latines* 62: 128-42.

Minow, Martha. 1998. 'Between Vengeance and Forgiveness: Feminist Responses to Violent Injustice.' *New England Review of Law* 32: 967-81.

Mitsis, Phillip. 1999. 'The Stoic Origin of Natural Rights.' In Katerina Ierodiakonou, ed., *Topics in Stoic Philosophy*. Oxford: Clarendon Press, 153-77.

Moeller, Susan D. 1999. *Compassion Fatigue: How the Media Sell Disease, Famine, War and Death*. London: Routledge.

Monsacré, Hélène. 1984. *Les larmes d'Achille: Le héros, la femme et la souffrance dans la poésie d'Homère*. Paris: Albin Michel.

Moore, James William et al., eds., 1997. *Moore's Manual: Federal Practice and Procedure*, vol. 1. New York: Matthew Bender and Co.

More, Ellen Singer, and Maureen A. Milligan, eds., 1994. *The Empathic Practitioner: Empathy, Gender, and Medicine*. New Brunswick: Rutgers University Press.

Morris, Royce L.B. 1975. A Study in the Social and Economic History of Oxyrhynchus for the First Two Centuries of Roman Rule. Durham NC: diss. Duke University.

────── 1981. 'Reflections of Citizen Attitudes in Petitions from Roman Oxyrhynchus.' In Roger S. Bagnall et al., eds., *Proceedings of the XVI International Congress of Papyrology* (Chico, CA: Scholars Press) 363-70.

Morsbach, H. and W.J. Tyler. 1986. 'A Japanese Emotion: *Amae*.' In Harré 1986: 289-307.

Mortureux, Bernard. 1989. 'Les idéaux Stoiciens et les premières responsabilités politiques: le "De Clementia".' In W. Haase, ed., *Aufstieg und Niedergang der Römischen Welt* 2.36.3 (Berlin: De Gruyter) 1639-85.

Mulroy, David. 1973-74. 'Pity and Fear.' *Classical Bulletin* 50: 53-5.

Myers, Fred R. 1980. 'Emotions and the Self: A Theory of Personhood and Political Order among Pintupi Aborigines.' *Ethos* 8.1: 343-70.

Miller, William Ian. 1997. *The Anatomy of Disgust*. Cambridge MA: Harvard University Press.

Murphy, Jeffrie G. and Jean Hampton. 1988. *Forgiveness and Mercy*. Cambridge: Cambridge University Press.

Neill, Alex. 1993. 'Fiction and the Emotions.' *American Philosophical Quarterly* 30: 1-13.

Bibliography

Newton, Tim. 1998. 'The Sociogenesis of Emotion: A Historical Sociology?' In Gillian Bendelow and Simon J. Williams, eds., *Emotions in Social Life: Critical Themes and Contemporary Issues*. London: Routledge, 60-80.

Ničev, Alexandre. 1978. 'Questions éthiques et esthétiques chez Polybe: *Eleos* chez Polybe et Aristote.' *Revue des Etudes Grecques* 91: 149-57.

—— 1981. 'La catarsi tragica di Aristotele.' *Homonoia* 3: 59-79.

—— 1985. 'La notion de pitié chez Sophocle.' In Jacques Brunschwig, Claude Imbert, and Alain Roger, eds., *Histoire et structure: A la mémoire de Victor Goldschmidt* (Paris: J. Vrin) 61-3.

Nock, Arthur Darby. 1972. *Essays on Religion and the Ancient World*, ed. with introduction by Zeph Stewart, 2 vols. Oxford: Clarendon Press.

North, James. 1999 (8 February). Review of Moeller 1999. *The Nation* 268.5: 28-30.

Nussbaum, Martha C. 1993. 'Equity and Mercy.' *Philosophy and Public Affairs* 22: 79-125.

—— 1993a. 'Poetry and the Passions: Two Stoic Views.' In Jacques Brunschwig and Martha C. Nussbaum, eds., *Passions and Perceptions: Proceedings of the 5th Symposium Hellenisticum* (Cambridge: Cambridge University Press) 97-149.

Oatley, Keith. 1992. *Best Laid Schemes: The Psychology of Emotions*. Cambridge: Cambridge University Press and Paris: Editions de la Maison des Sciences de l'Homme.

O'Brien, Peter T. and David G. Peterson, eds., 1986. *God Who is Rich in Mercy: Essays Presented to Dr. D.B. Knox*. Homebush West NSW: Lancer Books.

Olasky, Marvin. 1996. *Renewing American Compassion*. New York: The Free Press.

O'Laughlin, Michael, trans. 1990. 'Evagrius Ponticus: *Antirrheticus* (Selections).' In Vincent L. Wimbush, ed., *Ascetic Behavior in Greco-Roman Antiquity: A Source Book* (Minneapolis: Fortress Press) 243-62.

Orelli, Kaspar von. 1912. *Die philosophischen Auffassungen des Mitleids: Eine historisch-kritische Studie*. Bonn: C. Georgi.

Ortony, Andrew, Gerald L. Clore, and Allan Collins. 1988. *The Cognitive Structure of Emotions*. Cambridge: Cambridge University Press.

Ostwald, Martin. 1979. 'Diodotus, Son of Eucrates.' *Greek, Roman and Byzantine Studies* 20: 5-13.

Owen, David. 1984. *A Future that Will Work: Competitiveness and Compassion*. New York: Praeger.

Parker, Robert. 1996. *Athenian Religion*. Oxford: Clarendon Press.

Peek, Werner. 1960. *Griechische Grabgedichte: Griechisch und Deutsch*. Berlin: Akademie-Verlag.

Pelling, Christopher. 1997. 'Aeschylus' *Persae* and History.' In Christopher Pelling, ed., *Greek Tragedy and the Historian* (Oxford: Clarendon Press) 1-19.

—— Unpublished. 'Aristotle's *Rhetoric* and Thucydides.' Talk presented at Oxford November 1993.

Pera, Rossella. 1980. 'Significato etico-politico della *clementia* nelle monete da Adriano a Marco Aurelio.' *Numismatica e Antichità Classiche* 9: 237-46.

Perdrizet, Paul. 1908. *La vierge de miséricorde: étude d'un thème iconographique*. Paris: Albert Fontemoing = Bibliothèque des Écoles Françaises d'Athènes et de Rome 101.

Perkins, Judith. 1995. *The Suffering Self: Pain and Narrative Representation in the Early Christian Era*. London: Routledge.

Bibliography

Pétré, Hélène. 1934. ' "Misericordia": histoire du mot et de l'idée du paganisme au christianisme.' *Revue des Etudes Latines* 12: 376-89.
Pine-Coffin, R.S., trans., 1961. *Saint Augustine: Confessions*. Harmondsworth: Penguin Books.
Planalp, Sally. 1999. *Communicating Emotion: Social, Moral, and Cultural Processes*. Cambridge: Cambridge University Press.
Pleket, H.W. 1981. 'Religious History as the History of Mentality: The "Believer" as Servant of the Deity in the Greek World.' In H.S. Versnel, ed., *Faith, Hope and Worship: Aspects of Religious Mentality in the Ancient World* (Leiden: E.J. Brill) 152-92.
Plutchik, Robert. 1991. *The Emotions: Facts, Theories, and a New Model*, rev. ed. Lanham MD: University Press of America.
Pohlenz, Max. 1956. 'Furcht und Mitleid? Ein Nachwort.' *Hermes* 84: 49-74.
Pollack, Malla. 1998. 'The Underfunded Death Penalty: Mercy as Discrimination in a Rights-Based System of Justice.' *University of Missouri at Kansas City Law Review* 66: 513-58.
Pomeroy, Sarah B., Stanley M. Burstein, Walter Donlan, and Jennifer Tolbert Roberts. 1999. *Ancient Greece: A Political, Social, and Cultural History*. Oxford: Oxford University Press.
Pritchett, W. Kendrick. 1991. *The Greek State at War*. Part 5. Berkeley: University of California Press.
Pulleyn, Simon. 1997. *Prayer in Greek Religion*. Oxford: Clarendon Press.
Radford, Colin. 1995. 'Fiction, Pity, Fear, and Jealousy.' *Journal of Aesthetics and Art Criticism* 5: 71-5 (reply to Neill 1993).
Rahmani, L.Y. 1981. 'A Magic Amulet from Nahariyya.' *Harvard Theological Review* 74: 387-90.
Rainolds, John. 1986 [orig. c. 1572]. *John Rainolds's Oxford Lectures on Aristotle's* Rhetoric. Edited and translated with commentary by Lawrence D. Green. Newark: University of Delaware Press.
Ramos Guerreira, Agustín. 1998. 'Consideraciones sobre la expresión de la posesión en latin.' In B. García Hernández, ed., *Estudios de Lingüística Latina. Actas del IX Coloquio Internacional de Lingüística Latina*, vol. 2 (Madrid: Ediciones Clásicas) 673-88.
Reilly, Alexander. 1997/98. 'The Heart of the Matter: Emotion in Criminal Defences.' *Ottawa Law Review* 29: 120-51.
Rhodes, Peter J. 1998. 'Enmity in Fourth-Century Athens.' In Paul Cartledge, Paul Millett and Sitta von Reden, eds., *Kosmos: Essays in Order, Conflict and Community in Classical Athens* (Cambridge: Cambridge University Press) 144-61.
Rigsby, Kent. 2000. 'Textual Notes on Epitaphs.' *Zeitschrift für Papyrologie und Epigraphik* 133: 113-16.
Robert, Louis. 1939. 'Inscriptions grecques de Phénicie et d'Arabie.' In *Mélanges Syriens Offerts à René Dussaud* II (Bibliothèque Arch. et Hist. 30) 729-38; reprinted in Louis Robert, *Opera Minora Selecta*, vol. 1 (Amsterdam: Hakkert, 1969) 601-10.
——— 1968. 'Enterrement et épitaphes.' *L'Antiquité Classique* 37: 406-48; reprinted in Louis Robert, *Opera Minora Selecta*, vol. 6. (Amsterdam: Hakkert, 1989) 82-124.
Roberts, Adam and Richard Guelff. 1982. *Documents on the Laws of War*. Oxford: Clarendon Press.

Bibliography

Roberts, W. Rhys. 1984 [orig. 1924]. Translation of Aristotle's *Rhetoric*. In Barnes 1984: 2152-269.
Rodley, Nigel S. 1999. *The Treatment of Prisoners under International Law*. Oxford: Clarendon Press.
Rolls, Edmund T. 1999. *The Brain and Emotion*. Oxford: Oxford University Press.
────── 2000. 'Précis of *The Brain and Emotion*', 'Open Peer Commentary,' and 'Author's Response.' *Behavioral and Brain Sciences* 23: 177-233.
Romilly, Jacqueline de. 1974. 'Fairness and Kindness in Thucydides.' *Phoenix* 28: 95-100.
Rosaldo, Michelle Z. 1984. 'Toward an Anthropology of Self and Feeling.' In Shweder and LeVine eds., 1984: 137-57.
Rosaldo, Renato I. 1984. 'Grief and the Headhunter's Rage: On the Cultural Force of the Emotions.' In Edward Bruner, ed., *Play, Text, and Story* (Washington, DC: Proceedings of the 1983 Meeting of the American Ethnological Society) 178-95.
Rosenwein, Barbara H., ed., 1998. *Anger's Past: The Social Uses of an Emotion in the Middle Ages*. Ithaca, NY: Cornell University Press.
Rostovtzeff, Mikhail. 1941. *The Social and Economic History of the Hellenistic World*, vol. 3, rev. edition 1953, ed. by P.M. Fraser. Oxford: Oxford University Press.
────── 1928. 'Ptolemaic Egypt.' In S.A. Cook, F.E. Adcock, and M.P. Charlesworth, eds., *The Cambridge Ancient History*, vol. 7: The Hellenistic Monarchies and the Rise of Rome, 1st ed. (Cambridge: Cambridge University Press) 109-54.
Rousseau, Jean-Jacques. 1967 [orig. 1762, 1754 respectively], ed. Lester G. Crocker. *The Social Contract* and *The Discourse on the Origin and Foundation of Inequality among Mankind*. New York: Washington Square Press.
Rubinstein, Lene. 2000. *Litigation and Co-operation: Supporting Speakers in the Courts of Classical Athens*. Stuttgart: Franz Steiner Verlag = Historia Einzelschriften 145.
Russell, D.A. and N.G. Wilson, ed. and trans., 1981. *Menander Rhetor*. Oxford: Clarendon Press.
Russell, Frederick H. 1975. *The Just War in the Middle Ages*. Cambridge: Cambridge University Press.
Sacks, Kenneth S. 1990. *Diodorus Siculus and the First Century*. Princeton: Princeton University Press.
Sakenfeld, Katharine Doob. 1978. *The Meaning of Hesed in the Hebrew Bible*. Missoula, MT: Scholars Press = Harvard Semitic Monographs 17.
Scanlon, Thomas Francis. 1980. *The Influence of Thucydides on Sallust*. Heidelberg: Carl Winter.
Schadewaldt, Wolfgang. 1955. 'Furcht und Mitleid?' *Hermes* 83: 129-71.
────── 1973. 'Humanitas Romana.' In Hildegard Temporini, ed., *Aufstieg und Niedergang der Römischen Welt* 1.4 (Berlin: De Gruyter) 43-62.
Scheler, Max. 1954 [orig. 1923]. *The Nature of Sympathy*, trans. Peter Heath. London: Routledge & Kegan Paul.
Scherer, Klaus R. 1986. 'Emotional Experiences across European Cultures: A Summary Statement.' In Klaus R. Scherer, Harald G. Wallbott, and Angela B. Summerfield, eds., *Experiencing Emotion: A Cross-Cultural Study* (Cambridge: Cambridge University Press and Paris: Editions de la Maison des Sciences de l'Homme) 173-89.

Bibliography

Schiesaro, Alessandro. 1997. 'Passion, Reason and Knowledge in Seneca's Tragedies.' In Braund and Gill 1997: 89-111.
Schofield, Malcolm. 1999. *Saving the City: Philosopher-Kings and Other Classical Paradigms*. London: Routledge.
Schopenhauer, Arthur. 1995 [orig. 1840]. *On the Basis of Morality*, trans. David E. Cartwright. Providence: Berghahn Books.
Schrijvers, P.H. 1978. 'La valeur de la pitié chez Virgile (dans "L'Enéide") et chez quelques-uns de ses interprètes.' In R. Chevallie, ed., *Présence de Virgile: Actes du Colloque des 9, 11, et 12 décembre 1976* (Paris: E.N.S. Tours) 483-95.
Scourfield, J.H.D. 1993. *Consoling Heliodorus: A Commentary on Jerome, Letter 60*. Oxford: Clarendon Press.
Screech, M.A., trans., 1991. *Montaigne: The Complete Essays*. Harmondsworth: Penguin.
Scruton, David L. 1986. 'The Anthropology of an Emotion.' In David L. Scruton, ed., *Sociophobics: The Anthropology of Fear* (Boulder: Westview Press) 7-49.
Shapiro, Joseph P. 1993. *No Pity: People with Disabilities Forging a New Civil Rights Movement*. New York: Random House.
Shay, Jonathan. 1994. *Achilles in Vietnam: Combat Trauma and the Undoing of Character*. New York: Athenaeum.
Shweder, Richard A. and Robert A. LeVine, eds. 1984. *Culture Theory: Essays on Mind, Self, and Emotion*. Cambridge: Cambridge University Press.
Sider, Robert D. 1971. *Ancient Rhetoric and Tertullian*. London: Oxford University Press.
Sihvola, Juha and Troels Engberg-Pedersen, eds. 1998. *The Emotions in Hellenistic Philosophy*. Dordrecht: Kluwer Academic Publishers.
Silk, Michael. 1987. 'Pathos in Aristophanes.' *Bulletin of the Institute of Classical Studies* 34: 78-11.
Singleton, D. 1983. 'Juvenal's Fifteenth Satire: A Reading.' *Greece and Rome* 30: 198-207.
Snell, Bruno. 1955. *Die Entdeckung des Geistes: Studien zur Entstehung des europäischen Denkens bei den Griechen*, 3rd ed. Hamburg: Classen.
Smith, Adam. 1976 [orig. 1759; 6th ed. 1790]. *The Theory of Moral Sentiments*, ed. E.G. West. Indianapolis: Hackett.
Solomon, Robert C. 1984. 'Getting Angry: The Jamesian Theory of Emotion in Anthropology.' In Shweder and LeVine 1984: 238-54.
—— 1990. *A Passion for Justice*. Reading MA: Addison-Wesley.
—— 1993. *The Passions: Emotions and the Meaning of Life*, rev. ed. Indianapolis: Hackett.
Sorabji, Richard. 1999. 'Aspasius on Emotion.' In Antonina Alberti and Robert W. Sharples, eds., *Aspasius: The Earliest Extant Commentary on Aristotle's Ethics* (Berlin: Walter de Gruyter) 96-106.
—— 2000. *Emotion and Peace of Mind: From Stoic Agitation to Christian Temptation*. Oxford: Oxford University Press.
Spacks, Patricia M. 1995. *Boredom*. Chicago: University of Chicago Press.
Stafford, Emma. 2000. *Worshipping Virtues: Personification and the Divine in Ancient Greece*. London: Duckworth and the Classical Press of Wales.
Stanford, W.B. 1983. *Greek Tragedy and the Emotions*. London: Routledge and Kegan Paul.
Stearns, Carol Zisowitz and Peter N. Stearns. 1986. *Anger: The Struggle for Emotional Control in America's History*. Chicago: University of Chicago Press.
Stears, Karen. 1998. 'Death Becomes Her: Gender and Athenian Death Ritual.'

Bibliography

In Sue Blundell and Margaret Williamson, eds., *The Sacred and the Feminine* (London: Routledge) 113-27.

Sternberg, Rachel Hall. 1998. *Pity and Pragmatism: A Study of Athenian Attitudes toward Compassion in 5th- and 4th-Century Historiography and Oratory*. Bryn Mawr, PA: Dissertation Bryn Mawr College.

Stevens, Edward B. 1941. 'Topics of Pity in the Poetry of the Roman Republic.' *American Journal of Philology* 62: 426-40.

Stoebe, H.J. 1971. '*rhm* pi. sich erbarmen.' In Ernst Jenni and Claus Vestermann, eds., *Theologisches Handwörterbuch zum Alten Testament*, vol. 2 (Munich: Chr. Kaiser Verlag) coll. 761-8.

Stith, Kate and José A. Cabranes. 1998. *Fear of Judging: Sentencing Guidelines in the Federal Courts*. Chicago: University of Chicago Press.

Stocker, Michael (with Elizabeth Hegeman). 1996. *Valuing Emotions*. Cambridge: Cambridge University Press.

Striker, Gisela. 1996. 'Emotions in Context: Aristotle's Treatment of the Passions in the *Rhetoric* and His Moral Psychology.' In Amélie Oksenberg Rorty, ed., *Essays on Aristotle's Rhetoric* (Berkeley: University of California Press) 286-302.

Strubbe, J.H.M. 1998. 'Epigrams and Consolation Decrees for Deceased Youths.' *L'Antiquité Classique* 67: 45-75.

Stylianou, P.J. 1998. *A Historical Commentary on Diodorus Siculus Book 15*. Oxford: Clarendon Press.

Sundby, Scott E. 1998 (September). 'The Intersection of Trial Strategy, Remorse, and the Death Penalty.' *Cornell Law Review* 83: 1557-98.

Tarn, W.W. 1948. *Alexander the Great*, vol. 2. Cambridge: Cambridge University Press.

Thoreau, Henry David. 1997 [orig. 1846-47]. *Walden*, ed. Stephen Fender. Oxford: Oxford University Press.

Thornton, Agathe. 1984. *Homer's Iliad: Its Composition and the Motif of Supplication*. Göttingen: Vandenhoeck & Ruprecht = *Hypomnemata* 81.

Todd, Stephen C., trans., 2000. *Lysias*. Austin, TX: University of Texas Press.

Turner, Bryan S. 1993. 'Outline of a Theory of Human Rights.' *Sociology* 27: 489-512.

Uhlig, Gustav, ed. 1883. *Grammatici Graeci*, vol. 1.1. Leipzig: Teubner.

Umbreit, Mark S. with Robert B. Coates and Boris Kalanj. 1994. *Victim Meets Offender: The Impact of Restorative Justice and Mediation*. Monsey NY: Criminal Justice Press (Willow Tree Press).

van der Ben, N. 1976. 'Aristotle, *Poetics*, 1449b27-8.' In *Miscellanea tragica in honorem J.M. Kamerbeek* (Amersterdam: A.M. Hakkert) 1-15.

van Wees, Hans. 1998. 'A Brief History of Tears: Gender Differentiation in Archaic Greece.' In Lin Foxhall and John Salmon, eds., *When Men were Men: Masculinity, Power and Identity in Classical Antiquity* (London: Routledge, 1998) 10-53.

Versnel, H.S. 1991. 'Beyond Cursing: The Appeal to Justice in Judicial Prayers.' In Faraone and Obbink 1991: 60-106.

Vickers, Brian. 1979. *Toward Greek Tragedy*. London: Longman's.

Volkmann, Hans. 1961. *Die Massenversklavungen der Einwohner eroberter Städte in der hellenistisch-römischen Zeit. Abhandlungen der Akademie der Wissenschaften und der Literatur zu Mainz*, Geistes- und sozialwissenschaftlichen Klasse, 3.

Walbank, Frank W. 1957. *A Historical Commentary on Polybius*, vol. 1. Oxford: Clarendon Press.

Bibliography

Wallace, Anthony F.C. and Margaret T. Carson. 1973. 'Sharing and Diversity in Emotion Terminology.' *Ethos* 1: 1-29.

Walton, Douglas. 1997. *Appeal to Pity: Argumentum ad Misericordiam*. Albany: State University of New York Press.

Wardy, Robert. 1996. *The Birth of Rhetoric: Gorgias, Plato and their Successors*. London: Routledge.

Webb, Ruth. 1997. 'Mémoire et imagination: les limites de l'*enargeia* dans la théorie rhétorique grecque.' In Carlos Lévy et Laurent Pernot, eds., *Dire l'évidence: philosophie et rhétorique antiques*. (Paris: L'Harmattan, 1997 = Cahiers de Philosophie de l'Université de Paris XII – Val de Marne 2) 229-48.

―――― 1997a. 'Imagination and the Arousal of the Emotions in Greco-Roman rhetoric.' In Braund and Gill 1997: 112-27.

Webster's New Dictionary of Synonyms: A Dictionary of Discriminated Synonyms with Antonyms and Analogous and Contrasted Words. 1968. Springfield, MA: Merriam.

Weinstock, Stefan. 1971. *Divus Julius*. Oxford: Clarendon Press.

Weissbrodt, David. 1988. 'Human Rights: An Historical Perspective.' In Peter Davies, ed., *Human Rights* (London: Routledge) 1-20.

West, Martin. 1987. *Euripides Orestes*. Warminster: Aris and Phillips.

West, Robin. 1997. *Caring for Justice*. New York: New York University Press.

White, John Lee. 1972. *The Form and Structure of the Official Petition: A Study in Greek Epistolography*. Missoula, Mont.: Society of Biblical Literature = Dissertation Series #5.

White, Stephen D. 1998. 'The Politics of Anger.' In Rosenwein 1998: 127-52.

Wierzbicka, Anna. 1999. *Emotions across Languages and Cultures: Diversity and Universals*. Cambridge: Cambridge University Press.

Wiles, David. 1997. *Tragedy in Athens: Performance Space and Theatrical Meaning*. Cambridge: Cambridge University Press.

Williams, B.A.O. 1993. *Shame and Necessity*. Berkeley: University of California Press.

Willink, C.W., ed., 1986. *Euripides Orestes*. Oxford: Clarendon Press.

Wiltshire, Susan Ford. 1992. *Greece, Rome, and the Bill of Rights*. Norman: University of Oklahoma Press.

Wispé, L. 1991. *The Psychology of Sympathy*. New York: Plenum.

Wisse, Jakob. 1989. *Ethos and Pathos from Aristotle to Cicero*. Amsterdam: A.M. Hakkert.

Wright, Martin. 1996. *Justice for Victims and Offenders: A Restorative Response to Crime*, 2nd ed. Winchester: Waterside Press.

Wright, M.R. 1997. ' "Ferox virtus": Anger in Virgil's "Aeneid".' In Braund and Gill 1997: 169-84.

Wuthnow, Robert. 1991. *Acts of Compassion: Caring for Others and Helping Ourselves*. Princeton: Princeton University Press.

Zanker, Graham. 1994. *The Heart of Achilles: Characterization and Personal Ethics in the* Iliad. Ann Arbor: University of Michigan Press.

Zeldin, Theodore. 1994. *An Intimate History of Humanity*. New York: Harper-Collins.

Zierl, Andreas. 1994. *Affekte in der Tragödie: Orestie, Oidipus Tyrannos und die Poetik des Aristoteles*. Berlin: Akademische Verlag.

Zweig, Stefan. 1982 [orig. 1939]. *Beware of Pity*, trans. Phyllis and Trevor Blewitt. Evanston, IL: Northwestern University Press.

Index

Achaean War, 85-8
Achilles Tatius, 16-17, 73-4, 118
Aelian, 143n19
Aeschylus: *Prometheus Bound*, 60-1, 71, 73
afterlife and pity, 69-70
Alexander Romance, 118
Alford, Fred, 71-2, 111
Allen, Danielle, 82
altar to Pity, 89
Ambrose, 156n51
Anaxagoras, 63
Andersen, Francis, 120
Andronicus, 157n12
anger: of Aeneas, 78-9; of Antigonus, 87; definition of (Aristotle), 81; as a disposition, 4; metaphors for, 102; versus pity, 78; and punishment, 82; of Scipio, 83-4; in trials, 41-2
animals: and emotion, 7-8; and empathy, 14; and pity, 17
antitimêsis (Greek = 'sentencing phase'), 35-6
appeal to pity: in civil petitions, 114-15; in law courts, 27-45
Appian: *Civil War*, 76; *Libyan Wars*, 54; on the Second Punic War, 92-3; on the Third Punic War, 93-4
Apsines, 27
Apuleius, 77, 118
Árdal, Páll, 13
argumentum ad misericordiam, 27, 29; *see also* appeal to pity
Aristophanes: *Thesmophoriazusae*, 72; *Wasps* 27
Aristotle: on anger, 81, 133; on cognition and emotion, 6; on the condition of pitier, 130-2; on courage, 135; definition of pity, 34, 37, 49, 106, 128; on desire, 135-6; on emotion, 129; on fear, 73, 133-4; inconsistency concerning appeals to emotion, 44-5; on love, 133; on oratory (aims of), 82; on pain and pleasure, 129; on *pathos*, 88; on *philanthrôpon*, 46-7, 88, 130; on pity as an emotion, 128-36; and self-pity, 64-5; *Nicomachean Ethics*, 51, 58-9, 80, 135; *On the Soul*, 8; *Poetics*, 46-7, 88, 130; *Rhetoric*, 18, 34-5, 37, 44-6, 49-50, 73, 81-2, 106, 128-9, 133-6
[Aristotle]: *Problemata*, 10; *On Virtues and Vices*, 47
Aspasius, 157n12
Augustine, 64, 69, 103, 112, 136, 144n1
Augustus, 100
Aulus Gellius, 78
autocompasión (Spanish = 'self-pity'), 3
Averill, J.R., 17

Barbalet, J.M., 146n21
Bauman, Richard, 155n45
Bell, H.I., 114
Ben-Ze'ev, Aaron, 7-8, 59, 70, 88, 157n12
Boltanski, Luc, 51, 87, 145n9
Bowersock, Glenn, 119
brain: and emotion, 10-11; reptile, 14
Brutus, reputation for clemency, 76, 100
Burgess, Francis, 19
Burke, Edmund, 12
Burkert, Walter, 1, 151n8, 152n9

Index

Caesar, Julius, clemency of, 91, 95, 97-9
Cairns, Douglas, 33-5
Callimachus, 117
Callinus, 152n14
Calpurnius Siculus, 101
capital punishment, 31-3
captives, treatment of, 77
Cates, Diana, 59
Catilinarian conspiracy, 95
Catullus, 97, 153n26
Chariton, Callirhoe, 6
children and emotion, 14-15
Cicero: on clemency, 98-100; *On Invention*, 23, 27-8; *Letters to Brutus*, 100; *Letters to his Friends* 61; *For Ligarius*, 103; *On Old Age*, 97; *On the Orator*, 47, 157n9; *For Publius Sulla*, 97; *For Rabirius*, 145n7; *Tusculan Disputations*, 46, 49
Clausewitz, Carl von, 146n20
clemency, 1, 5; associations with autocracy, 99; and contempt, 12; as a disposition, 101-2; feigned, 99-100; and humaneness, 101; of Julius Caesar, 97-9; and leniency, 103-4; and pardon, 33-4; and pity, 91, 97-104, 119; in the Roman Empire, 100; Romans' reputation for, 96; and social order, 101; syntax of, 101-2; as a virtue, 100-1, 118
clemens (Latin = 'clement'), 102
clementia (Latin = 'clemency'), 97, 101
cognition: and emotion, 6, 8-10, 37, 86, 157n12; Posidonius on, 94-5
compassio (Latin = 'compassion'), 13, 58, 106
compassion, 1; among animals, 8; definition of, 105-6; fatigue of, 22; in modern society, 21-2; as opposed to pity, 59-60; *see also sun-*
confidence, 131, 135
consolation (genre), 63-4
contempt: and clemency, 12, 97-9; and pity, 2, 12, 101, 105
courage, 135

Crossly, David and Peter Wilson, 29
Crotty, Kevin, 61-2
culture and emotion, 16
Curtius, Quintus: *Alexander the Great*, 23, 101

Damasio, Antonio, 6
Darwin, Charles, 6
dead, pity for, 62-4, 67
deliberative versus forensic oratory, role of pity in, 82
democracy and pity, 111-12
Demosthenes 42, 79, 94
Denham, Susanne, 14
Descartes, René, 137n7, 155n43
desert and pity, 13, 30, 34-5, 38-40, 46-9, 57, 81; Aristotle on, 129-30; Diodorus on, 91; Polybius on, 84-8
desert versus pity, 85-6, 93-4
desire to help, and pity, 135-6
Dio Cassius, 86, 117
Dio Chrysostom (Dio of Prusa), 113, 153n25
Diodorus of Sicily (Diodorus Siculus), 58, 71; on Alexander the Great, 149n36; on divine pity, 117; on norms of war, 77; on the Sicilian expedition, 88-91; on Sulla's clemency, 97
Dionysius of Halicarnassus, 54, 72
disgust, 11-12
display of emotion, 20
disposition versus emotion, 4-5
distance between pitier and pitied, 60-1, 65, 72
Domine miserere (Latin = 'Lord have pity'), 105
Donnelly, Jack, 75-6, 88
Dover, Kenneth, 105
Dreitzel, H.P., 20-1
Drew-Bear, Thomas and Christian Naour, 117
Duris of Samos, 147n24

Eisenberg, Theodore et al., 31-2
Ekman, Paul, 7
Eleoi ('Pities'), 28
eleêmôn (Greek = 'disposed to pity'), 4-5
eleêmosunê (Greek = 'pity', 'act of charity'), 106, 119-20

Index

eleos (Greek = 'pity'), 53-4
Elias, Norbert, 19-20
Elster, Jon, 6, 137n3
emotion(s): Aristotle on, 128; and the brain, 10-11; which block pity, 131-2; classification of, 3-4; and cognition, 6, 8-10, 37, 94-5, 157n12; and culture, 16; definitions of, 4; display of, 20; evolution of, 6-7; inadequacy of term, 8; and language, 1-2; metaphors for, 102; multiple senses of, 3; and pain or pleasure, 129; and parts of speech, 3; as passive, 121; pity as, 3; as process, 10; progressivist view of, 19-21; versus reason, 5-6, 29, 37, 44; in reasoning, 37; versus reflexes, 8; restraint of, 19-21; social construction of, 17; and social roles, 16-17; Stoic hostility to, 48; in trials, 28; universality of, 7; vary over time, 1-3; as virtues (if used rightly), 121
emotional coincidence, 14, 50
emotional contagion, 14
empathy, 1, 12; in animals, 14; in children, 14-15; versus pity, 72
Ennius, 102, 126
enslavement in war, 76, 87
enthymeme, 44-5
envy: Aristotle on, 66; opposed to pity, 46; paired with pity, 65-6
epicedia (funeral lament), 64
Epictetus, 113
Epicureans, 113, 123
epieikeia (Greek = 'clemency', 'humanity') 80-1, 89, 91, 97, 104
Epirotes, 84-5, 149n35
Euripides: *Alcestis*, 109; *Cyclops*, 66, 115-16; *Electra*, 109, 157n6; *Hecuba*, 125; *Hippolytus*, 66-7; *Medea*, 56; *Heracles*, 59, 138n21; *Orestes*, 51, 54-8, 79; *Trojan Women*, 54, 60, 108-9
evaluation in emotions, *see* cognition
evolution of emotions, 6-7

fago (Ifaluk = 'compassion/love/sadness'), 2
family and pity, 61-2, 67

fear: and the brain, 11; and pain, 134-5; and pity (in Aristotle), 133-5; in tragedy, 2, 158n14
Fears, Rufus, 153n27
feeling, 4
Ferwerda, R., 59, 111, 152n9
Fessler, Daniel, 149n39
forensic versus deliberative oratory, role of pity in, 82
forgiveness, 1, 39-40
Fowler, Don, 17, 138n10
friendship and pity, 58-60, 73-4
funerary inscriptions, 62-4

Gardiner, H.M. et al., 155n44
gaze, *see* observer
Geertz, Hildred, 16
Georgius Monachus, 69-70
Giordano, Manuela, 146n11
God: Christian, 120, 122-4; Jewish, 120, 124; Muslim, 124
gods: in Homer, 109-11; invulnerability of, 112-13; and justice, 115-16; and pity, 49, 116-19; in tragedy, 106-9
Gomme, A.W., 81
gratitude, 38
Gregory of Nyssa: *On the Beatitudes*, 68-9, 120-1, 128
grief versus pity, 63-4
Griffiths, Paul, 8
guilt: and mercy, 33, 38, 94; and pity, 34-5, 39; *see also* innocence, merit
guilty plea, 35

harm, perception of, 128-9
Harries, Jill, 144n2
have, as non-transitive verb, 71
helplessness and pity, 22-3
Herodotus, 145n6
hesed (Hebrew = 'compassion'), 120, 154n38
historiography: and pity, 87-8; and surprise or wonder, 147n24
Homer: divine pity in, 109-11; *Iliad*, 61-2, 78-9, 125-6; *Odyssey*, 110-11
Horace: *Art of Poetry*, 101-2, 14
human rights, 75-6
humaneness, 47, 84, 88-91, 94, 123-4; Latin terms for, 99;

177

Index

Romans' reputation for, 114; *see also humanitas, philanthrôpia*
humanitas (Latin = 'humaneness'), 101, 123-4; *see also* humaneness, *philanthrôpia*
Hume, David, 12-13, 37

identification: between pitier and pitied, 12-13, 15, 60, 71-3; between reader and literary characters, 72-3; between writer and literary characters, 72
Ifaluk, 2
ignorance, pity for, 119
imagined pity, 62
indignation opposed to pity, 46, 66
innocence as condition for pity, 43; *see also* guilt, merit
inscriptions; funerary, 62-3; pity in, 116-17
intimates excluded from pity, 50-1, 56-7
Inwood, Brad, 11
iracundus (Latin = 'irritable'), 4
iratus (Latin = 'angry'), 4
irrational pity, 85-6
Isidore of Seville, 112
Isocrates 50, 46, 81

Jacobs, Harriet, 16-17
James, Susan, 139n5
Jerome, 64
judgment in emotions, *see* cognition
jury nullification, 33-4, 41-2
justice, and pity, 92-3, 96-7, 113-14, 123; versus pity in civil petitions, 114-15; and prayer, 116; and sympathy, 37
Juvenal: *Satire* 15, 122-3
kharis (Greek = 'gratitude', 'favour'), 38, 41
Kirchmeier, Jeffrey, 31
kurie eleêson (Greek = 'Lord have pity'), 105, 118

Lactantius, 121-4
language and emotion, 1-2, 7-8
Lattimore, Richmond, 62-3
Lazarus, Richard et al., 9
LeDoux, Joseph, 10-11, 137n10
lek (Balinese = 'shame'), 2

leniency and clemency, 103-4
Levene, David, 73, 86
Lewis, Thomas et al., 14, 73
Libanius, 81
Livy, 77, 47, 101; on mildness or clemency, 95-6; on Second Punic War, 95-6
logic and emotion, 29
logos (Greek = 'reason') versus passion, 6
love: Aristotle's definition of, 133; for family, 51; and pity, 58-60, 67; pity leading to, 73-4
Lucan, 99
Lucretius, 67-8, 122
Lutz, Catherine, 2
Lyons, William, 9
Lysias 37-42, 71

Malebranche, Nicolas, 16
malu (Malay = 'shame'), 149n39
manners and emotion, 19-20
Marcus Aurelius, 119
McCoskey, Denise, 16-17
Melville, Herman, 22-3
Menander (comic poet), 81, 117
Menander (rhetorician), 62-3
mercy, 1, 33, 38
merit and pity, see desert
metaphors for emotion, 102
Mettius Fufetius, punishment of, 77-8
Middle Ages, emotion in, 20
Miller, William, 11-12
mimetic behaviour, 14
misericordia (Italian = 'pity'), 146n17
misericordia (Latin = 'pity'), 96; as 'charity', 106; etymology of, 112
misericordia (Spanish = 'pity'), 3
misericors (Latin = 'disposed to pity'), 4-5, 102; etymology of, 112
mitigating circumstances, 32-3
Mitleid (German = 'sympathy'), 13
modes of eliciting pity, 27-8
Montaigne, Michel de, 142n13
mood, 4
Morris, Royce, 114-15, 153n23
Murphy, Jeffrie, 104
Myers, Fred, 21
Mytilenaean debate, 80-3, 90, 111

Index

nemesis, see indignation
neural pathways of emotion, 11
norms of war, 77, 86, 96

Oatley, Keith, 10, 37
observer, pity in relation to, 60-1, 72
oiktos (Greek = 'pity', 'lament'), 53-4
oiktos (Modern Greek = 'pity', 'contempt'), 137n4
oiktros (Greek = 'pitiful'), 2-3, 53
Olasky, Marvin, 21-2
ômotês (Greek = 'savagery'), 87, 89
opposite of pity, 18, 45-6
orgê (Greek = 'anger'), 7, 42, 87
Owen, David, 22

pain: and emotion, 129; and fear (Aristotle), 134-5; gods invulnerable to, 112-13, 155n44; mixed with pleasure, 157n4; and pity, 112, 129, 134-5; as sensation, 129
pardon, 30, 33-4, 80; and pity, 96
parricide, punishment for, 77-8
passio (Latin = 'emotion'), 121
pathos (Greek = 'emotion'), 3, 121; versus reason, 6
perception, *see* sensation
persuasion and the emotions, 17
petitions to civil authorities, 114-15
phantasia (Greek = 'perception'), *see* sensation
philanthrôpia (Greek = 'humaneness'), 47, 86, 88-9, 91-2, 94
philanthrôpon (Greek = 'humane'), 47, 84, 130
philia (Greek = 'love'), 133
Philo, 120-1
Philodemus: *On Anger*, 9
Philostratus: *Heroïcus*, 68; *Life of Apollonius*, 68, 140n17
Phylarchus, 85-8
physiology of emotions, 6-7
pietas (Latin = 'piety', 'pity'), 151n3
Pintupi, 21
pitiable, 132
pitiableness, 94
pitié (French = 'pity'), 66
pitier, condition of, 130-2
pitilessness, 2, 125-6

pity: and the afterlife, 69-70; altar to, 89; versus anger, 78; appeal to, 27-45; and aversion, 11-12; and the brain, 11; capacity for, 125-6; and clemency, 91, 97-103, 119; and compassion, 59-60, 63, 65, 89, 133; and condition of pitier, 130-2; and contempt, 2, 12, 101, 105; critique of (in Greek trials), 40, 42-4; for the dead, 62-4, 67; definition of (Aristotle), 34, 37, 64-5, 106; and desire (to help), 135-6; and democracy, 111-12; and desert, 13, 30, 34-5, 38-40, 46-9, 57, 81, 91, 129-30; versus desert, 93-4; and distance between pitier and pitied, 60-1, 65, 72; as an emotion, 3-4; emotions opposed to, 131-2; as ephemeral, 101; evocation of, 132; excess of, 22; and the family, 61-2, 67; like fear (in Aristotle), 133-4; and friendship, 58-60, 73-4; and God (Christian), 120, 122; and God (Jewish), 120; and the gods, 49, 106-12, 115-19; versus grief, 63-4; and guilt, 34-5, 39; and harm (perceived), 128-9; and helplessness, 22-3; and historiography, 87-8; and humaneness, 89-91, 94, 123-4; and identification, 12-13, 60, 71-3; and identity of situation, 14, 50; for ignorance, 119; imagined, 62; and innocence, 43; in inscriptions, 116-17; not among intimates, 50-1, 56-7; irrational, 85-6, 88; and justice, 92-3, 96-7, 113-14, 123; kinds of (two), 15, 45-6; and love, 58-60, 73-4; and mercy, 94; as misleading, 18; modes of eliciting, 27-8; as moral quality, 125-6; and the observer, 60-1, 72; for oneself, 64-71; opposite of, 18, 45-6; in oratory (forensic versus deliberative), 82; and pain, 112-13, 129, 134-5; and persuasion, 18; in petitions to civil authorities, 114-15; Polybius on, 83-8; and prayer, 105, 110-11, 116-18; in primitive societies, 21;

179

and rational soul, 121;
reciprocation of, 80-1; and related
terms, 1; and relation between
pitier and pitied, 12, 60, 65, 131;
and remorse, 32-6, 93; reputation
for (Greek), 81; reputation for
(Roman), 91; between similar
people, 50-1, 80-1, 111; and
slavery, 16-17, 23, 87-8; social
function of, 122-3; and
supplication, 78-9; syntax of, 102;
in the theatre, 69; and tragedy,
71-2, 136; versus vengeance, 90-1;
and vulnerability, 49-50, 52-3, 90,
92, 106, 125, 130; and the weak,
17, 79; among women, 16-17; for
women, 17
Planalp, Sally, 14-16
Plato: *Apology of Socrates*, 36, 42-3;
Epistles, 112; *Protagoras*, 46
Pliny the Elder, 17
Pliny the Younger: *Letters* 47-8, 64,
104; *Panegyric*, 100
Plutarch: *Consolation to Apollonius*,
63; *How a Young Man Should
Listen to Poetry*, 72-3, 113; *Life of
Nicias*, 148n35
Plutchik, Robert, 4
politics of pity, 119
Pollack, Malla, 33
Polybius: on Achaean War, 85-8; and
epieikeia, 149n35; on Epirotes and
Illyrians, 84-5; on pity and desert,
83-8; on Second Punic War, 83-4;
on self-pity, 70
Posidonius, 94-5
power and emotion, 16
praotês (Greek = 'mildness'), 87
prayer: and justice, 117; and pity,
105, 110-11, 116-18
primitivist view of pity, 21
Pritchett, W. Kendrick, 76-7, 82
process and emotion, 10
progressivist view of the emotions,
19-21
proofs in trials, 44
propatheia (Greek = 'protoemotion'),
11
protoemotion, 11
Punic War, Second: in Appian, 91-2;
in Livy, 95-6; in Polybius, 83-4

Punic War, Third: in Appian, 92-3

Radford, Colin, 142n14
rahamim (Hebrew = 'pity'), 120
reader's identification with literary
characters, 72-3
reason versus emotion, 5-6, 29, 37
reciprocation of pity, 80-1
reflexes, 8
remorse, 30, 32-6, 93
reptile brain, 14
reputation for pity: Greek, 81;
Roman, 91
restorative justice, 139n6
restraint of emotion, 19-21
rhetoric and the emotions, 17
rights, civic, 114-15
Rigsby, Kent, 63
Rodley, Nigel, 75
roles and emotions, 16-17
Rolls, Edmund, 138n16
Roman reputation: for clemency, 96;
for humaneness, 114; for pity, 91
Rosaldo, Michelle, 2
Rostovtzeff, Mikhail, 114, 145n5
Rousseau, Jean-Jacques, 21
rules of evidence: in ancient Athens,
29; in sentencing, 32-3; in United
States, 28

Sakenfeld, Katherine, 154n38
Sallust, 95
Salzburg, Stephen et al., 28
savagery, 87
Scheler, Max, 14, 68
Schopenhauer, Arthur, 13
Scruton, David, 17
self-love, 65
self-pity, 3, 64-71; and Aristotle, 64-5;
in English, 70-1
Seneca: *On Anger*, 4, 6, 14, 71; *On
Clemency*, 47, 96-7, 103-4, 145n3;
On Remedies for Chance Events,
63; *On Benefactions*, 103
sensation, 129
sentencing: in classical Athens, 35-6;
in the United States, 31-3
Septuagint, 120
sharing of pain and pleasure, 58-60;
see also sun-
shield of the virtues, 100

Index

Sicilian expedition, 88-91
similarity and pity, 50-1, 80-1, 111
slavery: as pitiable, 87; and pity, 16-17, 23, 111
Smith, Adam, 59-60
social construction of emotions, 17
society, pity in, 122-3
Socrates, 36, 42-3
Solomon, Robert, 9, 12, 37
Sophocles: *Ajax*, 60, 107-8, 138n21; *Electra*, 142n9; *Oedipus at Colonus*, 109; *Philoctetes*, 51-3, 55, 79; *Women of Trachis*, 54, 108, 138n21
Stanford, W.B., 72
Statius, 64
status and emotion, 16-17
Stocker, Michael, 126
Stoics: on emotions as cognitive, 6; hostile to emotions, 48, 113; Lactantius' critique of, 121-2
suicide after defeat in war, 76
Sulla, L. Cornelius, 97
sullupeisthai (Greek = 'feel pain with'), *see sun-*
sumpatheia (Greek = 'sympathy'), 58, 63
sumponein (Greek = 'struggle together'), 55, 57-8; *see also sun-*
sunalgein (Greek = 'feel pain with'), *see sun-*
sun- (Greek prefix = 'together with'), 57-8; in compounds signifying sharing of pain and pleasure, 58-60, 63, 65, 89, 133; of authors or readers in relation to literary characters, 72
Sundby, Scott, 32-3
sungnômê (Greek = 'forgiveness', 'understanding'), 30, 39-41, 80, 92
supplication and pity, 78-9
sympathy, 1, 12-13, 15-16; and justice, 37; versus pity, 72; versus sympathize, 3

Tacitus, 97
Tarn, W.W., 76
Tertullian, 124, 155n44
theatre and pity, 69, 71-2
Thoreau, Henry David, 71

Thrasymachus, 28
Thucydides, 80-3
timôria (Greek = 'punishment', 'vengeance'), 82
torture, 17, 87, 111
tragedy: and fear, 158n12; and pity, 71-2, 109, 136
trial procedure: in ancient Athens, 29, 34-5; in the United States, 28, 31

universality of emotions, 7

Valerius Maximus, 101
vengeance, 82, 90-1
Versnel, H.S., 154n31
victims' rights, 29
Virgil: *Aeneid*, 77, 153n26; on anger of Aeneas, 78-9
virtue, pity as, 121, 125-6
volunteer work, 22
vulnerability: and calculation, 130-1; of the gods, 106-9; and pity, 49-50, 52-3, 90, 92, 107-8, 125, 130-1

Walbank, Frank, 147nn23, 25
Walton, Douglas, 29, 72
war, consequences of, 76
weak, pity for, 17, 79
Weinstock, Stefan, 97-8
Weltschmerz, 22
White, Stephen, 20
Wierzbicka, Anna, 1, 3, 7, 70, 102-3
Wiles, David, 2
Williams, Bernard, 87
Wiltshire, Susan Ford, 145n3
women: pity among, 16-17; pity for, 17
writer's identification with characters, 72

Xenophon: *Apology of Socrates*, 36; *Cyropaedia*, 147n22
Xenophon of Ephesus, 118

Zanker, Graham, 126, 137n2
Zeldin, Theodore, 22
Zweig, Stefan, 15